Foundations of Cataloging

Foundations of Cataloging

A Sourcebook

Edited by
Michael Carpenter
and
Elaine Svenonius

1985
Libraries Unlimited, Inc. • Littleton, Colorado

LIBRARIES UNLIMITED, INC.
P.O. Box 263
Littleton, Colorado 80160-0263

Consulting Editor: Lois Mai Chan

Companion reader: *Theory of Subject Analysis: A Sourcebook,* edited by Lois Mai
Chan, Phyllis A. Richmond, and Elaine Svenonius.

Library of Congress Cataloging in Publication Data
Main entry under title:

Foundations of cataloging.

    Includes index.
    1. Cataloging--Addresses, essays, lectures.
I. Carpenter, Michael, 1940-   . II. Svenonius,
Elaine.
Z693.F68   1985   025.3'2   85-10333
ISBN 0-87287-511-3

Libraries Unlimited books are bound with Type II nonwoven material that meets
and exceeds National Association of State Textbook Administrators' Type II
nonwoven material specifications Class A through E.

Contents

v

The Most Concise AACR2
Michael Gorman

Cataloging and the New Technologies
Michael Gorman

The Catalog as Access Mechanism: Background and Concepts
Patrick Wilson

Index

Foreword

Recent decades have seen a great deal of activity in the field of descriptive cataloging, leading to the publication and implementation of *Anglo-American Cataloguing Rules*, second edition *(AACR2)*. *AACR2* represents the culmination of more than a century of cataloging principles and practice. Much of the literature that embodies the most cogent ideas and thoughts in the field of descriptive cataloging has gone out of print or is not generally accessible. In order to make that literature available to professionals and students in the field of cataloging, this collection of writings on the theory and philosophy of cataloging, selected from the writings of authors from Sir Anthony Panizzi to present-day scholars, was assembled. To assist in the study of these writings and to provide a proper context for them, each selection is preceded by a brief introduction written by the editors.

The editors of this volume, Michael Carpenter and Elaine Svenonius, have been active in the field of cataloging theory. Carpenter is the author of *Corporate Authorship: Its Role in Library Cataloging.* Svenonius is the author of numerous articles on subject analysis and descriptive cataloging, including "AACR2: Main Entry Free?" (*Cataloging & Classification Quarterly,* 1984).

The present volume is intended to be a companion to *Theory of Subject Analysis: A Sourcebook,* edited by Lois Mai Chan, Phyllis A. Richmond, and Elaine Svenonius.

Lois Mai Chan

Preface

Purpose

This anthology is addressed to teachers and students of cataloging. Its purpose is to bring together outstanding contributions to the literature on cataloging theory of the last 150 years. It seems particularly appropriate now, as we enter the online age, to offer for review the best thinking of the past on the design of cataloging codes. A question that begs for answer is whether the principles underlying past catalog code design suffice for the design of codes for online systems.

Definition and Scope

The most general question that can be asked of a code of rules used to describe and provide access to bibliographic records is, Why this code rather than one designed in a different manner? Some reasons must be given and these reasons, taken collectively, constitute the basis of a code. The selections in this sourcebook all deal with decisions that are made in code design and the reasons for them. Some of the questions raised in these selections are:

1. What are the objectives of a catalog? What are the best means to achieve these objectives? Do the means differ in the manual and online environments?

2. What attributes of a catalogable entity should be included in the descriptions that comprise bibliographic records?

3. What is authorship? Is authorship the primary attribute to be used in identifying bibliographic entities?

4. What are the advantages and disadvantages of standardization in cataloging? To what extent is standardization even possible?

5. What is the role of the main entry in fulfilling the functions of the catalog? Is the main entry needed in online catalogs?

6. What criteria have been used for making form of name decisions in the past? Are they still relevant today?

7. What bibliographic relationships need to be built into a catalog to make it more than just a finding list? Has thinking on this matter changed over the last 150 years?

Criteria for Selection

An attempt was made to include in this sourcebook readings that provide intellectual depth and matter for thought. Most of the selected readings are well known; a few, however, are little read but included as gems that deserve to be known. Panizzi's letter to Lord Ellesmere, for example, reflects in miniature the whole of the Anglo-American cataloging experience. Inevitably, the selections have an Anglo-American bias; particularly notable by their absence are representatives of the Indian and German schools. Some restriction was necessary to keep the volume to a manageable size, and, since it was felt that the literature written in English and about the Anglo-American tradition would be of most immediate interest, it is this writing that is represented. The volume includes relatively few recent contributions. This is a consequence of the fact that much recent writing is devoted to the engineering of online catalogs and to the mechanics of interface, rather than to the more philosophical issues of the purposes of the catalog and the means to achieve these.

Organization

Because many of the selections in the volume treat of more than one of the themes that characterize the literature on cataloging foundations, it was not possible to make an intellectual grouping of the selections. Instead the selections are arranged in chronological order. The aim of the introductions to each selection, the lists of further readings following them, and the index is to bring together related issues and ideas.

MC

ES

Rules for the Compilation of the Catalogue

British Museum

Editor's Introduction

Why should rules for a dead catalog be of interest today? Because the history of cataloging shows that controversies recur, although why these controversies should be perennial is not clear.

The ninety-one rules, as they are often called, were formulated for the compilation of the printed catalog of the printed books in the British Museum, the first and only volume of which appeared in 1841. The rules are set in the context of a catalog in which *main entry* stands for the one principal entry for a book. References are made to this principal entry, and the rules explain the different classes of references.

Although many writers have claimed that these ninety-one rules are a revolutionary achievement, examination of the historical record reveals that they are a natural outgrowth of trends in cataloging theory known to their writer, Panizzi. This fact should not detract from their importance; all modern codes descend from them.

The ninety-one rules appear to represent publications of corporate bodies as a certain class of anonymous publications. This equivocation about the rationale for corporate entry has permeated discussions about cataloging to the present day. In these rules, corporate entry can be used as a default (rule 34) or as a means of organizing publications of certain classes (rule 80). The provisions of rule 80, calling for entry of the publications of learned societies under the heading "Academies," is an example of the use of bibliographical form in the determination of main entry; other examples are found in rules 81 and 82, and possibly 79. Rule 79 calls for the bringing together of the various parts of the Bible, and may represent the ancestor of modern uniform title headings.

Panizzi's rules continue practices found as far back as the catalogs for libraries in medieval monasteries. In their turn, Panizzi's rules and the catalogs based on them are reflected in practices still found in AACR2. Among these practices are the punctuation of headings, the use of qualifying phrases after the names of certain classes of titled persons, the provision of book sizes (albeit in a form no longer readily understood), and, more importantly, the very depth of the description of a bibliographical object. How did these practices develop into conventions? Was it through the force of custom, or do the rules reflect something intrinsic about bibliographical objects?

MC

Further Reading

Predeek, Albert. "Antonio Panizzi und der alphabetischen Katalog des Britischen Museums." in *Festschrift Georg Leyh,* 257-82. Leipzig: Otto Harrassowitz, 1937.

An excellent study of the circumstances surrounding composition of the rules.

McCrimmon, Barbara. "Whose Ninety-one Rules? A Revisionist View." *Journal of Library History* 18 (Spring 1983): 163-77.

Claims that Panizzi wrote the rules only under pressure from the Trustees.

Panizzi, Anthony. "Mr. Panizzi to the Right Hon. the Earl of Ellesmere.—British Museum, January 29, 1848." In Great Britain. Commissioners Appointed to Inquire into the Constitution and Government of the British Museum, *Appendix to the Report of the Commissioners Appointed to Inquire into the Constitution and Management* [sic] *of the British Museum,* 378-95. London: Her Majesty's Stationery Office, 1850.

Reprinted in this volume.

Rules for the Compilation of the Catalogue

I.   Titles to be written on slips, uniform in size.
The entries of works in the collection of George the Third presented by George the Fourth to the Nation to be distinguished by a crown.

II.   Titles to be arranged alphabetically, according to the English alphabet only (whatever be the order of the alphabet in which a foreign name might have to be entered in its original language) under the surname of the author, whenever it appears printed in the title, or in any other part of the book. If the name be supplied in MS. the work must nevertheless be considered anonymous or pseudonymous, as the case may be, and the MS. addition deemed merely a suggestion to which the librarian will attach such importance as he may think proper, on his own responsibility, in supplying the author's name between brackets, as hereafter directed.
In the alphabetical arrangement, initial prepositions, letters or articles to be taken in connection with the rest of the name.

III.   If more than one name occur in the title, by which it may appear that the work is the production of more than one person, the first to be taken as the leading name.

IV.   The works of sovereigns, or of princes of sovereign houses, to be entered under their Christian or first name, *in their English form.*

V.   Works of Jewish Rabbis, as well as works of Oriental writers in general, to be entered under their first name.

VI.   Works of friars, who, by the constitution of their order, drop their surname, to be entered under the Christian name; the name of the family, if ascertained, to be added in brackets. The same to be done for persons canonized as well as for those known under their first name only, to which, for the sake of distinction, they add that of their native place, or profession, or rank. Patronymics, or

Reprinted from British Museum, *The Catalogue of Printed Books in the British Museum* (London, 1841), 1: v-ix.

denominations, derived from the ancestors or names of other persons, to be used as surnames.

VII.   The respondent or defender of a thesis to be considered its author, except when it unequivocally appears to be the work of the Præses.

VIII.   When an author uses a Christian or first name only (either real or assumed), such name to be taken as a heading; and if more than one be used, the first to be preferred for the principal entry. The surname or family name, when known, to be added in brackets after the first name.

IX.   Any act, resolution, or other document purporting to be agreed upon, authorized, or issued by assemblies, boards, or corporate bodies, (with the exception of academies, universities, learned societies, and religious orders, respecting which special rules are to be followed,) to be entered in distinct alphabetical series, under the name of the country or place from which they derive their denomination, or, for want of such denomination, under the name of the place whence their acts are issued.

X.   Names of persons that may have been altered by being used in various languages, to be entered under their vernacular form, if any instance occur of such persons having used it in any of their printed publications. With respect to places, the English form to be preferred.

XI.   Works of authors who change their name or add to it a second, after having begun to publish under the first, to be entered under the first name, noticing any alteration which may have subsequently taken place.

XII.   Foreign names, excepting French, preceded by a preposition, an article, or by both, to be entered under the letter immediately following. French names preceded by a preposition only, to follow the same rule; those preceded by an article, or by a preposition and an article, to be entered under the initial letter of the article. English surnames, of foreign origins, to be entered under their initial, even if originally belonging to a preposition. Foreign compound surnames to be entered under the initial of the first of them. In compound Dutch and English surnames the last name to be preferred, if no entry of a work by the same person occur in the catalogue under the first name only.

XIII.   German names, in which the letters *ä, ö,* or *ü* occur, to be spelt with the dipthong *ae, oe* and *ue* respectively.

XIV.   Surnames of noblemen, though not expressed in the book, to be ascertained and written out as the heading of the entry. A person who has assumed titles not generally acknowledged, to have the words "calling himself," between brackets, to precede the assumed title.

XV.   The same rule to be followed with respect to archbishops and bishops.

XVI. Christian names, included in paretheses, to follow the surname, and all to be written out in full, as far as they are known. In case of doubt on this or any other point, when the librarian is directed to supply any information in cataloguing, a note of interrogation to follow in such a position as to indicate clearly the point on which any doubt is entertained.

XVII. An author's rank in society, in cases in which he enjoyed any eminent honorary distinction, or office for life, not lower than that of knight, admiral, or general, to be stated in italics. Younger sons of dukes and marquesses, and all daughters of dukes, marquesses and earls, when not enjoying a distinct title, to have the designation *Lord* or *Lady* prefixed to the Christian name. All other younger branches of the nobility to have the word *Hon.* prefixed. The words *Right Hon.*, in the same situation, to distinguish privy councillors. Knights to be indicated merely by the appellation *Sir* prefixed to their first name. Titles of inferior rank, whether ecclesiastical, military, or civil, to be given only when necessary to make a distinction between authors having the same surname and Christian name.

Proper names commencing with Mc. or M' to be entered under Mac, *with cross-references from the other forms.*

Where a person is referred to in a title-page by a description sufficiently clear to render his or her identity obvious, the proper name of such person to be adopted as a heading, whether the work be historical or otherwise.

XVIII. The title of the book next to be written, and that expressed in as few words, and those only of the author, as may be necessary to exhibit to the reader all that the author meant to convey in the titular description of his work; the original orthography to be preserved. The number of the edition to be stated when appearing in the title.

In cataloguing sermons, the text always to be specified. The date at which preached to be inserted when it differs from that of publication.

XIX. Any striking imperfection in a book to be carefully noted; and any remarkable peculiarity, such as that of containing cancelled or duplicate leaves, &c., to be stated.

XX. When the book is without a title-page, its contents to be concisely, but sufficiently, stated in the words of the head-title, preceded by the word *begin. (beginning)* in italics; if there be no head-title, in those of the colophon, preceded by the word *end. (ending);* and when the want of title is owing to an imperfection, the words taken from either head-title or colophon to be included between parentheses. If both head-title and colophon be wanting or insufficient, then some idea of the work to be briefly given in English, between brackets, and the edition so accurately described as to be easily identified without fear of mistake.

XXI. Whenever one or more separate works are mentioned in the title of any publication, as forming part of it, the same to be particularly noticed in cataloguing the principal publication; and, if not mentioned in the title-page, this information to be added to the title between brackets or parentheses, as the case may be.

XXII. All works in Oriental characters or languages, except Hebrew, to be separately catalogued in a supplementary volume, according to special rules to be framed. The Bible and its parts, however, in whatever language or characters, to be entered in the general catalogue as hereafter directed.

XXIII. Works in more languages than one, accompanied by the original, to be entered in the original only, unless the title be accompanied by a translation or translations, in which case such translation also to be given. If no original text occur, the first language used in the title to be preferred. In all cases the several languages used in the book to be indicated at the end of the title, in italics.

XXIV. Works with a title in a language different from that used in the body of the book to be entered according to the above rule, merely stating at the end of the title in italics in what language the work is written.

XXV. The number of parts, volumes, fasciculi, or whatever may be the peculiar divisions of each author's work, to be next specified, in the words of the title.

XXVI. When nothing is said in the title respecting this point, if a work be divided into several portions, but the same pagination continue, or, when the pages are not numbered, if the same register continue, the work to be considered as divided into parts; if the progressive number of the pages or the register be interrupted, then each series of pages or letters of the register to be designated as a volume.

XXVII. Then the place where the book was printed; and in particular cases, as in the instance of early or very eminent typographers, the printer's name to be specified. Next the date: when no date or place is specified, then either or both to be given, if known to, or conjectured by, the librarian; but in these instances to be included in brackets. The form to follow, whether fol., 4to, 8vo, &c.

XXVIII. If an early printed book, and in Gothic or black letter, the circumstance to be mentioned at the end of the title, thus:—G. L. or B. L.

XXIX. If printed on vellum, satin, on large or fine paper, or if an editio princeps of a classical or very distinguished writer, who flourished before 1700, or if privately printed, or a fac-simile or reprint of an early edition; if only a small number of copies were struck off, or if there be any manuscript notes, these peculiarities to be stated.

XXX. If the author of the manuscript notes be known, this information to be added between brackets. If the volume belonged to some very distinguished personage, the fact to be recorded in few words at the end of the entry, also between brackets.

XXXI. An editio princeps to be designed by the words *ED. PR.*, in italic capitals, at the end of the title. Manuscript notes to be indicated in italics at the end of the title, previous to the size of the volume, as follows:—*MS. NOTES.* If the notes be remarkably few, or the reverse, the circumstance to be noticed by prefixing to the above the word *FEW* or *COPIOUS.* Works printed *ON VELLUM* to be distinguished by these words, in small italic capitals, at the end of the title. The letters *L.P.* or *F.P.* in the same situation, to indicate copies on large or fine paper.

XXXII. Works published under initials, to be entered under the last of them; and should the librarian be able to fill up the blanks left, or complete the words which such initials are intended to represent, this to be done in the body of the title, and all the supplied parts to be included between brackets.
The rules applicable to proper names to be extended to initials.

XXXIII. When the author's name does not appear on the title or any other part of the work, the following rules to be observed. Anonymous publications relating to any act, or to the life of a person whose name occurs on the title of a work, to be catalogued under the name of such person. The same rule to be followed with respect to anonymous publications addressed (not merely dedicated) to any individual whose name occurs on the title.

XXXIV. When no such name of a person appears, then that of any assembly, corporate body, society, board, party, sect, or denomination appearing on the title to be preferred, subject to the arrangement of Rule IX.; and if no such name appear, then that of any country, province, city, town or place so appearing, to be adopted as the heading.
Articles to be inquired of within an ecclesiastical district to be entered under the name of such district.

XXXV. If no name of any assembly or country, to be preferred as above, appear on the title, the name of the editor, (if there be any,) to be used as a heading; or, if no editor's name appear, that of the translator, if there be one. Reporters to be considered as editors.

XXXVI. Adjectives formed from the name of a person, party, place or denomination, to be treated as the names from which they are formed.

XXXVII. If two names occur seeming to have an equal claim, the first to be chosen.
Reports of civil actions to be catalogued under the name of that party to the suit which stands first upon the title-page.
In criminal proceedings the name of the defendant to be adopted as a heading.
Trials relating to any vessel to be entered under the name of such vessel.

XXXVIII. In the case of anonymous works, to which none of the foregoing rules can be applied, the first substantive in the title (or if there be no substantive, the first word) to be selected as the heading. A substantive, adjectively used, to be taken in conjunction with its following substantive as forming one word; and the same to be done with respect to adjectives incorporated with their following substantive. The entries which may occur under the same heading to succeed each other in strict alphabetical order.

XXXIX. Whenever the name of the author of an anonymous publication is known to, or conjectured by, the librarian, the same to be inserted at the end of the title, between brackets.

XL. Works without the author's name, and purporting to comment or remark on a work of which the title is set forth in that of such publication, to be catalogued under the same heading as the work remarked or commented upon.

XLI. In the case of pseudonymous publications, the book to be catalogued under the author's feigned name; and his real name, if discovered, to be inserted in brackets, immediately after the feigned name, preceded by the letters *i. e.*

XLII. Assumed names, or names used to designate an office, profession, party, or qualification of the writer, to be treated as real names. Academical names to follow the same rule. The works of an author not assuming any name but describing himself by a circumlocution, to be considered anonymous.

XLIII. Works falsely attributed in their title to a particular person, to be treated as pseudonymous.

XLIV. Works of several writers, collectively published, to be entered according to the following rules, [and the separate pieces of the various authors included in the collection to be separately entered in the order in which they occur; excepting merely collections of letters, charters, short extracts from larger works, and similar compilations.]

> *That part of the foregoing rule which is inserted between brackets has not been acted upon, in order to accelerate the printing of the catalogue.*

XLV. In any series of printed works, which embraces the collected productions of various writers upon particular subjects, such as Ugolini Thesaurus Antiq. Sacrarum, Gronovii Thesaurus Antiq. Græcarum, the work to be entered under the name of the editor.

> *Works of several authors published together, but not under a collective title, to be catalogued under the name of the first author, notwithstanding an editor's name may appear on the work.*

XLVI. If the editor's name do not appear, the whole collection to be entered under the collective title, in the same manner as anonymous works.

> *In cataloguing collections without an editor's name, and having a collective title, the heading to be taken from such collective title without reference to that portion of the title which may follow.*

XLVII. General collections of laws, edicts, ordinances, or other public acts of a similar description, to be entered under the name of the state or nation in which or by whom they were sanctioned, signed, or promulgated. Collections extending only to one reign or period of supreme government by one person, as well as detached laws and douments separately enacted and issued, to be catalogued under the name of the person in whose name and by whose authority they are enacted or sanctioned; such names to be entered alphabetically under the principal entry of the state or nation, after the general collections. When more than one name occurs, the first to be preferred.

XLVIII. Collections of laws, edicts, &c., of several countries or nations to be catalogued according to rules XLV. and XLVI.

XLIX. The same to be done with respect to laws on one or more particular subjects, either merely collected or digested in some particular order, or used as text to some particular comment or treatise.

L. The names of translators or commentators to be stated in cataloguing and entering a work, if they occur in the title page; and when they do not occur, but are known to or conjectured by the librarian, to be supplied between brackets.

LI. The works of translators to be entered under the name of the original author. The same rule to be observed with respect to the works of commentators, if the same be accompanied with the text complete.

LII. Translations to be entered immediately after the original, generally with only the indication of the language into which the version has been made, in italics; but if any material alteration in the title have been introduced, so much of the title of the translation to be given as may be deemed requisite, or a short explanation in English added, between brackets.

LIII. Commentaries unaccompanied by the text, to be entered under the commentator's name; if without a name, or with an assumed name, then according to the rules laid down for anonymous or pseudonymous works.

LIV. No work ever to be entered twice at full length. Whenever requisite, cross-references to be introduced.

LV. Cross-references to be divided into three classes, from name to name, from name to work, and from work to work. Those of the first class to contain merely the name, title, or office of the person referred to as entered; those of the second, so much of the title referred to besides, as, together with the size and date, may give the means of at once identifying, under its heading, the book referred to; those of the third class to contain moreover so much of the title referred from, as may be necessary to ascertain the object of the reference.

LVI. Cross-references of the first class to be made in the following instances:
From the titles of noblemen, and from the sees of archbishops or bishops, to the family name, or the first name under which the works of such personages are to be entered according to the foregoing rules.

LVII. From the family name of persons whose works are to be entered under the Christian or first name, to such Christian or first name; excepting in the case of sovereigns, or princes belonging to sovereign houses.

LVIII. From any surnames either spelt, or in any way used, in a manner differing from the form adopted in the principal entry, to such entry.

LIX. From any of the names or surnames used by an author besides that under which the principal entry is made, to the one so preferred.

LX. From the real to the assumed name of authors; adding *pseud.* to the entry referred to in the cross-reference.

LXI. Cross-references of the second or third class, according to circumstances, to be made in the following instances:
From the names of editors, or of biographers who have prefixed an author's life to his works, (provided such names appear in the book,) to the principal entry.

LXII. From the names of authors of anonymous or pseudonymous works supplied in the title, as well as from the names of authors who have shared with another in writing a work, or have continued it, and also from the names of translators, commentators, or annotators, either appearing on the title, or supplied as above directed, to the main entry.

LXIII. From the name of any person the subject of any biography or narrative, to its author; stating briefly, in italics, after the name referred from, the peculiar designation of the biography in the work referred to; or, if this cannot be done, using the nearest English word, in brackets and italics, that may give an idea of the object of the cross reference.
In this description of cross-reference the first words of the title of the work referred to to be given, but not its date or size, so that the cross-reference may serve equally for all editions.

LXIV. From any name which may be reasonably conceived to have an equal claim to that selected for the principal entry, to such entry.

LXV. From any author, any whole work of whom or any considerable part of it may be the subject of a commentary, or notes, to the name of the commentator or annotator. No notice to be taken of the name of authors, fragments or inconsiderable parts of whose works are observed upon by the commentator or annotator.

LXVI. From any author whose works, or considerable part of them contained in a collection, are considered so important as to be distinctly specified in the entry of the collection itself, to the principal entry; the volume, or part of the collection in which the article so referred to is found, to be specified.

LXVII. From the names of authors whose entire works or any considerable part of them are included among the collected works of a polygraphic writer, or translator, to the principal entry.

LXVIII.   From the name of a state or nation to which a collection of laws, entered under any other heading, belongs, to the main entry.

From the name of the superior of any ecclesiastical district who promulgates articles for inquiry to the name of such district.

From the name of any party to a civil action to the principal entry.

LXIX.   Entries to be made in the following order:

Cross-references to be placed at the beginning of the entry, from which they are made, in the alphabetical order of the entries referred to.

LXX.   Collections of all the works of an author in their original language only, to be entered immediately after the cross-references; the editions without date, and those of which the date cannot be ascertained even by approximation, to precede all those bearing date, or of which the date can be supplied either positively or by approximation. The latter to follow according to their date, whether apparent in any part of the book, or supplied. Editions by the same editor, or such as are expressly stated to follow a specific text or edition, and editions with the same notes or commentary, to succeed each other immediately in their chronological order after the entry of that which is, or is considered to be, the earliest.

LXXI.   The text of the collected works, accompanied by a translation, to follow those having the text only, and in the same order.

LXXII.   The translations of such collected works into the Latin language only to precede those in any other language in the above order; the Latin translations to be followed by those in English. Translations in any other language to follow according to the alphabetical order of the name of the language in English. If the volume contain two or more translations, without the text, the entry to be made according to the alphabetical order of the first of the languages employed. Translations into the same language, and their   several editions, to be entered in conformity with the rules laid down for the entries of the originals.

LXXIII.   Collections of two or more works of an author to be entered in the order and according to the rules laid down for the collections of all the works of a writer, after the translations of the whole works; such partial collections to precede, as are known or are supposed to contain the largest number of an author's works.

LXXIV.   Selections, or collected fragments, from the works of an author, to follow the partial collections of his works, and to be entered according to the above rules.

LXXV.   Separate works of an author to succeed each other alphabetically; the several editions and translations of each of them to be entered in the same manner as directed for the collected works of a writer.

LXXVI.   Entire portions of a separate work to succeed the work from which they are taken, in the order above directed. If the whole work to which they belong do not occur, such portions to be entered after all the separate works, but according to the principles laid down for the latter.

LXXVII. Works not written by the person under whose name they are to be catalogued according to the foregoing rules, to be entered alphabetically as an appendix, and in chronological succession, when more than one article occurs in the same alphabetical series, after all the works of the person whose name is selected, if any occur in the catalogue. Volumes without date, or the date of which cannot be supplied, to be entered first.

LXXVIII. The same rule as to the alphabetical and chronological arrangement to apply to works entered under any other heading than the name of a person.

LXXIX. The Old and New Testament and their parts, to be catalogued under the general head "Bible," and arranged in the following order:—

1st. The Old and New Testaments in the original Hebrew and Greek only, chronologically arranged.

2d. The same, in polyglot editions, which include the original texts; beginning with those editions which contain most translations.

3d. The same, translated into other languages, but without the original; those editions to precede which contain most languages; then translations into one language only, arranged as directed in rule LXXII.

4th. Editions, with comments, to follow those having the text only, in the same order and according to the same principles. Bibles accompanied by the same comment to follow each other immediately in chronological succession.

5th. The Old Testament only to be next entered, according to the same principles and rules.

6th. Detached parts of the Old Testament then to follow, in the same order in which they are arranged in the English authorised version of the Scriptures, and to be entered as directed for the whole Bible.

7th. The Apocrypha, as declared by the Church of England, to be next catalogued and entered according to the same rules.

8th. The New Testament to be next catalogued, and then its parts, according to the foregoing rules.

9th. General cross-references to be made from the several names of the inspired writers, as well as from the names of the several parts of Scripture, to the general head "Bible." Particular cross-references to be made from the names of editors, commentators, translators, &c., to the precise entry under which the part of Holy writ referred from in the cross-reference occurs.

10th. The names of parts of the Bible, as well as of inspired writers, to be expressed in the form adopted in the authorised English version of the Scriptures.

LXXX. All acts, memoirs, transactions, journals, minutes, &c., of academies, institutes, associations, universities, or societies learned, scientific, or literary, by whatever name known or designated, as well as works by various hands, forming part of a series of volumes edited by any such society, to be catalogued under the general name "Academies" and alphabetically entered, according to the English name of the country and town at which the sittings of the society are held, in the following order. The primary division to be of the four parts of the world in alphabetical succession, Australia and Polynesia being considered as appendixes to Asia;

the first subdivision to be of the various empires, kingdoms, or other independent governments into which any part of the world is divided, in alphabetical order; and a second subdivision of each state to follow, according to the various cities or towns, alphabetically disposed, belonging to each state, in which any society of this description meets. The acts, &c., of each society, when more than one meet at the same place, to be entered according to the name under which the society published its first work, in alphabetical series; and the acts, memoirs, &c. of each society to be entered chronologically. Continuations to follow the original entry.

LXXXI. The same rule and arrangement to be followed for "Periodical Publications," which are to be catalogued under this general head, embracing reviews, magazines, newspapers, journals, gazettes, annuals, and all works of a similar nature, in whatever language and under whatever denomination they may be published. The several entries under the last subdivision to be made in alphabetical order according to the first substantive occurring in the title.

LXXXII. All almanacs, calendars, ephemerides of whatever description they be, as well as their companions, appendixes, &c., to be entered under the general head "Ephemerides." The several works under this head to be entered alphabetically according to the first substantive occurring in the title.

LXXXIII. There shall be cross-references from the name of any author, editor, or contributor to any of the above works, appearing in any of the title-pages of any of the volumes, as well as from the peculiar name or designation of any of the societies, from the place at which they hold their meetings, from any place forming part of the·peculiar name of a journal, almanac, calendar, &c., from the name under which such publications are generally known, to the main entries of such works.

LXXXIV. Religious and military orders to be designated by the English name under which they are generally known, and entries to be made accordingly.

LXXXV. Anonymous catalogues, whether bearing the title catalogue or any other intended to convey the same meaning, to be entered under the head "Catalogues," subdivided as follows:—1st. Catalogues of public establishments (including those of societies, although not strictly speaking *public*). 2d. Catalogues of private collections, drawn up either for sale or otherwise. 3d. Catalogues of collections not for sale, the possessors of which are not known. 4th. General as well as special catalogues of objects, without any reference to their possessor. 5th. Dealers' catalogues. 6th. Sale catalogues not included in any of the preceding sections.

LXXXVI. Catalogues of the first subdivision to be entered under the name of the place at which the collection exists, as directed for Academies: those of the second, under the name of the collector or possessor: those of the third in strict alphabetical order, according to the first substantive of the title: those of the fourth, to follow the same rule: those of the fifth, under the dealer's name: those of the sixth, strictly chronologically, supplying the year in brackets whenever omitted, but known to, or conjectured by, the librarian; and when it is impossible to ascertain the precise day and month, for catalogues coming under the same year, in strict alphabetical order before those having a precise date. Catalogues without any date, and the date of which cannot be supplied, to be entered at the beginning of this subdivision in strict alphabetical order, as just directed. With respect to mere dealers' and sale catalogues compiled since the beginning of the present century, such only to be catalogued and entered as may be considered of peculiar interest.

LXXXVII. Cross-references of the second class to be made from the name of the compiler of a catalogue (when supplied by the librarian, and other than the collector or possessor of a collection, a dealer or an auctioneer) to the principal entry.

LXXXVIII. Anonymous Dictionaries of any description, including Lexicons and Vocabularies, to be catalogued under the general head "Dictionaries," and entered in strict alphabetical order according to the first substantive in the title, with cross-references from the author's name, when supplied.

LXXXIX. The same rule to be applied to Encyclopædias, the name of the editor of which does not appear on the title, and which shall be catalogued under the general head "Encyclopædias," with a cross-reference from the editor's name, when supplied in the principal entry, to such entry.

XC. Missals, Brevaries, Offices, Horæ, Prayer Books, Liturgies, and works of the same description (not compiled by private individuals and in their individual capacity, in which case they are to be catalogued and entered according to the general rules laid down for other works,) to be entered under the general head "Liturgies," in one strict alphabetical series, according to the English denomination of the communion, sect, or religious order for whom they are specially intended; if drawn up for any particular church, congregation, or place of worship, then according to the English name peculiar to such church, congregation, or place of worship; if any work of this description occur not coming under either of these two classes, then the first substantive in the title to be preferred as a heading. Entries under the same heading to be made in strict alphabetical order.

XCI. Cross-references of the second class to be made from the peculiar name or designation of any of the churches, communions, sects, religious orders, or places of worship, as well as from the name under which any of the works mentioned in the preceding article is generally known, to the main entry.

Mr. Panizzi to the Right Hon. the Earl of Ellesmere. — British Museum, January 29, 1848

Sir Anthony Panizzi

Editor's Introduction

Sir Anthony Panizzi (1797-1879) was born in the duchy of Modena and educated as a lawyer, but his political activities caused his exile from Italy. After emigrating to England, he found employment in the British Museum where he worked as a cataloger, starting in 1831. In 1837 he was appointed Keeper of the Department of Printed Books, and in 1856 Principal Librarian. After his retirement, he was knighted.

During Panizzi's first year as Keeper, he was directed by the Museum's Trustees to write rules for the compilation of a new printed catalog. He produced the famed ninety-one rules (reprinted in this volume), which are the ancestor of all modern library cataloging codes. The rules were partially applied to the first volume of the projected printed catalog, which appeared in 1841. Because the catalog was compiled and published simultaneously, it was defective. For example, not all books could appear in proper alphabetical order. In addition, the required references were incomplete because the catalogers could not be aware of their need until they had come upon a book requiring them. The catalog was discontinued after the publication of the first volume.

Questions were asked in Parliament about what appeared to be a failure. As a result, the British government appointed a royal commission (Commissioners Appointed to Inquire into the Constitution and Government of the British Museum), whose task was supposed to be the impeachment of Panizzi for insubordination. Hearings were held from the commission's establishment from June 17, 1847, through 1849, and the commission's report was issued in 1850. During the hearings, characterized by lively interchanges between persons representing views still held by some writers today, Panizzi held his ground and was completely vindicated.

In addition to the widely distributed 1850 report and minutes of evidence, an appendix to the report, containing the exhibits presented to the commission, was issued in only twelve copies, two of which are believed extant today. Panizzi's letter to the commission's chairman, Francis Leveson-Gower, first earl of Ellesmere, is part of this appendix.

That the letter was written in the midst of an inquiry into the printing of a large manuscript catalog is clear; discussions about the thickness of slips would scarcely be heard today. Panizzi assumed that a catalog must have one principal entry per book, with references leading to that entry, lest the catalog become impossibly bulky. In the era of the online catalog, this assumption need no longer apply unless a book catalog is to be published.

Panizzi makes no attempt to envision a center for the production of cataloging copy available for distribution to other libraries; Panizzi's task, as he saw it, was to provide for the catalog of one large library. Panizzi was not writing rules to be followed by other libraries, and so he could claim that a superintendent could act as a final check on consistency. Because the superintendent could formulate rules to take care of new types of material, a systematic approach, guided by principles, to the formulation of rules is missing.

The letter represents Panizzi's attempt to make the nature of a catalog intelligible to the Earl of Ellesmere, a layman. Because of its didactic approach, the letter is an excellent introduction to the foundations of cataloging. It covers topics of recurring interest such as the optimal length of bibliographic description and its relation to the objectives of a library catalog, the function of main entry, the requirement for normalization of names (personal and corporate), the problems of transliteration, the role of forms of publication in the determination of entry, the status of works modified or adapted from differing originals, the treatment of anonymous works, the problem of title page transcription, the requirement for uniformity in application of cataloging rules, the nature of references, filing arrangements, etc. The terminology in which these topics are discussed differs from that used today, and sometimes Panizzi has to describe a concept for which he has no term. For example, the reader should not assume that *work* means anything other than *book* without checking the context of the word's use. As another example, Panizzi's discussion of variant forms of name seems awkward because there is no straightforward concept of an authority file in which to record established headings.

The issues discussed by Panizzi recur so frequently in cataloging theory that the reading of his testimony in the commission hearings has often been required in the education of catalogers. With this first reproduction of his letter, the reader can see the systematic expression of Panizzi's views.

MC

Further Reading

Great Britain. Commissioners Appointed to Inquire into the Constitution and Government of the British Museum. *Report of the Commissioners Appointed to Inquire into the Constitution and Government of the British Museum with Minutes of Evidence [and] Index.* 1850. Reprint. Shannon, Ireland: Irish Universities Press, 1969.

Includes the original hearings.

Brault, Nancy. *The Great Debate on Panizzi's Rules in 1847-1849: The Issues Discussed.* Los Angeles: University of California, The School of Library Service and the University Library, 1972.

A compilation of pertinent extracts from the testimony presented in the full hearings.

Miller, Edward. *Prince of Librarians: The Life and Times of Antonio Panizzi of the British Museum,* 108-51. Athens, Ohio: Ohio University Press, 1967.

A history of the events surrounding the compilation of the ill-fated catalog of 1841 and the hearings concerning it.

Mr. Panizzi to the Right Hon. the Earl of Ellesmere.—
British Museum, January 29, 1848

MY LORD,—I beg to call the attention of your Lordship and of the other Commissioners appointed to inquire into the state and management of the British Museum to a subject of the highest importance and not less difficulty—the new Alphabetical Catalogue of the collection of printed books preserved for public use in that institution. Your Lordship is no doubt aware of the complaints which have at various times been uttered on the subject; complaints which are not to be wondered at when we reflect, that while the importance of a catalogue and its usefulness are easily and generally felt, the difficulties which must be overcome in order to execute such a work in a satisfactory manner are hardly intelligible to those who have not been called upon to give to this subject the mature consideration which its admitted importance demands.

My object in addressing your Lordship is to show the existence of these difficulties—their gravity—their variety. When your Lordship and the other Commissioners are persuaded of their extent and have become familiar with their nature, you will be able to inquire effectively into the means adopted in the British Museum for the purpose of overcoming them, and appreciate justly the comparative weight of the complaints above alluded to and of the answers made to them.

I must confess to your Lordship that, deeply impressed as I am myself with the difficulties often alluded to, I am even still more impressed with the *difficulty* of communicating to others an equal sense of these difficulties. In attempting to do so, I must enter into minutiæ and details, not only apparently insignificant, but also not very easy to make plain in writing; and I must beg a more than ordinary degree of attention from those who will condescend to follow me through a narrow, rugged, uninteresting path, requiring a patience and labour which few will deem well bestowed on so vulgar a subject as an ALPHABETICAL CATALOGUE.

Almost every one who possesses a library of a few hundred volumes thinks himself competent to draw up a list of them; this he supposes is easily done by copying the titles; and such a list he takes for granted constitutes an alphabetical

Reprinted from Great Britain, Commissioners Appointed to Inquire into the Constitution and Government of the British Museum, *Appendix to the Report of the Commissioner Appointed to Inquire into the Constitution and Management of the British Museum,* (London: Her Majesty's Stationery Office, 1850), 378-95.

catalogue. We see every day alphabetical catalogues by booksellers, or of books to be sold by auction, brought out in print with a rapidity which warrants the conclusion that their compilation does not require great exertion: why should not the alphabetical catalogue of a public library, however extensive, be completed, ay, and printed, in a proportionately short time?

To avoid the necessity of having to answer these and other such arguments, it is requisite to state the question with some precision. The question is: What is the best plan of completing in an uniform and consistent manner, within the shortest time, regard being had to the due execution of the work, a full and accurate alphabetical catalogue of a collection of printed books for public use, containing not less than 500,000 works, and being the amalgamation of three or four separate large libraries, each of which has a catalogue drawn up on distinct plans, by various hands, at various times? No full and accurate catalogue approaching to this in extent has ever been duly executed, or even attempted: in estimating the difficulties to be overcome, and in suggesting how this can be accomplished within the shortest time, we have no experience to guide us. And even in alphabetical catalogues of much less magnitude, it has not been found easy to obtain fulness and accuracy, or even to aim at it; and therefore the convenient adjective "useful" has been adopted by those who did not feel disposed to attempt "a full and accurate" compilation of this nature, but knew at the same time that merely saying "alphabetical catalogue" might mean everything or nothing. But then, again, nothing can be more vague and indefinite than the specious adjective "useful." A few examples will put this in a very clear light.

I am in a small village, and I hear there is a circulating library of 500 volumes: I look at the catalogue, and I find the following laconic entry:—

I. Abælard's Works.

Under such circumstances, that catalogue is "useful." I probably should never have thought of asking for such a work in such a place without that "useful" catalogue. But would the catalogue of a very extensive library be called "useful" if drawn up in such a manner? And if not, would such an entry as the following be such as to entitle the catalogue drawn up on such a plan to the epithet of "useful"?—

II. ABAELARDUS. Opera et Epistolis ejus et Heloisae. 4°.

This is a more "useful" entry than the foregoing. We learn from it that this book is in Latin, that it contains the works of Heloisa besides those of Abælard, and that it is in quarto.

In another catalogue I find the same copy of the work catalogued thus:—

III. ABÆLARDUS. Opera ejus et Heloisæ Abbatissæ conjugis ipsius. 4°. *Par.* 1616.

This is still more "useful." I learn from it that Heloisa was Abælard's wife and an abbess; and, what is more to the purpose in a catalogue, that the book is printed at Paris in 1616.

In the two last-mentioned catalogues, under the same heading, the two following entries occur.

In the first:—

IV. Epistolæ ejus et Heloisæ, ed. a R. Rawlinson. *Lond.* 1718. 8°.

In the second:—

V. Epistolæ ejus et Heloisæ, cum codd. MSS. collat. per Ric. Rawlinson. 8°. *Lond.* 1718.

From these two entries I draw the conclusion that in the catalogues where these entries occur the name of the editor is mentioned.

Now let us suppose that in the course of my studies I see reference made to an apology of Abælard's doctrine by André Duchesne, prefixed to his edition of Abælard's works. As in the two catalogues above supposed no mention is made of Duchesne in the entry of the edition of his works therein recorded, I conclude that in neither of the libraries represented by those two catalogues is to be found Duchesne's apology, his name as editor not appearing. Wishing to consult that apology, I turn, therefore, to the catalogues of other libraries, and in one of them I find, under the heading Abælardus:—

VI. Opera, et Heloisæ, Conjugis ipsius, cœnobii Paraditensis Abbatissæ; cum præfatione Apologetica pro PETRO ABÆLARDO per FRANCISCUM AMBÆSIUM *(Andream Quercetanum)* et censura Doctorum Parisiensium, in lucem edita, studio ejusdem Andreæ Quercetani; cum indice. 4°. *Parisiis,* 1616.

Here is at last the volume I wish to consult, and here is a specimen of "useful" cataloging. Had the title been less full, and the name of Duchesne omitted from it, the catalogue would have been "useless," and I should not have known where to find what I wanted. Having access to the library in which the volume described in this "useful" catalogue was preserved, I requested to see it; but, alas! to my great disappointment, I found that this catalogue, with such full titles, was less "useful" than the others, or rather was "worse than useless," inasmuch as I had lost my time in asking for a book, and searching in it for what I wanted and was told it would contain, but which it did not. Having the volume in my hands I copied the title, which was as follows:—

Petri Abælardi, Sancti Gildasi in Britannia Abbatis et Heloisæ conjugis ejus, quæ post modum prima Cænobii Paraclitensis Abbatissa fuit, Opera; Nunc primum ex MMS. Codd. eruta, et in lucem edita, studio ac diligentia Andreæ Quercetani, Turonensis. Parisiis, sumptibus Nicolai Buon, via Iacobæa, sub signis Sancti Claudij et Hominis Siluestris. MDCXVI. Cum privilegio Regis.

The volume is in 4to. and has the name of Duchesne in the title as that of editor. Not one word of the "Præfatio apologetica per Franciscum Ambæsium," which does not, in point of fact, occur in the volume, any more than the "Censura Doctorum." There is a dedication by Duchesne; there is his preface "ad lectorem," in which D'Amboise is mentioned as owner of certain manuscripts used by the editor; there are "Testimonia"—not always very flattering—respecting the unhappy writers of the works; there are notes by Duchesne at the end of the volume, "ad historiam calamitatum Petri Abælardi," but no "præfatio apologetica," no "censura."

On making further inquiry I find a copy of the works of Abælard, with this title:—

Petri Abælardi Filosofi et Theologi, Abbatis Ruyensis, et Heloisæ conjugis ejus primæ Paracletenis Abbatissæ, Opera, nunc primum edita ex MMS. Codd. V. illust. Francisci Amboesii, equitis, Regis in sanctiore consistorio consiliarii, Baronis Chartræ, &c. Cum ejusdem præfatione apologetica; et censura doctorum Parisiensium. Parisiis, sumptibus Nicolai Buon, via Iacobæa, sub signis Sancti Claudij, et Hominis Siluestris. MDCXVI. Cum privilegio Regis. 4°.

On consulting this volume it proves to contain not only the "præfatio apologetica," but several other accessories which did not form part of that copy of the book which was catalogued as containing them.

This copy of the work having been lately added to the library which contained that of which the title was given under Nos. II. and III., as well as the other under No. VI., the three copies were re-catalogued in the following order: viz.—1st. the copy lately added; 2nd, the copy catalogued as above under Nos. II. and III.; and 3rd, the copy under No. VI.: the three stand thus:—

ABÆLARDUS (PETRUS).

P. A. et Heloisæ conjugis ejus opera. Edita ex MMS. Codd. F. Amboesii [André Duchesne?] cum ejusdem præfatione apologetica, et censura doctorum Parisiensium. *Parisiis,* 1616. 4°.

Another copy. [Imperfect. The title-page and first six pages of the preface wanting.]

P. A. et Heloisæ conjugis ejus opera; nunc primum ex MMS. codd. in lucem edita studio Andreæ Quercetani. [This is the same edition as the above, with the exception of the preface and the censura.] *Parisiis,* 1616. 4°.

These three entries are what I call "useful," being "full and accurate." The last is not so long as No. VI., which is, however, worse than useless, not being "accurate," that is to say, stating that the book contains what it does not. On the other hand, the two entries Nos. II. and III. are not "useful," being neither full nor accurate: not "full," because they do not state, as they ought, that the copy there described does contain part of the "præfatio apologetica," and of the "censura;" not "accurate," because if it do not contain the whole, it is because the book is imperfect, which an "accurate" catalogue ought to have stated. And, for the present omitting to make further remarks on these several entries, I content myself with observing that a "full and accurate" catalogue informs us that there are two sorts of copies of this edition: one with the "Præfatio apologetica," without the name of Duchesne, who, *it is said*, wrote it; and another, *without* that Præfatio, but *with* Duchesne's name.

I trust, my Lord, that you will agree with me that no catalogue of a large public library, like that respecting which the Royal Commissioners are to inquire, can be called "useful" in the proper sense of the word, but one in which the title are both "accurate," and so "full" as to afford *all* that information respecting the real contents, state, and consequent usefulness of the book which may enable a reader to choose, from among many editions, or many copies, that which may best satisfy his wants, whether in a literary or scientific, or in a bibliographical point of view.

By an alphabetical catalogue it is understood that the titles be entered in it under some "headings" alphabetically arranged. Now, inasmuch as in a large library no one can know beforehand the juxtaposition of these headings, and it would be impossible to arrange them in the requisite order, if they cannot be easily shifted, each title is therefore written on separate "slips" of paper or "cards," which are frequently changed from one place to another as required. It is self-evident, that if these "slips" or "cards" be not uniform, both in size or substance, their arrangement will cause mechanical difficulties which take time and trouble to overcome; and those on thicker material, as board, tear and wear off those on thin paper. Hence the titles of a catalogue on "slips" cannot be amalgamated with those of one on cards, nor can a change be made in either system, however desirable it might have been to follow a different plan from the beginning, without altering the whole. The entire mass of 300,000 slips, for instance, of old titles in an increasing library must be transferred to cards were it deemed necessary to alter from "slips" to "cards" for books that are daily added to such a library. It would not answer to keep the old slips and adopt cards for the additions. A slip is less expensive, takes up less room, in thickness at least; and if it be broader or longer than a card it affords more room for "full" titles and for "accurate" information. It wears out sooner, is not so easily shifted, and is more easily destroyed or mislaid.

Even at first, therefore, and when a new catalogue of a new collection is about to be commenced, it requires to be considered whether the catalogue is to be very extensive and carried on for years and years, and the same slips preserved and continued—whether the titles are to be "full and accurate" or otherwise, and whether there may be no difficulty in finding accommodation for keeping these titles in good order and perfect safety. The space that these titles will occupy, in proportion with the material on which they are drawn up, is not an insignificant point in a vast collection. Titles which on "slips" occupy 360 square feet, three inches deep, will require 1500 square feet, of the same depth, on moderately thick cards of the size of the slips.

It is to be considered that it is not every part of a room that is available for the preservation of arranged titles on slips or cards. They must be preserved in some place fitted up for the purpose of keeping them in the order in which they are to remain, that they may be easily accessible either for use or for additions; but accessible only to those few persons who are responsible for the completeness of the catalogue as well as for its accuracy; it being manifest that if, through ignorance, carelessness, or love of mischief, a few bundles of loose titles be either disarranged or destroyed, the most ludicrous as well as the most serious mistakes may be the consequence, and the work of many years and of many persons may be thrown into irremediable confusion in a quarter of an hour by the first individual who has the inclination as well as the opportunity of so doing.

The name of Alphabetical Catalogue is now universally applied to that kind of catalogue in which the titles of books are arranged in the alphabetical order of the surname of the author, which surname is taken as a heading; and whenever no surname of the author occurs, some other word is taken as a heading (as I shall have presently the honour of stating at some length), which is arranged in its proper place with the surnames of authors, in alphabetical order. These headings, the necessity of which is manifest in an alphabetical arrangement, are not necessarily requisite in a classed catalogue, where the divisions and subdivisions of the classes may be totally independent of the alphabet. For instance—to arrange in an alphabetical catalogue the edition of Abælard's works, printed in 1616, above referred to, it was necessary to put the heading "Abælardus" to it, which fixed the order in which the title was to be arranged in a catalogue containing only AAGARD'S works in Aa, and none before ABANO—that is to say, between AAGARD and ABANO. The same might be said if, in a classed catalogue, what are called "Fathers" were to be arranged alphabetically, according to their names or surnames in that class. But, if the FATHERS be arranged not in the alphabetical order of names or surnames, but in a chronological order, according to the time when they flourished, then Abælard's works would require no heading but the title only; and a "class-mark" (for instance, "Fathers, XII. cent.") in a corner, to show the "class" and section to which the book belongs. Thus, ex. gr., No. VI.

would be inserted, it may be, between that of a work of Hugo de Sancto Victore and that of the works of St. Bernard, the three having lived in the twelfth century, and they would stand thus:—

Ven. P. HUGONIS DE SANCTO VICTORE quæstiones in epistolas D. Pauli Apostoli, nunc primum editæ studio Nicolai Buscoducenis. *Lovanii, Theodoricus Martinus Alostensis,* 1512, in 4°.

PETRI ABÆLARDI, S. Gildasi Abbatis, et HELOISAE conjugis ejus, cœnobii Paraclitensis Abbatissæ, opera nunc primum ex MSS. codd. eruta, et cum præfatione apologetica pro Petro Abælardo per FRANCISCUM AMBŒSIUM (ANDREAM QUERCETANUM), et censura doctorum Parisiensium, in lucem edita studio ac diligentia ejusdem Andreæ Quercetani. *Parisiis, Nicol. Buon.* 1616, in 4°.

D. BERNA[R]DI, Abbatis Clarevallensis, opera omnia, accuratissime recognita studio et labore IUDOC CLICHTHOVEI. *Parisiis, Claudius Chevallonius.* 1540, in fol.

These entries are here arranged in proper order, in consequence of the directions given in the class-mark ("Fathers, XII. cent."), which forms no part of the title, and they require no heading, a circumstance to which I shall have occasion to allude hereafter.

The alphabetical order of surnames and other headings must be on an uniform plan—that is to say, the order of whatever alphabet is once adopted ought to be strictly adhered to throughout. In any catalogue, but more particularly in that of a large library, the *slightest* deviation from the strictest and most uniform alphabetical arrangement renders it impossible to find what is required; and, by want of accuracy in this apparently trifling particular, a catalogue becomes useless. Suppose we place under ALFONSO what a student may properly expect to find under ALPHONSO; in a small catalogue ALPHO may be next to ALFO—in a large catalogue many and many pages and hundreds of entries may intervene between the two. And with respect to the variations in the order of an alphabet, if the principle be adopted of placing the letter D in the fourth and G in the seventh place, D ought always to precede G, even in headings which originally belonged to a language, like Greek, in which G precedes D; and thus, for instance, DIODORUS ought always to precede DIOGENES.

These remarks will not be deemed unimportant by those who know that an extensive library contains thousands of works in other languages than Greek, differing even more than this does from the Latin alphabet, in all of which the application of this principle is of great consequence.

And here, my Lord, it may not be out of place to notice the difficulties which arise in expressing, according to the English alphabet, the sounds of letters which occur in foreign names, but which have no fixed equivalent in that alphabet, or express in a very peculiar manner the sounds occurring in other languages. The Russian Ж is sometimes represented by Zh or J. The Ч in the same tongue is represented by Ch or Tsch; Щ is represented by *Shch* or *Schtsch*. In modern Greek B represents both V and B; and the latter, that is English B, is sometimes represented by $M\pi$.

The manner of proceeding in the compilation of a catalogue is well deserving the attention even of those who are not bound to execute such a work. The name of an author, the title of a work, its imprint, size, &c., are all matters of fact to be learned correctly from the book itself and nowhere else. Each volume of which a library consists must, therefore, pass through the hands of the compilers of its catalogue, in order that these facts may be carefully and accurately ascertained. It is manifest that if a collection of books has never been catalogued or inventoried in any way whatever, there is no other method of making a complete catalogue of its contents than by taking down every book, in the order in which it stands on the shelves, and writing out its title in a correct and accurate manner. But if any catalogues, lists, or inventories exist, is there any shorter method of compiling a "full and accurate complete catalogue, on an uniform and consistent plan," of such a collection, than that of taking down the books in the order in which they are placed on the shelves? If the catalogue is to be alphabetical, why should not all the books which are to be under A be catalogued on slips before those under B, and then arranged, transcribed, or printed, and made useful at once, and so on with all the other letters?

In order to appreciate fully the advantages and disadvantages of the two systems, it is necessary to enter into the details of the execution of each.

When I proceed to catalogue the books in the order in which they stand on the shelves, I place myself before the press which is to be catalogued, and the volumes are taken down by myself or an attendant, and laid before me on a table in the same order in which they are placed in the press. If there be old titles on slips in existence, they are placed in the volumes by an attendant, who can easily find them, provided the whole mass of titles be arranged beforehand in the same order as the books to which they refer. If titles on slips do not exist, it depends on the manner in which the old titles were drawn up to decide whether it is worth while to have them under the eye whilst the new titles are in the course of preparation. Old titles drawn up like those marked No. I. and II., are of no use whatever; titles drawn up like No. VI. may be useful. That title supplies some information respecting the editor and annotator of the work, and directs the cataloguer's attention to the apologetical preface, and to the name of D'Amboise assumed (or said to be assumed) by Duchesne. Even although, when compiling a new catalogue aiming at "accuracy," all these points cannot be taken for granted as true and ascertained, it is of infinite advantage to have the cataloguer's attention called to them as doubts for investigation. In all cases in which, in the compilation of a new "full and accurate" catalogue, it may be desirable to make use of the old titles, this can only be done by having them in slips, because, even when catalogues in volumes are in existence, they are in use for other purposes, and because to have to turn to the entries in such volumes is an unnecessary waste of the time of the cataloguers, who can be better employed while the titles are being transcribed, if necessary, from the volumes on to slips.

If I proceed to catalogue, first, the books which must come under letter A, then those which come under B, and so on, I attempt what it is absolutely impossible to carry out in a complete manner. How can I know, till the whole library is catalogued, which work will be under A and which under Z? and if I cannot know this till the work is gone through, how can I, beforehand, select A, then B, &c.? But, it is urged, suppose we have an alphabetical catalogue already, with the old titles we may find works under A, under B, &c. No doubt the works which were under A in the old catalogue will be found, but will these be part of the same letter in the *new* catalogue assumed to be in the course of compilation? It is with the preparation of the titles for *this* work that we are *now* occupied, and it is impossible, from the very circumstance of a new catalogue being wanted, that the headings of the titles in the old should be generally the same. It is therefore manifest that many titles under A will have to be transferred to other letters, and that a still greater mass of titles under the other letters will have to be transferred to letter A, but not discovered—and therefore not transferred—till the whole of the other letters are gone through. Add to this the trouble, or in other words, the expense, of sending men all over the library to hunt for works under the letter in the course of cataloguing, taking them to the cataloguers, replacing them, and adopting proper precautions with the view of being able to ascertain—what always takes time—where the book is to be found, supposing a reader asks for it, whilst out of its place for the purpose of being catalogued.

In a large public library, daily frequented by a large number of readers, it is of the greatest importance to interfere as little as possible with their convenience; and nothing is calculated to interfere with it so much as the not finding a volume where it ought to be. The plan of going to the books, and having few of them only removed, and that close to their fixed and known place, interferes the least with the readers, and with the general service and good order of a library. It is, moreover, the only way of having a really *complete* catalogue of the whole collection, as nothing is required but to proceed regularly from press to press, and from shelf to shelf, and from book to book. No book can be omitted: it is impossible. But going first through letter A, then B, &c., makes it certain, not only that every one of these letters will be incomplete till the whole collection is gone through, but that if any work be omitted in the old catalogues, lists, or inventories, by which alone, and not by searching the library itself thoroughly, the material existence of a work is ascertained, that same work will then be omitted, and its existence in a collection be totally unknown till a thorough search takes place in the manner first proposed —viz. looking through the collection itself in a regular and detailed manner.

As observed before, the headings in an alphabetical catalogue are generally according to the surname of the author. But, even when the author's name occurs, difficulties meet us as to how to adopt a heading. I want to consult a work the title of which is exactly as follows:—

Camera ed iscrizioni sepulcrali de' liberti, servi ed ufficiali della casa di Augusto, scoperte nella via Appia, ed illustrate con le annotazioni di Monsignor Francesco Bianchini Veronese l'anno MDCCXXVI. *Roma, Salvioni*, 1727, fol.

I look under BIANCHINI, and I find the work in the catalogue of a library to which I have access. Wishing to see another work of the same author, I consult the same catalogue and I do not find it; the title of it is:—

Hesperi et phosphori nova phenomena, sive observationes Circa Planetam Veneris. . . . editæ a Francisco Blanchino Veronensi. *Romæ, Salvioni,* 1728, fol.

I conclude that it is not in the collection. A student, however, who had seen it there, but was at a loss where to find the former work, which I had seen and he could not discover, informs me that it is entered under BLANCHINUS, whilst the first, I inform him in return, was entered under BIANCHINI. To avoid, therefore, making two authors of one, and save trouble to the readers, it is desirable to enter all the works of the same author under the same name; but in the case proposed should we prefer BIANCHINI or BLANCHINUS? The former might be deemed preferable, being the original vernacular form, but then we must adopt ALCIATI and TOMMASO D' AQUINO, instead of ALCIATUS and THOMAS AQUINAS. If the reverse be adopted, shall we have GROTIUS and not GROOT, and

CANDIDUS instead of WHITE? But occasionally persons have two surnames, as in Audin-Rouvière, Albergati-Capacelli, Cervantes-Saavedra, Baumgarten-Crusius, and so on. Which of them is to be prefered? ANTONIO ALCALA GALIANO calls himself GALIANO; his uncle DIONISIO ALCALA-GALIANO used both surnames together and joined them by a hyphen. And what is to be done with authors who change their surname? It also occurs very often that works are to be catalogued written by persons who, instead of using their family surname, take that of a title or of a see, or who write under their family surname, then under one adopted, and lastly under one or two titles. Lord Francis Leveson Gower, Lord Francis Egerton, the Viscount Brackley, and the Earl of Ellesmere are all one person; and Charles James Blomfield, Charles James Bishop of Chester, and Charles James Bishop of London are all one likewise. Nor is the case dissimilar of women, who may write under their maiden as well as under their husband's family's surname, if they marry.

Saints, sovereigns, and friars of some orders are known by their first or Christian name only, and the two latter use that alone. The case is occasionally the same with great artists, as Rafael, Michel-Angelo, &c. Some of these take their name from a country, as Correggio and Spagnoletto; others from some peculiarity, as Bronzino. Few people know that the family surname of Saint Bonaventura is Fidenza, or that of Saint Bernardino is Albizeschi. No one knows who Brother Cherubin d'Orleans was, although Brother Paolo da Venezia is well known. And with respect to sovereigns, or princes of sovereign houses, has Joseph King of Spain the same right to sink his family name Buonaparte or Bonaparte (Buonarroti or Bonarroti, Buonamici or Bonamici?) as Charles XIV. of Sweden that of Bernadotte? And what shall we do with Teodoro (in English he is Theodore, and in Russian Theodore would be Feodor) King of Corsica, James III. of England, Hentry V. of France, and Charles V. King of Spain? But in the case of first or Christian names, are we to preserve them in their original form? All the French LOUIS will continue to be so and not Lewis; PAUL of Russia will be PAVEL; ALBERT of Brandenburg or of Austria must be ALBRECHT. And for countries are we to say VENEZIA or VENICE; NAPOLI or NAPLES; MUNICH or MÜNCHEN; VIENNA or WIEN?

There are books, moreover, which, although apparently with an author's name and surname or either, yet in reality want both. CLERICUS may be a clerk or clergyman, and may be CLERK or LECLERK; JUSTUS BARONIUS may be the name of a relation of the great annalist, or a name assumed by a person of a totally different family; BUTTERMAN may be the real name of a locksmith or one assumed by Louis XVI.; and VOLTAIRE'S name may appear on the title of a work written by CONDORCET, or that of HUME on that of one written by VOLTAIRE himself. It is not always possible to distinguish when a name is real or imaginary, or when a work is really by the author it pretends to be by or is apocryphal. And even although one person who has made researches may know it, it is not to be expected that it will be as well known to those who have only seen the book or seen it quoted under the apocryphal name. But suppose it is quoted under the author's real name?–

Reflexions d'un Citoyen Catholique sur les Lois de France relatives aux Protestans; par M. de Voltaire. 8°. *Maestricht,* 1778.

Those who do not know it is by Condorcet will find it with Voltaire's other works if the book be catalogued as the real production of Voltaire; but in this case, if quoted as Condorcet's, one who does not know the assumed name under which it was published will be unable to discover it. On the other hand, if under CONDORCET, it will never be found by those who know of it only as one of Voltaire's productions. Do not works written "by a late Archbishop of Malines," "by the titular Archbishop of Armagh," "by the Author of Waverley," &c., offer difficulties?

But works are sometimes published under initials only. Are we to consider these as names or initials of names, or are they to be passed over altogether? Suppose they are not passed over altogether (if passed over, the work will have to be considered purely and simply as anonymous), in what part of the alphabet are they to be entered, under the first or the last letter if there be more than one? In most languages the surname or family name comes after the first name; not so in Hungarian, nor always so in Italian and other languages. If we adopt the first letter, we most likely enter a book under the initial of a Christian name, and possibly under that of a title.

Las Obras del famoso poeta D. J. D. M. 4°. *Madrid,* 1800.

If I enter it under *D.,* I enter it under the intial of *Don.* On the other hand, an Englishman suspects a doctor of medicine under D.M. In this case, however, the initials mean DON JUAN DE MENA, and M is the initial of the surname of the author. And even in English M.D. may mean *Medicinæ Doctor,* as well as MICHAEL DRAYTON; W. S. may stand for *Writer to the Signet,* as well as for WILLIAM SHAKSPERE or WALTER SCOTT; and even M.A. or A.M. for *Magister Artium* or *Artium Magister* (car on dit l'un et l'autre) as well as for MARK AKENSIDE or ALEXANDER MALCOLM. But what if these initials be preceded by other initials, and either set be printed in distinct type? do the initials D.D. mean *Doctor Divinitatis* (very strange Latin by the bye) either in the series T.S.G. *D.D.,* or in that *R.A.* D.D. in the following titles? "An Appeal to the Public for the Erection of Floating Chapels in our principal Seaports, by *R.A.* D.D., 8vo., *Liverpool,* 1846," and "The Claims of Lay Impropriators to Tithe, according to the Canon as well as Statute Law, by T.S.G. *D.D.* 12mo. *London,* 1818." If librarians knew for certain which initial stood for the name, and if every reader were to be supposed possessed of the same knowledge, the question would be easily settled, and the work placed under that initial; but if a work by H. D. B. E. M. is not known to be by BUNAU, one would never look for it under B in a catalogue which professes to place this class of books either under the first or under the last of these initials, although the cataloguer might know that the meaning of these initials is *Henricus de Bunau Eques Misnicus.* The cataloguer ought to follow his rule strictly, and place the books either under H or under M, but never under B, as he would thus assume a previous knowledge in the generality of readers that cannot be in fairness expected from them.

There are works, the authors of which are well known, whose surnames, from a variety of causes, it is very embarassing to select as headings under which to put the work to be catalogued. The BIBLE is generally considered one work, although a collection of many, mostly with an author's name. Which, if any, is to be preferred? And if no name of the author of any part of the Bible can be preferred, what name or word ought to be adopted for an alphabetical arrangement in cataloguing the Scriptures? Works published by learned or other societies are of a peculiar nature also for the purpose now under consideration. Transactions and Memoirs of

Academies are collected works of several authors; the same may be said of Reviews, Magazines, and other periodical publications. If such headings be adopted as *Academies* and *Periodical Publications*, the question arises very often in practice what is an Academy and what is a periodical publication? Was the College of Surgeons and Barbers an academy or learned society? What constitutes a periodical publication? Are the street-directories, the law-list, the annuals, periodical publications? Almanacs and calendars are periodical publications of a peculiar sort; some are published with an author's name, some with a name that may at one time have been that of the author, some anonymously. Occasionally they are printed with other works of an undefined nature, such, for instance, as directories and law-lists; and the Racing Calendar or Newgate Calendar is a very different publication from the Oxford or Cambridge Calendar.

With respect to the acts, orders, records, resolutions, &c., of other societies than such as may be properly included among those designated as "learned," the question is not less extended. Political societies come first, and their legislative enactments claim precedence. An act of Parliament or any other law becomes the act of a political society, and binds its members from the moment that the sovereign authority, to whom the laws and constitution of that society give the power, sanctions such an act and completes it. The acts of Parliament become so only by the sanction of the monarch; so does a law in France, &c. In despotic countries the head of the state alone makes laws. Although therefore it is true that the monarchs in England and in France, as well as in Russia, have a great share in making the laws, and are, in a greater or less degree, their authors, it is, nevertheless, true that such an authorship is not to be compared to that of the writings which are penned by these high persons in their private capacity. Again, Queen Anne's speeches in her Parliament are not hers in the same sense and manner as her letters to Mrs. Masham. Lambertini is not the author of the bulls which he issued as Pope, in the same manner as he is the author of so many learned works on canon law; and neither of these authorships is of the same class as that of the same personage when publishing laws as a temporal sovereign.

Many of the rules which are adopted for the high acts of nations may be adapted to the acts of certain minor corporations. There are some societies, however, which require special rules; and then the question may ultimately arise, what is a society to which these rules, whatever they be, may be applied?

Religious societies or corporations, besides publishing their statutes, regulations, &c., issued books of a totally different description, such as missals, breviaries, prayer-books, &c., as also works strictly like acts of academies and learned societies. And with respect to prayer-books, they are often issued, not under the name of the sect for whose use they are framed, but under the name of the place of worship where these sects meet, or for which such books are intended. It often occurs that many of the works hitherto mentioned, as well as many others anonymous in the strictest sense of the word, are either published singly with slight modifications, or adapted to certain purposes, or collected in the same manner, or merely collected without any alteration, with or without an editor's name. Take the case of the following work:—

Lord Campbell's Libel Act (6 & 7 Vict. cap. 96), with an Introduction on the Law of Oral Slander; commentaries upon each section of the Act; forms of indictments, pleas, &c.; and an Appendix containing extracts from the evidence given before the Select Committee of the House of Lords. By John Humffrey Parry. 12mo. *London*, 1844.

This book contains the whole of the act and something more; supposing it contained only the act and Mr. Parry's comments on it, would it be right to catalogue it as the act itself alone would be catalogued; and if not how? Is there no difference between one of Shakspere's plays with notes and an act of Parliament with notes? Such publications as the *Code Forestier, Code Municipal, Code du Notariat,* being collections of laws on forests, municipal corporations, notarial acts, &c., in France digested and arranged on a certain system, and published with or without an editor's name, are certainly essentially different publications from the *Code Civil* or the *Bulletin des Lois.* The collections of Graevius, of Muratori, &c., contain the text of certain separate works published in a series of volumes, sometimes abridged, but without any other alteration besides. Are they to be catalogued under the collector's name? Where are we to place the "Rerum Britannicarum Scriptores," printed at Heidelberg in 1587, without an editor's name? And the "Scriptores rei rusticæ" beginning so; the "Opera agricolationum" beginning so; and the editions beginning simply "M. Catonis ac M. Terentii Varronis de re rustica libri," &c., followed by the other authors' names—every one of these editions being without an editor's name? And what is a collection? Are Aratas' and Eratosthenes' astronomical works printed together a collection? If not, do they become so if Hyginus, for instance, be added to them? Is "Pindari Olympia, Pithia, Nemea, Isthmia: Cæterorum octo lyricorum carmina Alcæi, Sapphus, Stesichori, Ibyci, Anacreontis, Bacchylidis, Simonidis, Alemanis," a collection? If not, does it become so by having "nonnulla etiam aliorum"?

I have avoided, as carefully as I could, touching on a most important and numerous class of books which are published without any name, either real or fictitious, in any part of the book, without either initials or the name of a corporate body. How are these to be disposed of in alphabetical order with the names of authors? This question is the most important that can be propounded in the compilation of an alphabetical catalogue. The problem is, to submit to rules, intended for names of authors, works without such names. M. Barbier, in his preface to the second edition of his most useful work, "Dictionnaire des ouvrages anonymes et pseudonymes," makes the following observations on the subject:—"I had to choose between the two principal methods hitherto adopted for indicating anonymous and pseudonymous works. The first consists in following strictly the first words of each title; the second in selecting the principal word in the title, that is to say, the word which makes the subject of the work the soonest known. The first is the simplest and safest: neither the compiler of the catalogue nor those who have to make use of it can be mistaken. To show at once its merit, it will be enough to say that it was adopted by Audiffredi in the magificent catalogue of the Casanate Library. ... Bibliographers who have followed the other method are not consistent with themselves; they sometimes adopt the first word of the title, and sometimes prefer the principal one." It is more difficult than may appear, to those who have not had experience, to find in the title-page the word that makes the subject of a work the soonest known. Sometimes there are several words which seem to have an equal claim to be preferred: for instance—

Proposal of a Duty upon Soap instead of a £12 a-ton upon Wine. Fol.
Is it to be under *soap, wine,* or *duties?*
The Duties at this present time on all Merchandize. 12mo. *London,* 1714.
Under *duties,* or under *merchandize?*

Dissertations théologiques et dogmatiques:–I. Sur les Exorcismes et les autres Cérémonies du Baptême. II. Sur l'Eucharistie. III. Sur l'Usure. 8°. *Paris,* 1727.

Under *exorcisms, baptism, eucharist,* or *usury?*

The present State of Politicks in Europe, with some Observations on the present Posture of our Affairs. 8°. *London,* 1739.

This is the title of a work chiefly relating to the convention concluded in 1739 between Great Britain and Spain. If we are to peruse the book, and find out the word which ought to be preferred as a heading, we try to digest, according to subjects, a catalogue intended and assumed to have been compiled according to authors' names. The reader who wants to know what is the subject of the book is assumed to possess the very information which he wants. Who would look for such a work under CONVENTION, for instance, except one who knows that it relates to that act with Spain? I may be told that *Convention* is the last word that would occur to any one, even if he knew the subject of the work; but this makes my case stronger: it may be the last that might occur to a reader, and the first or only one striking a cataloguer. I shall add two titles only, without saying more, and allow any one's ingenuity to guess under what heading they are or ought to be found in the catalogue of the Museum.

The State and Condition of our Taxes considered. 8°. *London,* 1714.

Réflexions sur la Requeste de Denize ou Nizette. 4°. 1735.

Let it be supposed that in all these cases these works had been entered under the first word of the title, except an article, or, if deemed preferable, under the first substantive, there would be no difficulty. But it is objected: What if the reader do not know the correct title of the book? That is his fault, and not that of the library, the catalogue, or the librarian. An alphabetical catalogue presupposes that a person who wishes to consult a book written by an author, who has not chosen to conceal himself, knows that author's name; if the book be anonymous, it is not too much to expect that he knows its title correctly; and if he do know it at all, he is more likely to know the first words of it than any other. If the person who wishes to find a book do not look under the proper or correct heading, whether because he does not know the name of the author, when there is one, or the correct title, when there is no author's name, the fault is his own. If he look for the works of Villiers Duke of Buckingham under Sheffield Duke of Buckingham, or for those of Milton under Miltown, and is disappointed, there is no help for it. Nor can he complain if he do not find the "Essai sur le Luxe" (anonymously published by Saint-Lambert) under the same heading as the "Discours de la Nature et des Effets du Luxe" (anonymously published by Gerdil). An alphabetical catalogue supposes that he who wishes to make use of it knows exactly what he wants; if he do not, he must first procure that information, and then consult the catalogue in order to find whether what he wants is in the library to which he has access. The information here alluded to as required may be procured from other sources, but it is not to be expected that an alphabetical catalogue will supply it. Nor is it reasonable that those who do know precisely what they want should be put to inconvenience on account of those who do not. Now the convenience of Barbier's method for those who have the correct knowledge in question is plain and undeniable as it is simple and unerring.

Another method, not mentioned by Barbier, is that of placing the anonymous work to be catalogued under the name of the writer, if it happen to be known or conjectured by the cataloguer. But this is assuming that every reader knows or conjectures as correctly and exactly the same as the cataloguer. The following instance deserves consideration. Archbishop Wake wrote in 1700 his "Authority of Christian Princes over their Ecclesiastical Synods." He was answered by Samuel Hill, Archdeacon of Wells; and then appeared;—

A Vindication of the Authority of Christian Princes over Ecclesiastical Synods. 8°. *London,* 1701.

Under what heading is this to be put? If under the supposed author's name, then in Watt's Bibliotheca I find that this was written by Archbishop Wake himself, and I consider myself warranted in placing the work under WAKE. But a reader may chance to find that that same bibliographer, in another part of his work, has attributed the book to a Dr. Turner, and if that reader searches for it under this name in the catalogue compiled by a person who had as good authority for supposing it by Wake, he will be disappointed.

A principle once adopted ought never to be departed from. Barbier never departed from the simple principle of taking the first word—not an article or a preposition—excepting in the case *of panegyrics;* for instance, he places the "Eloge historique de FONTENAY" before the "Eloge de Bernard de FONTENELLE," because FONTENAY is before FONTENELLE, although in any other case he would have placed *Eloge de* in its strictly alphabetical order before *Eloge historique.* He does not, however, do so for lives, which seems inconsistent.

But the fact is that inconsistencies, embarrassments, uncertainties of all sorts seem to be unavoidable from the moment that we depart from the strictly pure, simple, and constant alphabetical order of words as they come. Rules may be drawn up to meet cases and to afford a clue by which to wade through the intricate labyrinth which is thus created; but the application of these rules becomes very difficult: in aiming at consistency we are driven into absurdities, and by arguing from analogies we become so refined that we become unintelligible. There is no case of anonymous works that seems more easy to solve than that of lives, as it appears to be so very easy to put the work under the name of the person whose biography forms the subject of it. The same applies to the case of sermons on the death of a person, panegyrics, &c. Then we extend it to any work relating to any act in the life of a person. "The Duke of Wellington at Waterloo," or "The Duke of Wellington at Verona," are books which may be or, perhaps, have been written, and which may be easily catalogued under WELLINGTON, or WELLESLEY *Duke of Wellington.* The same may be said of the parties to a trial, a lawsuit, &c. But the principle once adopted and having to be applied in connexion with, and regard being had to, other principles which may have been adopted for totally distinct cases, the complication and difficulties greatly increase and become perplexing. Let us suppose, for instance, that the name of a place be adopted as a heading in the same manner as is done with the name of a person and that "The Battle of Waterloo," supposing this the title of a book, were placed under WATERLOO, which seems the easiest, and many would think the most natural and only natural heading; how are we to act in a case like the following?—

An Account of the Battle of Waterloo, fought on the 18th of June, 1815, by the English and allied Forces commanded by the Duke of Wellington, and the

Prussian Army under the Orders of Prince Blucher, against the Army of France commanded by Napoleon Bonaparte. By a British Officer of the Staff. With an Appendix containing the British, French, Russian, and Spanish official details of that memorable Engagement. Fifth edition enlarged. 8°. *London,* 1815.

Is the name of the place where the battle was fought to prevail over those of WELLINGTON, BLUCHER, and BONAPARTE? Another work is:—

An authentic Narrative of the Campaign of 1815; comprising a circumstantial Detail of the Battle of Waterloo. 8°. *London,* 1815.

Is the name "Waterloo" to be selected even in cases like this, when the work professes to be on the campaign of 1815, of which the battle of Waterloo is only a part? But it has what is technically called a half-title, thus:—"French circumstantial Account of the Battle of Waterloo;" and this adds to the complication, as the question arises, how far a half-title differing from the title of a book is to be adopted in cataloguing?

Again:—

French Account of the last Campaign of Buonaparte, by an Eye-witness. Translated by Captain Thornton. With a Plan of the Battle of Waterloo, sketched by the Translator. 8°. *London,* 1816.

Are we to prefer the name of Buonaparte? In addition to the uncertainty created by so simple an extension of the rule from the names of persons to those of places, cases are rendered still more complex and uncertain if the rule as to proper names be extended to countries, nations, &c., and to the adjectives formed from them. Then we are perplexed in the above titles by "ENGLISH *Forces,*" "FRANCE," "PRUSSIAN *Army,*" and "FRENCH *Account.*" But if we go so far, what is to be done with the names of editors? of commentators? of translators? A commentator is in part the author of a book published with his comments and notes on the principal work, which shall be supposed anonymous, whilst the name of such commentator shall be supposed to be given in the book. And with respect to translators the case is peculiar. Although the original of a book be anonymous, if, when translated, it has the name of the translator, the book is not anonymous so far as regards the words in which the anonymous ideas are clothed. If by such reasons we were induced to admit the claims of editors, commentators, and translators, cases would become still more complicated and perplexing.

In considering this point it must not be forgotten that the problem is, how these difficulties are to be solved with a view to the compilation of an alphabetical catalogue. In a classed catalogue in which books are entered without individual headings under the class and peculiar subdivision to which the works are supposed to belong, the three books of which I have just given the titles would be placed, let us suppose, under "Military History," and in such a place in that class, division, or subdivision as might be generally adopted, exclusive, as we suppose, of headings. These three works would be placed together with such of the same class as have an author's name.

I have endeavoured to show how the variety and multiplicity of even the most analogous and consistent rules lead to embarrassment in this matter of anonymous works, and I think it superfluous to add more instances, founded on rules which seem to follow almost necessarily from the most simple ones, the moment that any departure from the single principle of the plain alphabetical order of the first word is allowed. And yet when this principle is not strictly carried out, some rules are requisite to direct the reader; for it must be evident that, however difficult it may be either to settle or to apply these rules, a catalogue is not improved by being drawn up without any rules at all, and leaving to caprice and chance all entries of anonymous publications. As a last consideration I beg to add that the enormous increase of time and expense which is the consequence of the slightest departure from the strict alphabetical arrangement under the first word, is a matter of too much consequence to be lost sight of. Having deeply reflected on the subject, I am of opinion that, in a library like that of the British Museum, the attempt to enter in a consistent, uniform, and intelligible manner the anony- mous works in an alphabetical catalogue, when once the adoption of the first word is abandoned, will cause an increase of trouble and expense of at least one-fifth on the whole.

I have hitherto, my Lord, considered only some of the difficulties that occur at the very beginning of cataloguing a work in nothing peculiar or extra- ordinary, and provided with an appropriate and clear title in the usual manner. But suppose a book without a title-page? or a book without a title at all? or with two title-pages. A book may be without a title-page, either because it is mutilated, or because it never had any. The copy of the works of Abælard, catalogued as shown above under that name (titles No. II. and III.), was imperfect; by not noticing this circumstance the cataloguer gave to the reader the trouble of sending for a book which he found of no service when brought to him. In early printed books there are no title-pages. How are we to proceed? Are we to catalogue such a book as if it had a title, either by making one ourselves, or by taking it from any any other part of the book—from the colophon, for instance, without making any remark on it? But what is to be done when there are two titles to a book—an absurd system general in German books, some of which push the absurdity so far as to have three or four title-pages occasionally? And supposing a book in several langu- ages, and the title in one only, or the title in as many languages as the work, or the title in one language and the body of the work with the head title in another, which language shall we prefer in cataloguing? I am here reminded, my Lord, of a difficulty with respect to names which I ought to have mentioned above. What is to be done with authors who are not consistent in spelling their own names? It is said that Sir W. Raleigh spelt his in sixteen different manners. Brathwaite, we can show, spelt his in six; and every one knows that Shakspere's has been written Shakspear, Shakespear, and Shakespeare. Which of these is to be adopted?

Let us suppose all these preliminaries settled at last; we come to the title. Is it to be written out at full length in the very words of the title-page, if there be one? If there be no title-page, how are we to proceed? Is the title to be made up, or ought it as far as possible to be taken from the book? and when a title is to be made, will it not be better to adopt certain signs by which it may be easily recog- nised that the title in the catalogue is not in the words of the book; and also to distinguish between the words when taken from the title-page and when taken from other parts of the volume? It is obvious that the strict adherence to the words of the title helps a reader at once to identify a book so as to make it impossible to mistake it for any other. A catalogue, in which the reader can rely on a scrupulous attention to these minutiæ, is invaluable, in so far as the student can rely on it without further inquiry as to the existence of a particular edition of a certain work, and spare himself the trouble of calling for many volumes which he sees from the title in the catalogue are not what he wants. How many books have not been supposed to exist owing to fictitious titles, and how many volumes have not been supposed unknown and unique having never been correctly described? How many books have not been supposed to exist in a library, which never were in it, and how many others have not been set down as wanting, although forming part of the collection, owing to inexact titles? All the trouble which I have above supposed to be occasioned to a reader who wanted to see Abælard's works with Duchesne's notes, as described above under titles marked II., III., and VI., was caused by carelessness in drawing up the several titles of the books catalogued—that is, by taking not the titles as they stood in the books, but as the cataloguer had found in existence somewhere.

Whence the difficulty, some persons will say, of copying a title-page exactly as it stands? Although a title ought to be given only in the words of the volume which is catalogued, it is not meant by that that all the words on the title-page should be faithfully copied. The title-page ought not to be always transcribed at full length as it stands, in cataloguing a book. It is not necessary to transcribe the information found in the title-pages of Abælard's works that he was "a philosopher and theologian," abbot at two several places; nor that Heloise was the first abbess of a certain convent after having been his wife; nor that D'Amboise was a "vir illustris" and privy-counsellor; nor that Duchesne was from Tours. All this may and ought to be omitted, generally speaking. There are, however, cases when all these particulars, of no importance in themselves, and not requisite in the great majority of cases, may be absolutely requisite for the "fulness and accuracy" of the title of a very rare or early printed book. And, *generally speaking,* even in common cases, if these words, otherwise insignificant, are the very first of the title, it may be desirable not to omit them. An old edition of some of Æsop's Fables, in Spanish, printed at Seville in 1526, begins thus:—"Libro del sabio et clarissimo Fabulador Ysopo, hystoriado et anotado." Now, although it be well known what an "Æsopus moralisatus" is, and although this be only a translation of it, yet it would be very wrong to omit the otherwise useless words "Libro del sabio et clarissimo Fabulador," and give the title only, as "Ysopo hystoriado." In like manner the title of Agnellus's or Andreas's work, "Vitæ Pontificum Ravennatum," is clear enough, full, and accurate; yet no one would omit the words by which it begins, "Liber Pontificalis." But to return to the instance of the works of Abælardus, it is important not to omit the words "nunc primum edita," as has been done in recataloguing the first of the three copies of this edition in the manner above stated. This is an error: the first edition of a work ought always to be especially noticed; if the title-page does not afford this information it ought to be added, as was done (very properly with a query) in the case of the name D'Amboise, under which some have supposed that André Duchesne had concealed himself. In a well-compiled catalogue the student ought not only to be warned of the additions to, but of the omissions from, a title. It is obvious that to omit only what is useless, and no more, requires great judgment; it is not perhaps so obvious, although equally true, that, in order not to infringe the rule of not altering any word in a title-page, it is often necessary to allow many otherwise useless words to remain. When those who catalogue abridge a title carelessly, they often not only alter the sense and affect the meaning of the author, but render him liable to the charge of ignorance. I have to catalogue the following work of Aristotle:—

Rhetoricorum Artisque Poeticæ libri atque etiam Problematum sectiones omnes.

I might omit the useless words *libri* and *sectiones*, and abridge this title thus:—

Rhetorica: Poetica: Problemata.

But then I alter the words of the title. I cannot say merely—

Rhetoricum Artisque Poeticæ atque etiam Problematum.

This will be considered so absurd as to be impossible. It is not so, however. To give an instance, I can only say that it is very common to see "Opere del Lodovico Ariosto," "Tragedie del Vittorio Alfieri," &c., a word, such as *Signor, Conte, &c.*, being omitted; which renders what is left as absurd as saying "a letter to *the* John Russell," omitting the word "Lord," which was in the title-page.

The title of a work being given, the place where it was printed, the date which it bears, and the size of the volume are to be added; they are the means of identifying a volume or an edition. If the place or date, or both, are wanting, it is desirable, when possible, to add them, because it may be an important fact in literary history to know where and at what time a certain book was printed. As to the size, it is the means, in the great majority of cases, of distinguishing an edition from any other. It is not often that the same work is printed in the same year, in the same place, and of the same size. In a good catalogue the editions from the presses of celebrated or early printers ought to be specified, and any other information given respecting the outward appearance of a work; as, for instance, the number of volumes of which it consists, the separately paged additions or appendixes, the material on which it is printed, that is to say, whether vellum, fine paper, large paper, &c.; the manuscript notes, which may render a volume infinitely more useful or more valuable in proportion to their extent, intrinsic merit, the reputation of the author, &c. There is, moreover, occasionally, some information which it is most important to give and which it is almost impossible, at all events very inconvenient, to introduce in the title. For instance: it is not always certain whether a book is complete or not, whether the date on the title-page is the bonafide date of an edition, or whether it is only an imposition—a new title being in fact prefixed to an old edition; whether the work catalogued be what it pretends to be, and by the author who claims it, or whether it may be doubtful, &c. To decide these points in the body of a title, or even to moot the question, is impossible. The first book printed at Milan by Valdarfer contains several tracts, which are enumerated by Panzer. The work "De Officiis" of St. Ambrose, Archbishop of Milan, and a necrology (passio) of two saints, Vitalis and Agricola, by the same author, being part of Valdarfer's publication, are in the British Museum in a separate form, each, to all appearances, a whole and complete book—one dated 1474, with the name of the printer and of the place where it was printed, the other without any date or name of either printer or place. There are two apparently distinct editions of what purport to be two several translations of the "Orlando Furioso;" one with the name of T. H. Croker at the end of the preface, printed in London, 1755, 4°; the other also printed in London, and 4° likewise, dated 1757, and purporting to be by W. Huggins. In point of fact, these translations and editions are one and the same. No one would think it right to omit this information; and as the most convenient means of introducing it, bibliographical notes are added to the titles.

These notes are far from being approved of by two classes of persons—those who cannot write them, and those who cannot appreciate them. They are required in some cases when one would expect it least. The first edition of Æschylus, printed by Aldus in 1518, purports to be of *six* tragedies; they are, however, *seven;* but, about 700 lines of the "Agamemnon" being omitted, the "Choëphoræ" is printed as part of the "Agamemnon." Aldus printed also, in 1498, the first edition of Aristophanes, containing nine comedies; Giunta, in 1515, printed also what in the title he called "Comædiæ Novem," but to this he added a "little book," containing two more ("Lysistrata" and "Thesmophoriazusæ"); so that he printed eleven comedies, two of which were now published for the first time. Are all these circumstances to be passed by unnoticed?

If all persons could agree in interpreting rules or principles always in the same manner—if all could agree in applying them—if by a strict adherence to any system it were possible not to pass over the name of a single author or of a single production, the finding whether a certain work is or is not in the library would present no difficulty. But this unanimity cannot be expected, nor can infallibility be expected either. Nor is it fair to expect that those who want to use a catalogue know correctly all the modes of spelling a name, or the various ways in which it was used by an author, or both surnames of those who have more than one, nor all the family names of all noblemen and all bishops, nor the Christian names of all saints and all friars, &c. To remedy the defects and inconveniences that may arise from such and many other causes, which will be presently dwelt upon more at length, cross-references have been introduced in all works of this description—that is, entries under other headings than the one under which the works are catalogued, referring those who make use of the catalogue to the entry which is wanted.

It might appear more useful, and when the difficulties of introducing proper cross-references, as I shall presently have the honour to show, are considered, even more easy, to repeat the entries. There is first of all this almost fatal objection to such a plan—that we should have nearly to double the catalogue. Every one of the editions of a work by one of the families of Albi—ex Albiis, Blanco, de Blanchis, Bianchi, Candidi, White, &c.—would have to be entered under every one of those names; every one of the editions of any one work by C. J. Blomfield entered under this name, as well as Charles James Bishop of Chester, and Charles James Bishop of London; every one of the editions of every work of Bacon under this name, as well as Verulam and St. Albans; every edition of every translation of Homer and Virgil (of these and of the following species of cross-references more will be said presently) under those names as well as under those of the translators. The same must be said for works with notes, and works continued, and works with appendixes and supplements from other hands than those of the principal or original or primary author. And the repetition of entries must take place for every one of the various ways in which the names of the translators, annotators, continuators, &c., are used. If this be not done, these re-entries will do more harm than good, as they will lead those who consult a catalogue into the same kind of mistake as that which has been mentioned under Bianchini and Blanchinus. Under such circumstances, therefore, no one will suggest re-entries, but such a system of cross-references as will give all the assistance without being liable to any of the objections which can be urged against re-entries.

It is self-evident that the more numerous these cross-references are the more useful a catalogue must be; it is also self-evident that, as between two catalogues, one drawn up and without any regard to principles or consistency, and another drawn up on an uniform and consistent plan strictly adhered to, cross-references are still more wanted in the former than in the latter; lastly, it is self-evident that, the larger the catalogue is, the more requisite it is to give precise cross-references, if they are to be as useful as one has a right to expect. There are cases when it would otherwise be very difficult and troublesome to derive any benefit from them.

This is the case when the cross-reference is not merely from one surname to another, or from a title, &c., to a family name, but when it is from a work to a work. The work of one author forms not unfrequently so integral a part of the work of another, that, without a cross-reference or a re-entering of the same work over and over again under different headings, one work would disappear, being, as it were, absorbed in another. Without cross-references Pope and Dryden, as translators of Homer and Virgil, would never appear under their own surnames. In the same manner Bentley's name would appear only under Horace for his magnificent work—the notes on that poet; the name of a continuator of a work left imperfect by a former author, that of the authors of a supplement, of appendixes, &c., would likewise not appear; and, what is more, the name of the author of a work, which, it may be, was never printed but in a collection, would be totally and entirely omitted. Now in such and other cases of a similar nature, it is causing too much trouble to him who consults a very large catalogue to give such a cross-reference as "Malone, *see* Shakspere; Bentley, *see* Horace; Maffei, *see* Virgil; Hieronymus, *see* Biblia; Theophrastus, *see* Aristotle; Planudes, *see* Æsop, &c. &c. &c. It will take hours sometimes before we find that particular entry which is wanted under the heading so vaguely referred to. To provide against this inconvenience and avoid the unnecessary increase of the catalogue, it has been imagined to have cross-references of different classes, adapted to the object for which each is intended, and so individualizing the entry referred to as to relieve the person who consults the catalogue from as much trouble as possible. An obvious way of individualizing the entries so as to refer to the precise one which is wanted would be to number them and to refer to that number in the entry from which the cross-reference is made. The progressive number, however, will be interfered with in an alphabetical catalogue by any addition made to the collection. Yet this plan may be of some use if the principal entries are to be immediately fixed and settled at once with a view to printing, certainly not a good catalogue, but the best that can be procured within a very short space of time.

It is impossible to individualize entries till after the heading of them as well as the whole entry is definitively settled. If we omit all the cross-references from a catalogue, and only the principal entries be introduced, and these be numbered, the manuscript or slips may be got ready with great rapidity, as the whole attention needs only at first to be limited to placing the entry under the correct number, which must not be altered. If nothing be done which throws the entry out of the regular series of numbers, on revising the manuscript and on correcting the press, great alterations may be introduced in the rest of the title. Such a catalogue may be, so far as it goes, and if compiled in strict accordance with good and consistent rules, a useful index of the contents of the library; and the cross-references made afterwards, not from the books but from the catalogue, an index to the catalogue itself. This is, however, an expedient which nothing but necessity ought to warrant a librarian in adopting, and which, in the case of an increasing library, will throw additional difficulties in the way of keeping the catalogue in order, difficulties which I am happy not to be obliged here to point out.

The principles of a catalogue being adopted, the question is, how they are to be carried out on an uniform and consistent plan, the work being of such magnitude that no man can hope to carry it out single-handed. We know what kind of headings we want, and on what principle; we know what principles have been adopted as to surnames, as to the language, is to the wording of the title, the imprint, the bibliographical remarks that it is desirable to make the importance of cross-references and of the system on which they are to be drawn up. How are we to ensure the carrying out of the principles adopted in these and in many more cases, which are not here enumerated, partly because it would be too long to enter into details with respect to them, and partly because the variety of cases is so vast, and on many occasions the difficulties are so unexpected and unforeseen, that it is impossible to estimate their nature and the means which may be required to overcome them? It has been imagined to draw up a certain code of rules, in which the principles adopted for all known cases should be embodied and digested in a clear, concise, and simple form. In coming to the determination of drawing up such a code of rules, those who have attempted it have acted, not from actual practice and from experience in such species of codification, but from analogy of what is done in other cases to ensure uniformity. There is no instance of a catalogue equal in extent to that of the British Museum collection of printed books having been attempted, and there is no precedent for rules being embodied to carry into execution even a compilation far inferior in extent. Hence, it is humbly submitted, the reason that there is no catalogue in existence (except one or two of so moderate a length that one person only could draw them up in a long course of years) which is compiled on a well-digested plan, uniformly, consistently, and strictly executed. If the work to be compiled be of so moderate a size as to be compiled from beginning to end by the same person in the best way he may think proper, according to his unfettered discretion, there is no necessity for any code of rules. He adopts what principles he deems proper, and carries them out as he thinks right. It will always be impossible to draw up rules so perspicuously as to enable all those who have to act on them to put on them the same interpretation in every instance. When practical rules are to be drawn up, as in the case under consideration, from theoretical principles only, it is to be expected that the causes of doubt in the interpretation will be greatly increased by ordering theories to be practically applied. The application is rendered still more perplexing if rules are drawn up by men having no practical knowledge of the subject, and whose crude theories are purely offsprings of their imagination, expressed in words the technical import of which these theorists do not understand.

It has therefore been found necessary in practice, in order to insure the due execution of such a vast work, to intrust it to one person only who should superintend it, as the only means of securing as much consistency and uniformity as can be expected in such a compilation, under such circumstances. It is the duty of such a superintendent to see that the rules are properly attended to, to decide to the best of his abilities dubious cases, interpreting the rules when either uncertain or obscure, providing for unforeseen cases, and as far as possible seeing that the precedents adopted in one case be strictly applied to all similar cases, so as to give the whole work that uniformity which is not less essential to the usefulness of a catalogue than accuracy. It is not what is best to be done in individual cases that ought alone to influence the adoption of a certain line of conduct, but what is best to be done in conformity with a general principle adopted. If, for instance, the principle adopted is that of entering the works of noblemen under their family name, it is not because MONTESQUIEU and WELLINGTON are more known under these titles than as SECONDAT and WELLESLEY that we ought to depart from the adopted maxim, and misdirect the student, who cannot foresee that we make a distinction between those two noblemen and a GAETANI Duke of SERMONETA, or a HOWARD Duke of NORFOLK; nor ought we to shrink more from AROUET de VOLTAIRE than from NAPIER of MERCHISTOUN.

My Lord, it can never be too frequently repeated that it is impossible to judge of the correctness of a title without seeing it with the book which it represents. It is not by intuition and *à priori* that we can say which of the titles of Abælard's works is correct, whether a volume is complete or not, anonymous or not, avowedly written by Smith, Smyth, or Smythe. To superintend a catalogue, therefore, it is necessary to revise every title, when drawn up, with the book, and see that it is done as it ought to be—that is, fully, accurately, and consistently. It is superfluous to say that as the work proceeds all parties become more fit to execute it properly. Experience teaches their duties to all. There is less to inquire in revising; on the great majority of cases there is no diversity of opinion; there are, however, many cases when titles require alteration, either because carelessly drawn up, or because some points have not been sufficiently attended to, or because mistakes have crept in, or because a wrong principle has been adopted. After the work has proceeded to a certain extent the superintendent may have the advantage of assistance in correcting any of these defects in a title; but if a case occur when a rule admits of doubt, or when it is obscure, when a precedent is to be created, the consequences of which it is impossible to foresee, when diversities of opinion arise, when cases unprovided for present themselves, when a new principle is to be introduced, then the superintendent must take on himself personally the responsibility of determining what is to be done, and of insisting on what he determines being done, as he alone, being responsible, ought to be the judge of what is best for the whole compilation. These, and these only, appear, from experience, to be the means of carrying on a work of such magnitude with as much despatch as is consistent with its due execution. It is clear that the object intended to be attained by the superintendent being assisted would be defeated if this assistance were to be extensive in point of numbers; it would be opening the way to the very evils which superintendence is meant to prevent; and no one but the person who is responsible for such a work ought to decide how far he can safely call for or rely on assistance in this respect.

My Lord, I trust that in what I have hitherto said there is abundant evidence of the necessity for that peculiar sort of revision and superintendence, in the compilation of a large catalogue drawn up by several hands, which I have endeavoured to describe; that is, strict, special, undivided, and uniform. It can hardly be supposed that, this being admitted, the question should ever have been mooted whether the titles might not be written out by several gentlemen, independent of each other, under a sort of general undefined superintendence of two persons, and afterwards be carefully and properly revised by one. This would be to allow the errors and inconsistencies of several hands to accumulate, and, when the whole mass were deliberately collected, then to ask one man to take down again, one by one, every book, compare it minutely with every title, and make what he can of the catalogue during his lifetime, leaving work for two generations more of revisers. It would be in fact to employ ten men for ten years, for instance, in drawing up an incorrect and inconsistent work, which would require a hundred years and three men in succession to correct. As prevention is better than cure, so is a constant and vigilant superintendence, exercised as the work proceeds, better than a future revision of what is wilfully allowed to be inevitably badly compiled.

I have endeavoured to lay before your Lordship what is required in order to compile a good catalogue of a large library *on slips.* Let us now suppose that such a catalogue is complete, that is, that all the titles are drawn up fully, accurately, and consistently. How is it to be rendered available to the public? We cannot allow the public, as we should an individual of careful habits, or persons responsible for the order of the *slips,* to have access to these titles, because they would soon be lost or misplaced, and sooner or later, according to the material on which they are written, destroyed. The plan then would be to arrange these slips in a certain order, and then to transfer them to volumes, either in print or manuscript.

I shall not trouble your Lordship with details with respect to arrangement, but content myself with pointing out how, especially in long articles, it is necessary to enter the titles coming under the same heading in some order, so as to render it less troublesome to refer to them and find what is wanted. A student ought to know where to find at once the collected and where the separate works of an author— where the translations and where the selections; the cross-references ought not to be mixed with the main entries of works. Then there are works which, although coming under the same heading as the works of an author, are not written by him; these ought not to be mixed with the others. And with regard to works under certain peculiar headings, as Bibles, Liturgies, Periodical Publications, &c., the arrangement of the entries under the chief heading, the division of this into sub-headings where necessary, and the order of the entries under these sub-headings, are matters which require uniformity, consistency, and accuracy, like all the other operations, and in like manner principles and rules for arrangement. In a large catalogue the student will be unable to find what he wants if the entries are not made accurately and consistently. The question whether the titles ought always and in every case to be entered at full length, as they are originally written out on slips, or whether, under certain circumstances, they should be abridged, is deserving great consideration.

In order to save room, it has been considered expedient to shorten titles on entering them when two follow each other wholly the same, excepting the imprint, or alike up to a certain point. In such cases either the whole of the second title or so much of it as is a mere repetition of the foregoing is omitted, and either a line substituted so far as is requisite to show how much is left out, or the words "alia editio" or "another edition," followed by whatever is not conformable to the title of the first in the title of the second entry. The substitution of either a line or the words "alia editio" instead of what is omitted requires great attention, and may be

the source of such errors as to render worse than useless the transcript of a catalogue, however well executed the original, on slips, may have been. I say "worse
than useless," because such a substitution may convey the impression that such a
work is wholly or partially a repetition of another, whereas in point of fact it may
be totally distinct, and thus students not only be misled in looking in vain for what
does not exist, but be moreover led to believe from the catalogue that certain
books exist that have never been printed. This source of error is avoided if no
abridgment of titles takes place; a system, however, which adds considerably to the
bulk of a long catalogue, but at the same time contributes considerably to its
utility, besides tending in so great a degree to secure its accuracy. It causes, moreover, a very great saving of time; for it is a far easier thing merely to arrange the
titles for transcription, according to the plan that may have been adopted, whatever
that may be, than to alter them in consequence of the place which they may
occupy in the transcript. These alterations may be of little extent in a small catalogue in which but few editions of the same work may occur, and consequently not
many omissions be requisite in the titles, but, when the number of these volumes is
great, the alterations required are by far greater in proportion than the comparative
difference between the number of volumes.

Connnected with the saving of time and the more or less rapid arrangement of
the titles on slips for further use, is the question, whether these titles for a catalogue such as I have had all along in view while I have been considering this question, that is to say, one unparalleled in extent as well as in fulness of titles, in special cross-references, in accurate and useful information—a catalogue which
probably contains more than a million of entries—a catalogue to be placed in the
hands of the public who have access to a library of 420,000 volumes and not much
less than 600,000 works—whether the titles of such a catalogue are to be printed or
merely transcribed in manuscript?

If it be determined to print such a catalogue, it seems to me that it must in
the first place be drawn up in manuscript on slips, that the slips must be arranged
for press in the precise and exact order and form in which they are to be printed,
and, lastly, that they be sent to press, the press corrected, and the copies struck
off. These steps in preparing and printing a catalogue may appear self-evident, and
the detail of them consequently superfluous; yet, my Lord, it has been contended
that a catalogue might and ought to be printed as fast as the titles could be got
ready in manuscript. Therefore it is that I urge again and again that no alphabetical
catalogue can be sent to press until the whole of the titles from A to Z are not only
written in a consistent, full, and accurate manner, but until they are consistently
and accurately arranged for press. The correctness of the very first entry may
depend on that of the last; and as no human being can know *à priori* whether the
very last work that comes to the hands of the cataloguer will have to be entered
under A or under Z, it is necessary to ascertain this by cataloguing the book first,
then to insert the title in its proper place, and then to print it when that part of the
catalogue is printed. By beginning to print before, we are certain to bring out a
hurried, ill-digested, disgraceful mass of titles of more or less of the works forming
a library, but certainly not of the whole: a mass destined to mislead the public,
both by what it contains and by what it omits. And this hurried, ill-digested, disgraceful, and imperfect mass of titles must take longer to print than if the whole
were ready and fit to be put in the printer's hands, as the printing must be delayed

by the preparation of what is technically called "copy." This copy may be as care-lessly prepared as any one can imagine,–hundreds and hundreds of titles may be purposely omitted in order to proceed rapidly in bringing out something, and mis-lead the public by offering them as the catalogue of the books in a library what is the catalogue of only part of it–yet even then the preparation of "copy" will take time and delay the printing, which, if all the "copy" was got ready beforehand in a proper manner, would proceed with ten or twenty times the rapidity, to say nothing of accuracy and completeness.

It is very material to the preparation of the titles for a catalogue, after the whole of them have been written out in a proper manner, to know whether these titles are to be merely transcribed–and if transcribed, in what manner–or whether they are to be printed.

The printing of the catalogue of a vast increasing library has been so often considered a very desirable performance, that those who doubt it are looked upon as ignorant or interested parties. It is undoubtedly true that a full, accurate, and complete catalogue of a library, well arranged and well printed, is very convenient to consult. But the first question which arises is,–how can the printed catalogue of an increasing library be complete? Suppose we have a million of titles quite ready for press according to a certain plan, and that the printing of them begins, who is to superintend the press? Of course those who are conversant with the subject, trained to the work, well acquainted with the principles on which the publication is to be carried out, and who are, as they were during the compilation of the manuscript, under the superintendence of one person responsible for the due execution of the work. A catalogue containing one million of titles will consist of fifty folio volumes of the size of parliamentary papers, each volume containing 500 pages. The fifty volumes will therefore contain about 25,000 folio pages. How long will it take to carry through the press such a work in an accurate and creditable manner? Cer-tainly less than if the printing of the first entries in letter A had begun before those under AD were ready; yet it must take considerable time. Meanwhile, and whilst this huge work is printing, the library increases; what is to be done to render avail-able the titles of these additions? Insert them in manuscript in one, two, or three copies of the catalogue for the use of the library and of the students who wish to consult it; but of what use are the fifty printed volumes if they are not even evi-dence of what the library contains at the very moment they issue from the press? Print a supplement. Well; but the supplement itself is imperfect the very moment it is published. And what will catalogue, supplement, supplement of supplement, and the great-great-grandchildren of the race be twenty years after the birth of the eldest? And how many volumes shall we have to consult before we have ascertained whether a certain work was or was not in the library within a year or two of the time when the inquiry is made?

In point of fact, however, the inquiry will very seldom, if ever, be made out of the library itself, of which the catalogue is a description, if books are not lent out of it. This is the case at the British Museum. Of what use will it be to know in Yorkshire or in the Highlands that the British Museum possesses the Edinburgh and Quarterly Reviews, Moore's and Murphy's Almanacs, Forcellini's and Stephanus' Lexica, Valpy's Latin Classics, and Rymer's Fœdera? True, I am told, this is not of great use; but it is important to know that the first Homer, and first Horace, and Chaucer's Canterbury Tales by Caxton, and the first edition of the Bible in Latin or

English, and so on, are in the Museum. The argument therefore is, that, because it is important and may be useful to perhaps ten men in the provinces to know that there are ten or twelve or twenty thousand rare books in the library of the British Museum, the catalogue of which may be drawn up in two volumes, it is necessary to print forty-eight volumes more. Even the catalogue of rarities would be of more use to book-collectors than to literary or scientific men. Any one engaged in a work or pursuit of importance, who feels the want of consulting a large library, and who has the means and leisure of visiting the capital for that purpose, does not want to consult merely a rare book, the existence of which in the British Museum he wishes to ascertain before he determines on his journey. He wants to consult more than one book, and these not all rare: he is sure that the great majority of them at least must be in the British Museum. He needs no printed catalogue of the whole library to be perfectly certain of that. The plea for printing the catalogue of the whole of an enormous library, like that of the British Museum, is the great advantage that it will confer on students, and I contend, my Lord, that it confers hardly any— certainly none commensurate with the expense. I contend also that, if the catalogue of a large increasing public library is to exist *only in print*, the public will be injured by it; and that they would be infinitely more benefited by a good catalogue in manuscript, well kept up, than by one printed. If the library belongs to a nation so extravagantly fond of spending money as to wish that that part of the public which does not attend at the library, nor read in it, or even know of its existence (and the latter class, my Lord, is more numerous than is generally supposed), should never-theless have the opportunity of knowing what books were in it up, say, to twenty years previous, its catalogue may be printed—(what is to bring within reach of this class of persons a catalogue in fifty or sixty folio volumes?); but for the more use-ful purpose of making the contents of a vast increasing public library readily accessible to those who attend such an institution in order to make use of its treasures, the catalogue on the spot ought to be in manuscript.

A printed catalogue, kept up with manuscript additional entries, is, in fact, a catalogue divided into two alphabets, one printed, the other manuscript. The great advantage which those who have to make use of it derive from the manuscript additions being bound up in the same volume with the printed part is, that they are not obliged to make search in two volumes. There is, however, this disadvantage— that to keep the manuscript additions as near as possible to the printed pages (which are otherwise bound up at so great a distance from each other as to cause considerable trouble in finding them), the manuscript entries must not be far apart; not being far apart, the interval between some of them is soon filled up, and then the difficulty arises of preserving the strict alphabetical order. No one can think of departing from it—the objections are too clear and self-evident. For the purpose of inserting an entry between two others, if there be no space in the exact spot which the new entry must occupy without infringing upon the alphabetical arrangement, we must have recourse either to erasing one or more of the entries—supposing there is room either above or below them, where one or more can be removed—and in this case, to enter one title, we must, 1st, erase one or more of the titles already entered; 2nd, re-enter them in a new place; 3rd, enter the additional title. If there is no more room for additional entries, even by erasing one or two of the former ones, the contents of a whole sheet must be transcribed on two, three, or four sheets, and so we are driven to recopy perhaps forty titles to make room for one. The more manuscript leaves are inserted between the printed pages, the more are these pages placed asunder, and the less easy is it to find them. Between ARGELATUS and ARGENTUS there may be twenty entries in a printed page; the additional entries in manuscript may amount to forty more; if we put only two on each side of a manuscript leaf, the last printed entry under ARGENTUS, in one page, is ten manuscript leaves off from the next entry, ARGENVILLE, which is at the top of the printed page immediately following.

The amount of manuscript entries must depend on—1st, the completeness of the printed part of the catalogue; 2nd, the additions made to the library. If, by going to press before the whole manuscript of a catalogue be ready, we omit printing a number of entries, we must add such entries in manuscript—so that ultimately the more haste the less speed; and, if we print the catalogue of a library which we double whilst printing it, the rapid additions to the collection will greatly increase the number of the manuscript additions of titles to the catalogue.

I beg for a moment, my Lord, to apply these abstract views to the actual case of the British Museum Collection of Printed Books. Suppose a Catalogue (I apply the word "Catalogue," for want of another, to a compilation which would not certainly have deserved it) of that collection had been printed by the end of 1844, what would have been the consequence? 1st, A large number of titles, now at the disposal of those who have to consult our catalogue, would have disappeared, as that part of the alphabet containing the heading under which they would have had to be placed would have been printed before the titles were drawn up. 2nd, All the additions to the library since 1838 (for instance, and probably much earlier) could not of course have been inserted. 3rd, All the additions since 1844—that is, during the time that the library has been increased at a rate of which there is no example, and which ten years ago we never even contemplated—would also have to be added. In conclusion, out of a million of titles, of which the catalogue of such a collection will now consist, possibly four hundred thousand might have been printed in a manner disgraceful to the institution, discreditable to the officers, and the very reverse of useful to the students; while six hundred thousand titles, at least, would have to be added in manuscript, and these, too, incorrectly, as it is impossible ever to add correctly and accurately to an incorrect and inaccurate catalogue. I cannot now diverge into this branch of the subject, but I might easily satisfy your Lordship of the correctness of this position. I shall here merely observe, that the difficulties which it is requisite to overcome in making these manuscript additions, even in a tolerable manner, the time and expense which are required, and the trouble that, under any circumstances, it entails upon those who have to consult such a catalogue, are beyond conception, and will hardly be understood, except by those who will have patience enough to inquire minutely into the practical details of this most important part of the subject. I trust that your Lordship and the other Commissioners will have that patience, and will apply it to the point. Here lies the real ground of complaint against the Catalogue of the Museum; it is only to be regretted that the rashly-proposed remedies have greatly increased the evil.

It has been suggested that, instead of attempting to add manuscript entries to a printed catalogue, the whole of the additions should be entered by themselves in a manuscript catalogue, entirely distinct from that which is printed. But this manuscript supplement would oblige persons to consult two volumes of the catalogue—one printed, the other in manuscript—in the great majority of cases, before they could ascertain whether the work or works they wanted were or were not in the library. This is a serious objection under any circumstances, but more particularly if the catalogues are kept in a public reading-room, accessible to all classes of readers, some of whom are particular in taking as little trouble as possible for themselves, and none whatever for the accommodation of others. There is another objection which I must notice. All those cross-references, which need not be repeated in the manuscript additions to a printed catalogue when these additions are bound up together with it, must be repeated in the manuscript part when it is in distinct volumes. A library under these circumstances has in fact not one catalogue only, partly in print and partly in manuscript, but a portion of such a library has a distinct catalogue in print, and the other part a totally distinct one in manuscript.

On examining, in a large library, a volume of a catalogue partly printed and partly in manuscript, and on my pointing out in it the practical difficulties that occurred in endeavouring to keep up with such a catalogue, one of two gentlemen, a great partisan of a printed catalogue, who was listening to the objections which I urged against the system, asked; Why should not these printed entries be transcribed and incorporated with the rest? I answered; Why should they be printed at all, if we are to transcribe them? He smiled then; but has ever since continued to descant on the great importance of a printed catalogue of a large increasing library. In his theoretic visions he has wholly forgotten the common-sense view he took on considering the subject practically. No doubt a good, well-arranged, and well kept-up catalogue wholly in manuscript is what is wanted in a large increasing library. No page ought to contain more than three entries at first: these three entries should be at full length—not abridged—but as they stand on the slips. The pages should be of a moderate folio size, and no more than two additional entries should ever be made in them. There ought to be no more than five entries on a page; when another title, making the sixth entry in a page, is to be inserted, the whole leaf should be retranscribed on the original plan. One volume of seven hundred pages (three entries each page) would contain 2100. Five hundred such volumes would contain one million and fifty thousand entries, with space to increase the whole to one million seven hundred and fifty thousand. I do not by any means pledge myself to the absolute perfection of the details here hastily suggested; I foresee, for instance, that several leaves would have to be recopied, whilst pages in other parts of the alphabet would remain in their original state. I should therefore wish to consider and reconsider the plan well, and see part of a volume of such a catalogue compiled before finally adopting it: but, whatever modification the details might require, there is no doubt in my mind that the catalogue of a large library, largely increasing, ought to be in manuscript.

The vast number of volumes of such a catalogue will, of course, be a great subject for mirth to those who will not understand that it is no uncommon thing for large libraries to have large catalogues. Let them go and see what is the number of volumes of the catalogue of such libraries as Göttingen, Berlin, Dresden—all inferior in extent to the British Museum collection of printed books—and when they have found what is done in Germany, they may probably not object to it in England. To those who want to make use of a catalogue which is accessible to the public, or even to a large number of persons, there is nothing so inconvenient as to have it bound in a small number of volumes. Two or three or more persons are more likely to be prevented from consulting the same volume at the same time if that volume contain, for instance, the whole of letter A, than if letter A is divided into ten parts; for then one person can consult *Ac,* the other *Af,* the other *Ar,* &c., at the same moment; so that, care being taken that the volumes are of such a size as to be easily replaced in their proper order by paying the slightest attention to the alphabet, a catalogue in five hundred volumes will be more accessible to many persons at the same time than one in fifty, and the latter much more than one in five. The first volume of the New Catalogue of the British Museum, incomplete as it is, was originally divided into sixteen interleaved volumes. One of them became so thick by manuscript additions, that it had to be taken to pieces and rebound in two volumes, so that the whole first volume is now bound in seventeen. That not too much blank space was left in these volumes is proved by the fact that already not only is it necessary to erase and retranscribe some of the manuscript entries, in order to make room for new ones, but entire leaves have to be retranscribed and additional ones inserted. If the twenty-four letters of the alphabet were divided only into seventeen volumes each, the whole would make 408 volumes. But letter A is not one of the longest, and some time hence even the seventeen volumes of that letter will become twenty or more.

Long as this communication is, I can assure your Lordship and the other Commissioners that the subject is very far indeed from being exhausted. I have matter and difficulties at hand to produce, that might easily more than triple what I have already written; and even then more would remain to be said, owing, partly to omissions on my part, and partly to the large number of difficulties unforeseen or unknown till they actually happen, and which occur daily. I have only been able to mention some of the most striking difficulties, and those of the most common occurrence; I have not brought forward any minor difficulty, or one so rarely happening, as to deserve to be looked upon only as an exception.

If I have succeeded in convincing those for whom my observations are intended that the compilation of an alphabetical catalogue of a vast increasing library is a matter not only requiring great attention, but learning and powers of mind, then the Commissioners will, my Lord, be able to appreciate the hasty assertions often made on the subject, and the incorrect views taken of it even by men of science and of learning. I hope the Commissioners will be on their guard against general opinions and vague statements, and that the explanation of the grounds for such opinions and the particulars of these statements will be insisted upon, so as to make it possible to sift them and appreciate their value. Whenever, for instance, the Commissioners are told that there are good catalogues of large increasing libraries printed and well kept up in manuscript for the use of the readers; that so many titles a-day can be prepared; that titles prepared for a classed catalogue can be used at once for an alphabetical catalogue; that titles drawn up by one person without any revision may be sent direct to the printer; that the superintendence and responsibility of one person are not necessary; then I earnestly and respectfully beg of the Commissioners to have specimens of such titles, of such compilations laid before them; and then the hollowness of such statements and the futility of such evidence will be easily exposed. If these specimens be not produced, then the *causa scientiæ* must be inquired into, and the practical knowledge of him who ventures on such dangerous, and to him probably unknown, ground ascertained. As to persons who see no difficulties, who speak of immaculate catalogues, who laugh at rules, at method, at principles, at accuracy, at consistency, and at such other bibliographical *follies*, they are not worth listening to, my Lord, any more than a blind man, or a man who will not look, when he descants on the faults of a painting, or the art of colouring in general.

I have, &c.

A. PANIZZI.

The Earl of Ellesmere,
  &c.   &c.   &c.

Smithsonian Catalogue System

Charles C. Jewett

Editor's Introduction

A bequest by the English chemist James Smithson led to the establishment in the United States of the Smithsonian Institution in 1846. The purpose of the Smithsonian was to promote the "increase and diffusion of knowledge among men,"[*] but an inevitable controversy arose over the means to achieve this. The controversy was dramatic. One of its leading protagonists was Charles Coffin Jewett, newly appointed Librarian and Assistant Secretary at the Smithsonian. Jewett felt the role of the Institution should be to develop a great national library, one that would incorporate within it a union catalog of the holdings of all public libraries in the United States. This he envisioned as the first step in a course that would lead eventually to a universal catalog. "How much this would promote the progress of knowledge... how much, by rebuking the rashness which rushes into authorship, ignorant of what others have written, and adding to the mass of books, without adding to the sum of knowledge."[†]

---

[*]*Dictionary of American Library Biography* (Littleton, Colo.: Libraries Unlimited, 1978), s. v. "Jewett."

[†]Charles C. Jewett, *"Smithsonian Catalogue System,"* in *On the Construction of Catalogues of Libraries and of a General Catalogue and Their Publication by Means of Separate, Stereotyped Titles with Rules and Examples,* 2d ed. (Washington, D.C.: Smithsonian Institution, 1853), 9-10.

In following his vision, Jewett was impassioned and eloquent. Unfortunately, he was also impolitic. His opponent was his supervisor, Joseph Henry, a scientist who felt the role of the Smithsonian should be to provide scientists with the monies needed to carry out their research. The controversey over how to spend Smithson's bequest is emblematic of the antagonism between the two cultures, Jewett representing literature, and Henry, science. It reached its denouement with Jewett's dismissal from the Smithsonian.

The following excerpt is from the introductory matter to the code of rules developed by Jewett for the Smithsonian, and embodies an expression of his vision of a universal catalog and the two primary means to realize his vision. The first is a technological innovation, the use of stereotyped plates; the second is a program of action, cooperative cataloging.

Jewett opens his discussion on stereotyped plates by observing that the costs of printing were such that libraries could not keep their book catalogs current even by making use of supplements. The expense of updating, he argues, could be obviated if each bibliographic record were stereotyped on a separate plate; this would enable the mass production (words Jewett never used) of catalogs. This process would be so inexpensive that every library could afford to have different versions (a classed version as well as an alphabetic version, for example) of its unique catalog. More significantly, the use of stereotyped plates would facilitate the making of union catalogs. Then, as now, technological innovation was seen as effecting economies by expediting the exchange of bibliographic data.

A technological advance that promises to reduce cataloging effort tends to be accompanied by a concern for standardization. If the bibliographic records of one institution are to be used by another, they must be constructed according to a uniform style. For Jewett, a code of cataloging rules exists to promote uniformity, and he formulated what might be called a principle of standardization: "The rules for cataloguing must be stringent, and should meet, as far as possible, all difficulties of detail. Nothing, so far as can be avoided should be left to the individual taste or judgment of the cataloguer." Cataloging theory since Jewett has vacillated between the legalistic position reflected in the lines quoted above and the position represented by Cutter, which holds that cataloging is an art that applies a few highly generalized rules by analogy to specific cases.

ES

**Ibid., 8.

Further Reading

Cutter, Charles A. *Rules for a Dictionary Catalog.* 4th ed., rewritten. Washington, D.C.: Government Printing Office, 1904.

Selections reprinted in this volume. Argues for user convenience, as opposed to standardization and consistency, presenting the opposite theoretical approach to catalog code design.

Osborn, Andrew D. "The Crisis in Cataloging." *Library Quarterly* 11 (October 1941): 393-411.

Reprinted in this volume. Presents a caricature of the legalistic school of cataloging.

Lubetzky, Seymour. *Cataloging Rules and Principles.* 1-8. Washington, D.C.: Processing Department, Library of Congress, 1953.

Oppressed by the sheer number of rules required to legislate practice for every bibliographic contingency, Lubetzky asks the famous question: "Is this rule necessary?"

Smithsonian Catalogue System

Difficulties in Publishing Catalogues

Few persons, except librarians, are aware of the nature and extent of the difficulties, which have been encountered, in attempting to furnish suitable printed catalogues of growing libraries; difficulties apparently insurmountable, and menacing a common abandonment of the hope of affording guides, so important, to the literary accumulations of the larger libraries of Europe.

It is, of course, entirely practicable to publish a complete and satisfactory catalogue of a library which is stationary. But most public libraries are constantly and rapidly increasing. This circumstance, so gratifying on every other account, is the source of the difficulties alluded to.

While the catalogue of such a library is passing through the press, new books are received, the titles of which it is impossible, in the ordinary manner of printing, to incorporate with the body of the work. Recourse must then be had to a supplement. In no other way can the acquisitions of the library be made known to the public. If the number of supplements be multiplied, as they have been in the library of Congress, the student may be obliged to grope his weary way through ten catalogues, instead of one, in order to ascertain whether the book which he seeks be in the library. He cannot be certain, even then, that the book is not in the collection, for it may have been received, since the last appendix was printed. Supplements soon become intolerable. The whole catalogue must then be re-arranged and reprinted. The expense of this process may be borne, so long as the library is small, but it soon becomes burdensome, and, ere long, insupportable, even to national establishments.

There is but one course left—not to print at all. To this no scholar consents, except from necessity. But to this alternative, grievous as it is, nearly all the large libraries of Europe have been reluctantly driven.

More than a century has passed, since the printing of the catalogue of the Royal Library at Paris was commenced. It is not yet finished. No one feels in it

Reprinted from Charles C. Jewett, *On the Construction of Catalogues of Libraries and of a General Catalogue and Their Publication by Means of Separate, Stereotyped Titles with Rules and Examples,* 2d ed. (Washington, D.C.: Smithsonian Institution, 1853), p. 3-19.

the interest which he would, if he could hope to have its completeness sustained, when once brought up to a given date.

Dr. Pertz, chief librarian of the Royal Library at Berlin, declares, that to print the catalogue of a large library, which is constantly increasing, is to throw away money. His opinion is founded upon the supposed impossibility of keeping up the catalogue, so as continually to represent the actual possessions of the library.

The commissioners, lately appointed by the Queen of England, to inquire into the constitution and management of the British Museum, have, in their report, expressed an opinion decidedly against the printing of the catalogue at all, and principally on the ground that it must ever remain imperfect.

One of the witnesses, (the Right Honorable J. W. Croker,) examined before the commissioners, thus strongly states the case with respect to printing:

"You receive, I suppose, into your library every year some twenty thousand volumes, or something like that. Why, if you had a printed catalogue dropped down from Heaven to you at this moment perfect, this day twelve-month your twenty thousand interlineations would spoil the simplicity of that catalogue; again the next year twenty thousand more; and the next year twenty thousand more; so that at the end of four or five years, you would have your catalogue just in the condition that your new catalogue is now [the manuscript part greater than the printed part]. With that new catalogue before your eyes, I am astonished that there should be any discussion about it, for there is the experiment; the experiment has been made and failed."

Not one European library, of the first class, has a complete printed catalogue, in a single work. The Bodleian Library is not an exception. It may be necessary to search six distinct catalogues, in order to ascertain whether any specific book were or were not in the collection, at the close of the year 1847.

This is, surely, a disheartening state of things. It has been felt and lamented by every one who has had the care of an increasing library.

Plan for Obviating These Difficulties

As a remedy for this evil, it is proposed to STEREOTYPE THE TITLES SEPA-RATELY, and to preserve the plates or blocks, in alphabetical order of the titles, so as to be able readily to insert additional titles, in their proper places, and then to reprint the whole catalogue. By these means, the chief cost of re-publication (that of composition) together with the trouble of revision and correction of the press, would, except for new titles, be avoided. Some of the great difficulties, which have so long oppressed and discouraged librarians, and involved libraries in enormous expenses, may be thus overcome.

Application of the Plan to the Formation of a General Catalogue

The peculiar position of the Smithsonian Institution suggested the application of this plan, on a wider scale, and for a more important purpose, than that of merely facilitating the publication of new and complete editions of separate catalogues.

It had been proposed to form a general catalogue of all the books in the country, with references to the libraries where each might be found. The plan of stereotyping titles, separately, suggested the following system for the accomplishment of this important purpose:

1.　　The Smithsonian Institution to publish Rules for the preparation of Catalogues.

2.　　Other institutions, intending to publish catalogues of their books, to be requested to prepare them in accordance with these rules, with a view to their being stereotyped under the direction of the Smithsonian Institution.

3.　　The Smithsonian Institution to pay the whole *extra* expense of stereotyping, or such part thereof as may be agreed on.

4.　　The stereotyped titles to remain the property of the Smithsonian Institution.

5.　　Every library, acceding to this plan, to have the right of using all the titles in the possession of the Institution, as often as desired, for the printing of its own catalogue, by the Smithsonian Institution; paying only the expense of making up the pages, of press-work, and of distributing the titles to their proper places.

6.　　The Smithsonian Institution to publish, as soon as possible, and at stated intervals, a General Catalogue of Libraries coming into this system.

Advantages to be Derived from this System of Preparing Catalogues

The plan of stereotyping the titles, separately, would be of great value to every increasing library, independent of any general system. Such a library, in the first issue of its catalogue, would be obliged to incur an additional expense for stereotyping, which we may, for the present, state at fifty per centum above the price for composition. But, in the first reprint, both these expenses would be saved; so that the whole cost of the two editions would, in this respect, be twenty-five per cent less, if stereotyped.

Moreover, it would be necessary to print only a comparatively small number of copies, when the book, in a more perfect state, could be reproduced so easily; much would therefore be saved in paper and press-work. Besides, the arrangement of the titles, for a reprint, would pass from the hands of the librarian to those of the printer. The proof-reading, also, would have been done, once for all. In keeping up such a catalogue, the attention and labor of the librarian would have to be bestowed only upon additional titles.

Reckoning, thus, the expense of stereotyping as a part of the diminished cost of the first reprint, the saving, for every subsequent repetition, would be equal to the whole original cost of composition and proof-reading, for the part already stereotyped, and a considerable part of that of paper, press-work, and rearrangement. It is, therefore, demonstrable that the economy of the plan would be very great, to every library publishing and reprinting its catalogues, even without connection with the system proposed.

But, in connection with a general system, the advantages of this plan would be greatly increased, inasmuch as the same books are to be found in many libraries. If the titles, which have been stereotyped for one library, may be used for another having the same books, the saving to the second would be equal to the whole cost of composition and stereotyping of the titles common to the two, added to that of preparation of such titles.

At least one quarter of the titles in any two general libraries, of ten thousand volumes and upwards, may safely be supposed to be the same. The saving, from this source, to the second library, would, therefore, go far towards defraying the extra expense of stereotyping. A third institution, adopting the plan, would be likely to find a very large proportion of its titles identical with those already stereotyped, and the amount saved by the use of these titles, would, perhaps, be sufficient to counterbalance the whole extra expenditure for stereotyping. At any rate, the extra expense would be constantly and rapidly diminishing, and would, probably after the fourth or fifth catalogue, cease entirely. The Smithsonian Institution would not, therefore, be required to assume the charge of an enterprise, which might involve it in great and increasing expense, but merely to organize, and to guide a system, which will almost immediately pay its own way, and will soon save large sums of money to our public libraries.

That the aggregate economy of this plan would be very great, may be seen from the following statement:

In fifteen thousand pages, mostly in octavo, of catalogues of public libraries in the United States, there were found to be more than four hundred and fifty thousand titles. But, according to the best estimate which could be made, these catalogues contained not more than one hundred and fifty thousand *different* titles. Two-thirds, at least, of the whole cost of printing these catalogues (except the extra expense incurred by stereotyping the titles which differed) might have been saved, by following this plan.

Having shown its economy when employed by single libraries, and its greater economy, in connection with a general system, it is proper to suggest a few, among the many benefits to the cause of knowledge, which the general adoption of this method would seem to promise.

It can hardly be necessary to dwell, at length, upon the benefits to be expected from a general printed catalogue of all books in the public libraries of America. By means of it, every student in this country would be able to learn the full extent of his resources for investigation. The places where books could be found, might be indicated in the catalogue. A correspondence could be kept up between this Institution and every other library in the country. A system of exchange and of loans might, with certain stringent conditions, be established, or, when the loan of a book would be impracticable, extracts could be copied, quotations verified, and researches made, through the intervention of the Institution, as effectually to the purpose of the student, in most cases, as a personal examination of the book. All the literary treasures of the country might thus be made measurably available to every scholar.

Again, this general catalogue would enable purchasers of books for public libraries, to consult judiciously for the wants of the country. So poor are we in the books which scholars need; so long, at best, must we remain in a condition of provincial dependence in literary matters; that a responsibility to the whole country rests upon the man, who selects books for any public library.

An important advantage of this sytem is, that it allows us to vary the form of the catalogue, at will, from the alphabetical to the classed, and to modify the classification as we please. The titles, separately stereotyped, may change their order at command. If, for example, it were required to print a separate list of all books in the country, on the subject of *meteorology,* it would merely be necessary to check off, in the general catalogue, the titles to be used, leaving to the printer the rest of the work.

Another highly beneficial result would be, the attainment of a much higher degree of *uniformity* than could otherwise be hoped for. The rules for cataloging must be stringent, and should meet, as far as possible, all difficulties of detail. Nothing, so far as can be avoided, should be left to the individual taste or judgment of the cataloguer. He should be a man of sufficient learning, accuracy and fidelity, to apply the rules. In cases of doubt, reference should be made to the central establishment, to which the whole work should be submitted, page by page, for examination and revision. Thus, we should have all our catalogues formed substantially on one plan. Now, even if the one adopted were that of the worst of our catalogues, if it were strictly followed in all alike, their uniformity would render catalogues, thus made, far more useful than the present chaos of irregularities. The best possible system ought, however, to be the object of our aim.

It is an important consideration, that this plan would greatly facilitate the formation of an American bibliography, or a complete account of all books published in America.

By law, a copy of every book, for which a copyright shall be secured, in this country, is required to be delivered to the Smithsonian Institution, and to be preserved therein. It is hoped, that additional legislation, on this subject, will soon lighten the burdens of publishers, and secure the observance of this law, *in all cases.*

The collection of books thus obtained and preserved, will present a complete monumental history of American literature, during the existence of the law. It is needless to enlarge upon its value, in this point of view. If, now, a list of these publications, as they come into the library, should, month by month, be published in a *Bulletin,* and the titles immediately stereotyped, the expense would be but trifling of issuing, every year, a catalogue of books copyrighted in America, during the year, and printing, every five years, a general catalogue of American publications, up to that limit. Thus, monthly bulletins, annual lists, and quinquennial catalogues would furnish full and satisfactory records of American publications.

Another general consideration is, that this project looks towards the accomplishment of that cherished dream of scholars, a *universal catalogue.* If the system should be successful, in this country, it may eventually be so in every country of Europe. When all shall have adopted and carried out the plan, each for itself, the aggregate of general catalogues, thus formed—few in number—will embrace the whole body of literature extant, and from them, it will be no impossible task to digest and publish a universal bibliography. How much this would promote the progress of knowledge, by showing, more distinctly, what has been attempted and accomplished, and what yet remains to be achieved, and thus indicating the path of useful effort; how much, by rebuking the rashness which rushes into authorship, ignorant of what others have written, and adding to the mass of books, without adding to the sum of knowledge; how much, by giving confidence to the true and heroic student, who fears no labor, so that it bring him to the height at which he aims—the summit of learning, in the branch to which he devotes himself; are objects which deserve the hopeful attention of all who desire their attainment.

Distinction between a Catalogue and a Bibliographical Dictionary

A catalogue of a library is, strictly speaking, but a list of the titles of the books, which it contains. It is not generally expected to give any further description of a book than the author gives, or ought to give in the title-page, and the publisher, in the imprint, or colophon; except the designation of form, which is, almost universally, added.

A bibliographical dictionary is supposed to contain, besides the titles of books, such descriptions, more or less extended, drawn from all available sources of information, as may be necessary to furnish means of identifying each work, of distinguishing its different editions, of ascertaining the requisites of a perfect-copy, of learning all facts of interest respecting its authorship, publication, typography, subsequent casualties, alterations, etc., its market value, and the estimation in which it is held.

A catalogue is designed to show what books are contained in a particular collection, and nothing more. Persons in want of further information, are expected to seek for it in bibliographical dictionaries, literary histories, or similar works.

Inasmuch, however, as bibliographical works are not always accessible, or known to the investigator, additions are, not unfrequently, made to the titles, in catalogues, of such notices as belong more appropriately to bibliographical dictionaries, as above described. These, of course, impart to such catalogues greater value and usefulness.

As bibliographers, we cannot indeed but wish, that the catalogue of every library were a bibliographical dictionary of its books. Practically, however, we must restrict our efforts, within the limits of probable accomplishment. There is no species of literary labor so arduous, or which makes so extensive demands upon the learning of the author, as that of the preparation of such works. The most which one man can hope to effect, in this department, is to examine and describe books, in some special branch of knowledge, or books of some particular class, as *paleotypes*, books privately printed, a selection of books most esteemed by collectors, &c. It is too much to expect, that every librarian can find time, or possess learning, for such a description of all books under his care. Besides, this would be a waste of labor and of money. The same description would be prepared and printed, a hundred or a thousand times.

It is doubtless desirable, that such results of *original* investigations of librarians, as are not to be found in any of the bibliographical dictionaries, should be given, in the catalogues which they publish. In other cases, also, as will appear hereafter, it may be important to give, in a catalogue, fuller and more accurate descriptions of books, than are to be found upon their title-pages; but the principle should be established, and ever borne in mind, that a catalogue, being designed to be merely a list of titles, with imprints and designations of size, all additional descriptions should be limited and regulated by explicit rules, in order to give uniformity and system to the work, and to restrict its bulk and cost, within reasonable bounds.

Preparation of Titles so as to Serve
for Both General and Particular Catalogues

It is proposed to prepare and stereotype catalogues of particular libraries, in such a manner, that the titles can be used, without alteration, for constructing a General Catalogue.

This requires, that the title of every book be such, as will apply to every copy of the same edition.

If the edition be different, the book is to be considered different. In almost every instance, the title also, is different. There are, indeed, cases, where the title of a book is the same, in two editions, while the body of the work is more or less altered. Such instances are, however, of rare occurrence. They are, or should be, recorded in bibliographical works. They could only be described by one, who should place the two books side by side, and compare them together. In general, titles vary with the editions. We may, therefore, in using a title transcribed from one copy of a book, for other copies, avoid trouble by preparing and stereotyping a new title for every distinct edition; treating new editions as new books. So that, if copies of various editions of a work exist in several libraries, each will appear with a distinct title, in the General Catalogue.

This method of forming a general catalogue requires, further, that *peculiarities of copy,* which it may be desirable to note in preparing the catalogues of particular libraries, should not be stated within the titles; but, if at all, in notes appended to the titles, and entirely separate from them.

One copy of the same edition of a book may be on vellum, another, on paper; one may be in quarto form, another in octavo; one may have cancelled leaves, another, the substituted leaves, another, added leaves; some may contain autographs; some, valuable manuscript notes; others may be bound by Roger Payne, etc., etc. These are peculiarities of copy, and they may be as numerous as the number of copies in the edition. They are not noticed in title-pages, and, consequently, would not modify the entries in a catalogue, which takes cognizance of titles alone.

The printed matter, which constitutes the book, as a literary production, is not altered, in any of these cases, except in that of cancelled, substituted, or added leaves. It is indeed true, that, occasionally, alterations are made in the body of a book, while it is passing through the press; that is to say, after a few copies have been struck off, some error may be discovered and corrected, or some word may be substituted for another. But, such changes are always slight, and can only be detected, by comparing two or more copies of a work together. In the case of cancelled leaves, it may, sometimes, be desirable to print in the general catalogue, the description of rare and important copies possessed by particular libraries. But these cases would occur comparatively seldom. The rule would be, to omit from the title to be stereotyped, all account of peculiarities, or defects of copies.

In cataloguing particular libraries, such peculiarities should be stated, upon the card, after the title, but separate from it. They may be printed, at the expense of such libraries, in the form of notes to their catalogues. The notes for any particular library may be made as extensive, as the means of the institution, and the learning and leisure of its librarian permit.

There is another particular, in which the catalogue title might vary, in different copies: that, of designation of size. The same book, in the same edition, may have copies in quarto, in octavo, and in duodecimo. The size of the printed page is, however, in all these cases, the same; otherwise, the edition is different. All difficulty, on this account, therefore, is obviated, and all confusion of editions prevented, by adopting, instead of, or in addition to the usual designation of *form*, as the indication of size, the measurement of the printed page, in inches and tenths. Other reasons for this mode of marking the size of books, with minute directions, will be given hereafter.

Form of the Catalogue

The titles constituting the catalogue may be variously arranged. They may be placed under the names of authors, and the names disposed in alphabetical order; they may be grouped in classes, according to subjects; or they may be made to follow the order of the date, or place of printing.

The two most common forms for catalogues, are the alphabetical and the classed. Much controversy has arisen respecting their comparative usefulness. It is not necessary to revive it here, since the system now proposed, renders it easy to vary the order of titles, so as to suit any desired form.

For the General Catalogue, however, it is, for several reasons, desirable to adopt the alphabetical arrangement.

It would be impossible to propose any system of classification, which would command general approval, or upon which a commission of competent bibliographers would be unanimous in opinion. A classification, founded upon the nature of things, though it has occupied the best thoughts of such men as Bacon, Leibnitz, D'Alembert, Coleridge, Ampère, and many others, has not yet been attained. Every classification which has been proposed or used, is more or less arbitrary, and consequently unsatisfactory, and liable to be altered or superseded.

If, however, it were possible to agree upon a system of classification, the attempt to carry it out would, in a work like that proposed, be fatal to uniformity. Where different men were applying the same system, their opinions would vary, with their varying intelligence and skill. This would lead to utter and irremediable confusion, and would eventually defeat all our plans.

Even were these objections obviated, the occurrence of fewer difficulties in constructing an alphabetical catalogue would still present a decisive argument in its favor. Even these are great. If increased, by an attempt at classification, they would soon lead to an abandonment of the work.

Another consideration of great weight is, that, in reprinting classified catalogues, and inserting additions, if the titles were kept in systematic order, the work of selecting those to be used, and of distributing them to their places, would have to be done by a person, who, besides being a practical printer, should be familiar with the bibliographical system adopted. This would be very expensive. Whereas, on the alphabetical plan, any printer could do the whole.

On general considerations, without special reference to those which are peculiar to this system of publishing, alphabetical catalogues are to be preferred;— catalogues in which all the works of each author are placed under his name, and the names of authors are arranged alphabetically; anonymous works being entered under the first word of the title, not an article or preposition. Such is now the general opinion of competent bibliographers and literary men.

The Edinburgh Review, in an able and interesting article upon the British Museum, holds the following language:

"It seems to have been almost universally agreed that the catalogue ought to be alphabetical. Some time ago the current of opinion among literary men seemed to be setting towards classed catalogues, or those in which the books are arranged according to subjects. We had hardly supposed that this illusion (as we hold it to be) had become so nearly obsolete as the evidence before us shows that it is: and this disappearance of a most injurious opinion, which never was entertained to any extent by the really experienced in bibliography, encourages us to hope that it will not be long before the *professional* persons just alluded to [librarians] will be admitted to know best on all the points which have been raised relative to the care of a large library."

The experience of all students, of all who use books, if carefully noted, will show, that, in a vast majority of cases, whoever wishes to refer to books in a library, knows the names of their authors. It follows, that this form of arrangement must be, in the main, the most convenient; and if any other be pursued, it can but accommodate the minority, at the expense of the majority.

Still, it is indisputable that, oftentimes, the names of authors are not known; that one knows, merely, what subjects he wishes to investigate.

It may be said, that a catalogue, being designed to be merely a list of books contained in a library, is not expected to furnish this information; and that references to all authors, treating of any particular subjects, may be obtained from bibliographical works, encyclopædias, and other sources of information. This is true. But, unfortunately, these sources of information are not generally known, or not readily accessible, even to men of considerable attainments and scholarship.

It becomes, then, a question of importance how far the wants of such persons are to be provided for. The following remarks on this subject are worthy of attentive consideration:

"On this, as on other points, we may observe that two descriptions of persons consult a catalogue—those who know *precisely* what book they are in search of, and those who do not. The first will find by any rule, so soon as they have learnt it; and will be glad indeed of a catalogue which preserves its consistency, even though 600,000 titles, running over four quarters of the globe, four centuries of time, and four hundred varieties of usage, should actually require *ninety-one*[1] rules of digestion. The second class could easily be suited, if all their imperfect conceptions tended to the same case of confusion: and, as being the majority, would have a right to the adoption of the one nearly universal misconception; which, being one, would furnish a rule. But it is truth which is single, while error is manifold; and consequently, it is clear to every common sense except that of men of letters claiming, as such, to be bibliographers, that one of two things should be done:—either the truth should be taken, when known, or in the event of it being possible to be wrong, the error should be the consequence of a digested and easily-apprehended rule, consistently applied throughout. If the framer of the catalogue be allowed to do as he likes, the consulter of it must do as he can. Now which of the two cases should be considered in preference,—those who know what they want or those who do not? The Doctor of Divinity already quoted, gives this as one of his rules: "Item, when anie man comith and wotteth not what he wold haue, then he (the keper of the Bokys) shall tell hym, and doe hym to understond hys besynesse.' This can be done, to a certain extent, by *cross-references.* But, all cross-references being concessions to want of accurate knowledge, it is plain that discretionary entries, with discretionary cross-references, would form a plan which puts entirely out of the question the convenience of the person who knows exactly what he wants; which kills both calf and cow for the less deserving son, without giving the power of making any answer to the complaint of the one who never fed on husks. Nothing is stranger in the course of the evidence before us, than the quiet manner in which the opponents of the existing plan take it for granted that no one ever goes with a precise knowledge of the title-page of the work he seeks, unless it be the coolness with which this accurate inquirer is told, as Mr. Carlyle said to those who write useful knowledge, that he is one 'whom it is not worth while to take much trouble to accommodate.'"

But it is convenient even for those to whom the principles and means of research are best known, to be able to ascertain, readily, what books, of those which they know to have been written upon the subjects of their investigation, are to be found in the particular libraries which they consult. This end may be attained in the following manner. In connection with the *catalogue* of each library, there should be an *index* of subjects. This index should also be alphabetical. Under each subject, the divisions which naturally belong to it, should be distinctly recognized. It may here be remarked, that the parts of any particular science, or branch of learning, may be clearly defined, and universally acknowledged, whilst the relation of this science, or branch of learning, to others, may not be clearly established. To use the words of a vigorous writer upon this subject: "Take a library upon one science, and it classifies beautifully, sketching out, to a nicety, the boundaries, which, it is too rarely noticed, are much more distinct between the parts of a subject, than between one subject and another. Long after the counties of England and Scotland were well determined, the debateable land was nothing but a theatre of war."

This index should be alphabetical, rather than classed, because it is easier to find a word, in an alphabetical arrangement, than in any other order of classification; and, besides, the subject of research may be one not admitted, as a distinct division, in any classification. Such indexes can hardly be expected, immediately, in connection with the general catalogue; though, it is to be hoped, that these valuable appendages will not long be, of necessity, omitted.

A method of securing uniformity in such indexes may, hereafter, be agreed upon, so that they may be combined and form an alphabetical index of subjects to the general catalogue. It is thought best, however, for the present, to limit our efforts to the procuring of good alphabetical catalogues, as a groundwork, to which other valuable aids to research, may, as opportunities offer, be superadded.

Necessity of Rules for the Preparation of Catalogues

The preparation of a catalogue may seem a light task, to the inexperienced, and to those who are unacquainted with the requirements of the learned world, respecting such works. In truth, however, there is no species of literary labor so arduous and perplexing. The peculiarities of titles are, like the idiosyncracies of authors, innumerable. Books are in all languages, and treat of subjects as multitudinous as the topics of human thought.

Liability to error and to confusion is, here, so great and so continual, that it is impossible to labor successfully, without a rigid adherence to rules. Although such rules be not formally enunciated, they must exist in the mind of the cataloguer, and guide him, or the result of his labors will be mortifying and unprofitable.

In this country, he who undertakes to prepare a catalogue, goes to the work under great disadvantages, in many respects. Few have had opportunity to acquire the requisite bibliographical knowledge and experience; and few libraries contain the necessary books of reference. A set of rules, therefore, seems peculiarly necessary for the assistance of librarians.

Minute and stringent rules become absolutely indispensable, when the catalogue of each library is, as upon the proposed plan, to form a part of a general catalogue. *Uniformity* is, then, imperative; but, among many laborers, can only be secured by the adherence of all to rules embracing, as far as possible, the minutest details of the work.

The rules which follow were drawn up with great care. They are founded upon those adopted for the compilation of the catalogue of the British Museum; some of them are, *verbatim,* the same. Others conform more to rules advocated by Mr. Panizzi, than to those finally sanctioned by the Trustees of the Museum. Many modifications and additions have been made, adapted to the peculiar character of the system now proposed. Some innovations have been introduced, which, it is hoped, may be considered improvements. The commissioners, appointed to examine and report upon the catalogue project, considered not only its general features, but, also, its minute details. To them, were submitted the rules for cataloguing, which were separately discussed, and, after having been variously amended and modified, were recommended for adoption.

It is too much to suppose that any code should provide for every case of difficulty which may occur. The great aim, here, has been to establish principles, and to furnish analogies, by which many cases, not immediately discussed, may be indirectly settled; and, it is believed, that the instances will be few, which cannot be determined, by studying the rules, with the remarks under them, and carefully considering the characteristics of this kind of catalogue.

It should be remembered that a principal object of the rules is to secure *uniformity*; and that, consequently, some rules, which may seem unnecessarily burdensome, and, in certain applications, even capricious, are, all things considered, the best; because they secure that uniformity, which is not otherwise possible of attainment, and without which, the catalogues could not be comprehended in a general system.

Notes

1.   These are not all that might be wanted. For example, the case is not provided for, though it has occurred, in which an author, in his title-page, invites the reader to make his choice between two ways of spelling his own name. Here, we are to presume, some of our witnesses would take the first method given, others would leave the cataloguer to comply with the author's request.

Rules for a
Dictionary Catalog: Selections

Charles A. Cutter

Editor's Introduction

Charles Ammi Cutter, a nineteenth-century Bostonian, was at Harvard studying for the ministry when he was offered a position as student librarian at the Harvard Divinity School. It was an experience that changed the direction of his life. After graduation, he joined the Harvard College library staff, and in less than a decade he was appointed librarian at the Boston Athanaeum. While at the Athenaeum, he completed a printed catalog of such excellence that it has been called "the most ambitious attempt ever made in the realm of cataloging, unique in its plan and superior in its execution."* Shortly thereafter he was asked by the Bureau of Education to prepare a status report on public libraries in the United States to commemorate the country's one hundredth year as a nation. The *Rules for a Dictionary Catalog,* parts of which are excerpted here, form part 2 of this report. It is a landmark work, being the first attempt to "set forth [cataloging] rules in a systematic way or to investigate what might be called the first principles of cataloging.†

---

*William P. Cutter, *Charles Ammi Cutter,* American Library Pioneers, no. 3 (Chicago: American Library Association, 1931), 23.

†Charles A. Cutter, *Rules for a Dictionary Catalog,* 4th ed. (Washington, D.C.: Government Printing Office, 1904), 3.

Two points might be noted in the "Preface to the Fourth Edition." The first is the well-known lament, "Still I cannot help thinking that the golden age of cataloging is over and that the difficulties and discussions which have furnished an innocent pleasure to so many will interest them no more."** The lament was occasioned by the commencement of the Library of Congress' printed card program. Despite this program, it would seem that discussions of cataloging persist and, no doubt, continue to furnish innocent pleasures to some. Indeed, it seems unlikely that even the wide availability of a standardized product in machine-readable form will render discussions of cataloging superfluous.

The second point to note in the *Preface* is Cutter's credo, "The convenience of the public is always to be set before the ease of the cataloger."†† The requirement to consider the user can sometimes conflict with a requirement for consistency. Whereas Jewett, in the interest of consistency, wanted to leave nothing to the "taste or judgment of the cataloguer,"*** Cutter opted for flexibility and sensitivity to users' needs. Today, faced with questions of how best to design online catalogs, a librarian may ask whether these opposing philosophies can be reconciled in a machine environment.

The section headed "General Remarks" contains Cutter's most cited text regarding the objects of the catalog. An early systems designer, Cutter understood the need to set forth the objectives of the system he was creating. Cutter's "Objects" have been restated by Seymour Lubetzky in his *Code of Cataloging Rules* and in the *Paris Principles.* Testimony to the importance of the "objects" is the fact that nearly every cataloging theorist, who writes in the Anglo-American tradition, cites them.

Cutter had as exacting a mind as anyone who has made cataloging a serious study, and he realized the need for definition in the construction of a code of rules. Many current

---

**Charles A. Cutter, "Preface to the Fourth Edition," in *Rules for a Dictionary Catalog,* 4th ed., rewritten (Washington, D.C.: Government Printing Office, 1904), 5.

††Ibid., 6.

***Charles C. Jewett, "Smithsonian Catalogue System," in *Smithsonian Report on the Construction of Catalogues of Libraries and of a General Catalogue and Their Publication by Means of Separate, Stereotyped Titles with Rules and Examples,* 2d ed. (Washington, D.C.: Smithsonian Institution, 1852), 8.

definitions derive from those that first appeared in Cutter's *Rules.* Examples are "Rule 98," which gives the definition of a collection and of an editor of a collection, and "Rule 133," which defines a periodical.

While Jewett is credited with being the first to suggest that bodies of men be considered authors, it was Cutter who elevated corporate authorship to the level of principle and in his arguments for corporate entry entrenched the "American way." These arguments, reprinted by Cutter from the *Library Journal* where they first appeared, are presented here under the rubric *2.Corporate.*

ES

Further Reading

Cutter, Charles A. "Library Catalogues." In U.S. Bureau of Education, *Public Libraries in the United States of America, Their History, Condition and Management: Special Report,* Part 1, 526-622. Washington, D.C.: Government Printing Office, 1876.

Describes, using a theoretical framework, different forms of catalogs represented in libraries in the United States, and presents advantages and disadvantages of each.

Miksa, Francis L. *Charles Ammi Cutter: Library Systematizer.* Littleton, Colo.: Libraries Unlimited, 1977.

Presents a biography of Cutter together with a selection of his writings and a complete bibliography.

Rules for a Dictionary Catalog: Selections

Preface to the Fourth Edition

On seeing the great success of the Library of Congress cataloging, I doubted whether it was worth while to prepare and issue this fourth edition of my Rules; but I reflected that it would be a considerable time before all libraries would use the cards of that library, and a long time before the Library of Congress could furnish cards for all books, long enough for the libraries to absorb another edition and use it up in that part of their cataloging which they must do themselves. Still I can not help thinking that the golden age of cataloging is over, and that the difficulties and discussions which have furnished an innocent pleasure to so many will interest them no more. Another lost art. But it will be all the better for the pockets of the public, or rather it will be better for other parts of the service—the children's room and the information desk, perhaps.

In the last two years a great change has come upon the status of cataloging in the United States. The Library of Congress has begun furnishing its printed catalog cards on such liberal terms that any new library would be very foolish not to make its catalog mainly of them, and the older libraries find them a valuable assistance in the cataloging of their accessions, not so much because they are cheaper as because in the case of most libraries they are better than the library is likely to make for itself.

The differences between these rules and those adopted by the Library of Congress are of two classes. The first class of differences is in trifles of punctuation, capitalization, the place of certain items on the cards, and the like. If one already has a catalog with a large number of cards, and merely inserts in it as many of the Library of Congress cards as possible, I see no reason for altering one's own style, either on the past accumulations or on the new cards that one is to write. The two kinds of cards can stand together in the drawers and the public will never notice the difference. But if one is commencing a new catalog, to be composed mainly of Library of Congress cards, I advise following the Library of Congress rules closely. It will save much trouble.

Reprinted from Charles A. Cutter, *Rules for a Dictionary Catalog,* 4th ed., rewritten (Washington, D.C.: Government Printing Office, 1904), "Preface to the Fourth Edition," 5-6; "General Remarks," 11-12; "Rule 98," 51; "Rule 133," 59-60; "2. Corporate," 39-41.

In the second class of differences, those relating to place of entry of the card in the catalog, or of choice of heading, we must note that it is very easy to alter the entry of a Library of Congress card, as there is room enough above the heading on the printed card to write in the one preferred. A librarian who already has a large catalog will therefore find no difficulty in continuing his present heading and need change only if he thinks the Library of Congress practice better. Nevertheless, as it is some trouble to look for differences of practice, and there is always a chance of overlooking one and so getting different entries for similar books, it would be well to adopt the Library of Congress rules unless there is some decided reason against them. The librarian who is just commencing his catalog has still more reason for this course. In the matter of capitalization, on which the advisory committee give no advice, the course I recommend was decidedly favored by the votes of the Catalog Section, at the meeting of the American Library Association at Magnolia in 1902. This course does not agree with the present practice at the Library of Congress.

The convenience of the public is always to be set before the ease of the cataloger. In most cases they coincide. A plain rule without exceptions is not only easy for us to carry out, but easy for the public to understand and work by. But strict consistency in a rule and uniformity in its application sometimes lead to practices which clash with the public's habitual way of looking at things. When these habits are general and deeply rooted, it is unwise for the cataloger to ignore them, even if they demand a sacrifice of system and simplicity.

The rules issued by the advisory catalog committee of the American Library Association are, according to the preface to the printed edition of these rules, expressly designed to be made for the use of a learned library. The old catalogs were not made for children, but the modern ones have to be especially in a circulating library, for the children are the library's best clients. That the committee has always understood the public's views, estimated correctly its power of changing them, and drawn the line in the right place between a conservative regard for custom and a wish to lead the public toward a desirable simplicity and consistency is too much to assume, but I have at least always looked for the reasons on both sides.

The increase in the number of rules is due chiefly not to making new rules, but to taking out from the long notes many recommendations that were in effect rules, and are more easily referred to and found in their present place. The changes are largely for the sake of greater clearness and of better classification.

Cataloging is an art, not a science. No rules can take the place of experience and good judgment, but some of the results of experience may be best indicated by rules.

· · · · ·

General Remarks

No code of cataloging could be adopted in all points by every one, because the libraries for study and the libraries for reading have different objects, and those which combine the two do so in different proportions. Again, the preparation of a catalog must vary as it is to be manuscript or printed, and, if the latter, as it is to be merely an index to the library, giving in the shortest possible compass clues by which the public can find books, or is to attempt to furnish more information on various points, or finally is to be made with a certain regard to what may be called style. Without pretending to exactness, we may divide dictionary catalogs into short-title, medium-title, and full-title or bibliographic; typical examples of the three being, 1°, the Boston Mercantile (1869) or the Cincinnati Public (1871), 2°, the Boston Public (1861 and 1866), the Boston Athenæum (1874-82); 3°, the catalog now making by the Library of Congress. To avoid the constant repetition of such phrases as "the full catalog of a large library" and "a concise finding-list," I shall use the three words Short, Medium, and Full as proper names, with the preliminary caution that the Short family are not all of the same size, that there is more than one Medium, and that Full may be Fuller and Fullest. Short, if single-columned, is generally a title-a-liner; if printed in double columns; it allows the title occasionally to exceed one line, but not, if possible, two; Medium does not limit itself in this way, but it seldom exceeds four lines, and gets many titles into a single line. Full usually fills three or four lines and often takes six or seven for a title.

The number of the following rules is not owing to any complexity of system, but to the number of widely varying cases to which a few simple principles have to be applied. They are especially designed for Medium, but may easily be adapted to Short by excision and marginal notes. The almost universal practice of printing the shelf-numbers or the class-numbers renders some of them unnecessary for town and city libraries.

Objects[1]

1. To enable a person to find a book of which either
   - (A) the author ⎫
   - (B) the title   ⎬ is known.
   - (C) the subject ⎭
2. To show what the library has
   - (D) by a given author
   - (E) on a given subject
   - (F) in a given kind of literature.
3. To assist in the choice of a book
   - (G) as to its edition (bibliographically).
   - (H) as to its character (literary or topical).

Means

1. Author-entry with the necessary references (for A and D).
2. Title-entry or title-reference (for B).
3. Subject-entry, cross-references, and classed subject-table (for C and E).
4. Form-entry and language-entry (for F).
5. Giving edition and imprint, with notes when necessary (for G).
6. Notes (for H).

Reasons for Choice

Among the several possible methods of attaining the OBJECTS, other things being equal, choose that entry

(1)   That will probably be first looked under by the class of people who use the library;

(2)   That is consistent with other entries, so that one principle can cover all;

(3)   That will mass entries least in places where it is difficult to so arrange them that they can be readily found, as under names of nations and cities.

This applies very slightly to entries under first words, because it is easy and sufficient to arrange them by the alphabet.

. . . . .

Rule 98

98.   COLLECTOR, collecting editor.

That is, the one who *is responsible for the existence of a collection.*

A collection is made by putting together, *with a collective title,* three or more works by different authors, so as to make one work.

Ex. Buchon's "Collection des mémoires."

. . . . .

Rule 133

133.   PERIODICALS are to be treated as anonymous and entered under the first word, not an article or serial number.

Ex. Popular science monthly, Littell's living age.

When a periodical *changes its title* the whole may be cataloged under the original title, with an explanatory note there and a reference from the new title to the old; or each part may be cataloged under its own title, with references, "For a continuation, *see* ," "For the previous volumes, *see* ."

Treat almanacs and other *annuals* as periodicals.

Do not confound periodicals with *serials.*

The four characteristics of a periodical are: (1) that it be published at intervals usually but not necessarily regular; (2) in general that the publication be intended to continue indefinitely; (3) that it be written by a number of contributors under the supervision of one or more editors; (4) that it consist of articles on various subjects, so that a set of the work does not form an organic whole. The 2d, 3d, and 4th criteria exclude works like Trollope's "The way we live now" (first published serially)," and the Encyclopædia Britannica." There are some exceptions to the 3d, as Brownson's quarterly review; and to the 4th, as Masters in art, Boston, 1900, etc., and the present Portfolio, London, which may be considered either as a periodical or as a serial.

Make a reference from the name of the editor when the periodical is commonly called by his name, as in the case of Silliman's Journal of science.

The *Memoirs, Proceedings, Transactions* of a society are periodicals in point of (1) occasional publication, (2) indefinite continuance, and—so far as they contain anything beyond the record of the society's meetings—of (4) variety of subject; but they lack the 3d characteristic, variety of authorship, inasmuch as the memoirs or other papers given in addition to "proceedings" proper may be considered as the work of the society acting through its members; the society, therefore, is the author, and the Transactions, etc., need not have title-entry. There are, however, some "Journals" published by or "under the auspices of" societies which are really periodicals, and should be so treated in entry, the society being not the author but the editor. Again, there are works which occupy a borderland between the two classes, in regard to which the puzzled cataloger should remember that it is not of much importance which way he decides, provided he is careful to make all necessary references. Examples of such doubtful cases are "Alpine journal: a record of mountain adventure and scientific observation. By members of the Alpine Club;" which contains nothing of or about the Club itself;—"Journal of the American Institute, a monthly publication devoted to the interest of agriculture, commerce, etc. Edited by a committee, members of the Institute," and "Journal of the Society of Arts and of The Institutions in Union," both of which are journals both in the sense of record of proceedings and of periodical publication.

Newspaper titles are troublesome. It is not uncommon for the name of the place to be included in the name on the first page (as The Boston Ægis), but to be dropped over the editorial column, or vice versa, or to be used for some years and afterwards dropped, or vice versa. The searcher can not always remember whether it is used or not. It would be well, therefore, to give under each name of a city the title of every newspaper published there which the library has.

. . . . .

2. Corporate

An article in the *Library Journal* (21:493-494) opposed the principle of Corporate authorship as a library superstition and recommended the practice of German libraries, who consider "all works issued by corporate bodies as anonymous, for the purposes of entry", when they have no individual author.

Part of my reply is here reprinted from the *Library Journal* (22:432-434):

"I think the American practice of regarding bodies of men as the authors of their own journals, proceedings, etc., and as collecting-editors of the collections issued by them, is preferable to the German practice of dispersing these works throughout the alphabet under the noun which happens to be first in the title.

"The American way is preferable for two reasons: first, because as a matter of fact these bodies *are* the authors not only of their own proceedings but also of their collections regarded as a whole; secondly, because as a matter of convenience, both in the enlargement of the library and in the service of the public, it is better that all the books connected with the name of a society or government should be brought together in one place. It is true that in a dictionary catalog this may be accomplished more or less inappropriately by entry under the name of the society as a subject; but in an author catalog it does not come about at all. If you want to find in Kayser's list of the books published in Germany in the last five years all the publications of a German learned body you must look under Abhandlungen, Almanach, Annalen, Arbeiten, Archiv, Aufsätze, Beiträge, Bericht, Bibliothek, Bulletin, Centralblatt, Correspondenzblatt, Ephemeriden, Erlaüterungen, Jahrbuch, Jahresbericht, Journal, Kalender, Magazin, Memoiren, Mittheilungen, Monatsblatt, Nachrichten, Preisschrift, Programm, Publicationen, Repertorium, Resultate, Sammlung, Schriften, Sitzungsberichte, Studien, Tageblatt, Tagebuch, Uebersicht, Verzeichniss, Versammlungen, Vierteljahrschrift, Vorlesungen, and Zeitschrift, because the works may be under any one of these; and if by racking your brain you remember all of them and have patience to look them all up, you yet are not sure that there is not something important hidden away under some other word which you may think of when it is too late—Verhandlungen, for instance.

"So much for societies. Government publications fall into two classes— onymous and anonymous. As to the first the Rules catalog all works which have an author under his name. But the Rules direct that if issued by the government they should also appear either in full or by a reference, according to circumstances, under the department of government which issues them. A small library may very well omit this; that is one of the many economies which are permissible to small libraries; but no large library is well catalogued unless it has lists (at least by refer- ence) of all the works for which each department has made itself responsible.

"As to the second class, the anonymous issues, I cannot see the advantage of entering them under the first word. Either (1) they are the journals, reports, etc., of legislative bodies, of which even my objector allows that the government is the author and puts them (unlike the Germans) under the country, or (2) they relate to the country, in which case the objector puts them also under the country, but in a subject division and not under the department, or (3) they do not relate to the country. As to (1) we agree; as to (2) I have no objection whatever to full entry under a country-subject heading alone, provided there is entry by reference under the name of the department. When they come on the same page the reference is perhaps unnecessary. The best place for the full entry depends on the object of the catalog.

"There remains only (3) the few anonymous works published by a depart- ment which do not relate to the country. Whether or not they ought to be entered under the first word like any other anonymous work, it seems to me that there should be an entry under the department which, even more than in the case of works issued with their authors' names, must be supposed to adopt the opinions of the work and assume responsibility for it.

"Before the 'Rules for a dictionary catalog' were made catalogs seemed to me to be chaotic collections of empirical entries. I tried to find a few simple principles around which all desirable practices could be grouped. One of those principles is corporate authorship and editorship. I have as yet seen nothing to convince me that it is not a good one, since it corresponds to fact, inasmuch as societies are the authors of their proceedings and the collectors of their series; it is convenient in practice for complete cataloging; and for incomplete cataloging it admits of econ- omies which produce all the effects of the objector's rejection of the principle with none of the disadvantages of his method.

"The German practice is to enter anonymous works under the first noun in the title. The practice advocated by my objector, however, was not this but title entry under the society's name, e.g. the writer enters, not under Proceedings of the Royal Society, as the Germans would do, but under Royal Society, Proceedings of, as a title entry. That is to say he takes the name of the society as it happens to appear on the title-page and inverts the title, so as to get at it first. If it appears as Academia Caesareo-Leopoldina, that work will be entered under Academia; if in another the same society appears as Kaiserliche-Königliche Akad.d.Wissenschaften, that work will be entered under Kaiserliche. One German academy would necessarily appear under (1) Académie Royale for its early 'Mémoires,' when the French influence prevailed in Germany, (2) Königliche Akademie for later works, and (3) Academia Litterarum Regia for one of its longest and most important publications. Of course one can partly get over this objectionable dispersion of works that ought to be entered together by putting all societies first under the name of the place where their headquarters are, but even then in those cities where there are many societies there will be a certain amount of mixing up of different ones and tearing apart the works of those which have put their names in different languages or in different forms on the title-page; and if this is avoided by adopting one form for all, what is that but an abandonment of the title-entry idea and a return to author entry?"

General Principle

45.   Bodies of men are to be considered as authors of works published in their name or by their authority.

The chief difficulty with regard to bodies of men is to determine (1) what their names are, and (2) whether the name or some other word shall be the heading. In regard to (2) the catalogs hitherto published may be regarded as a series of experiments. No satisfactory usage has as yet been established. Local names have always very strong claims to be headings; but to enter the publications of all bodies of men under the places with which the bodies are connected is to push a convenient practice so far that it becomes inconvenient and leads to many rules entirely out of harmony with the rest of the catalog.

Notes

1.   *Note to second edition.* This statement of Objects and Means has been criticized; but as it has also been frequently quoted, usually without change or credit, in the prefaces of catalogs and elsewhere, I suppose it has on the whole been approved.

The Development of Authorship Entry and the Formulation of Authorship Rules as Found in the Anglo-American Code

Julia Pettee

Editor's Introduction

How does one decide what rules to put in a catalog code? Perhaps the choice of rules should be based on past practice as this would incorporate conventional wisdom and insure a uniform approach over time. A different, more theoretical, answer might be that the choice of rules should be governed by certain external and agreed upon criteria, such as "furthering the objectives of the catalog" or "being consistent with cataloging principles." During the fifty years between the publication of the first edition of Cutter's *Rules* and the publication of the selection that follows, much effort was expended on rule making, but relatively little regard was paid to the principles underlying these rules. In 1936 Julia Pettee, head cataloguer at the Union Theological Seminary in New York, wrote the following article in which she traces the history of two fundamental principles underlying Anglo-American cataloging codes: the authorship principle and the literary unit principle. In so doing, she awakened catalogers from their dogmatic slumbers, and turned their attention to the objectives of the catalog.

The authorship principle dictates that personal entry should be given precedence over any other entry form whenever possible, Pettee sees this principle rooted in a psychological reality of the Western world, *viz.* that books are best known by their creators. Traditionally, certain kinds of bibliographic materials—periodicals, works published by corporate bodies or editors, and works published under pseudonyms or anonymously—have proved resistent to entry under author. The evolution of the authorship principle, as Pettee depicts it, is an attempt to stretch the idea of authorship to bring in "lambs outside the authorship fold."* In a footnote, she expresses concern over the expense of scholarship required to support such a principle, but immediately dismisses it: "It is not for us to stay the normal advance of the authorship idea."† Today, the normal advance of the authorship idea has been—if not stayed—at least slowed down. This tendency is due in part to the fracturing of the concept of author responsibility into a variety of different responsibility functions. Indeed, the reversals of this normal advance, exemplified by the recent expulsion of editors and corporate bodies from the domain of authorship, raises questions about the presumed psychological reality of the authorship principle and its supposed elasticity.

The literary unit principle was recognized as early as 1674 by Thomas Hyde in his Bodleian catalog,** but, Pettee observes, the principle did not assume a position of dominance until catalogs reached their third evolutionary stage. The first stage of catalog development reflected the purpose of catalogs as inventory lists; the second, their function as finding lists; and the third, most advanced, stage of catalog development reflects their function as bibliographic tools. A catalog that is a bibliographic tool serves users by assembling literary units, that is, it collocates all versions of a specific work.

In identifying the essential characteristic of contemporary catalogs as the assembling of literary units, Pettee was prophetic. Her influence can be seen in subsequent milestones in cataloging theory, particularly the papers written by Verona and Lubetzky during the fifties and sixties, which are

---

*Julia Pettee, "The Development of Authorship Entry and the Formulation of Authorship Rules as Found in the Anglo-American Code," *Library Quarterly* 6 (July 1936): 286.

†Ibid., 285, note 11.

**Thomas Hyde, "Praefatio ad Lectorem," in *Catalogus impressorum librorum Bibliothecae Bodlejanae in academia Oxoniensi* (Oxonii: E theatro Sheldoniano, 1674).

reprinted in this volume. Pettee ends her article by asking that new rules be developed in accordance with principles, and, once more prophetic, she warns of the specter of cataloging codes, allowed to grow in disregard of principles, becoming encyclopedias of pedantic distinctions.

ES

Further Reading

Verona, Eva. "Literary Unit Versus Bibliographical Unit." *Libri* 9 (1959): 79-104.

> Reprinted in this volume. Considers the role of main and added entries in assembling literary units.

Lubetzky, Seymour. "The Objectives of the Catalog." In *Principles of Cataloging. Final Report, Phase I: Descriptive Cataloging,* 11-15. Los Angeles: Institute of Library Research, 1969.

> Reprinted in this volume. Adopts the concept of literary unit, calling it "work" and, in terms of it reformulates Cutter's objectives of the catalog.

The Development of Authorship Entry
and the Formulation of Authorship Rules
as Found in the Anglo-American Code

Mr. Hanson's article on cataloging in the October, 1935, *Library quarterly*[1] raises a question much larger than the relative convenience and expense of title versus authorship entry for publications of corporate bodies. It brings up the two fundamental principles which underlie the Anglo-American code[2] upon which our American cataloging practice is based.

The author is the first concern of the American cataloger. He searches for anonymous authors. If he is dealing with corporate bodies, he seeks to identify and name the society, institution, or governmental body responsible for the document. If he has an anonymous classic, the search goes back to the source of the classic, and in lieu of author he establishes a form of name under which this literary unit is most correctly known. Only in the case of hopelessly anonymous works or works of multiple authorship, where personal authors are too many to be serviceable as an entry form, does he resort to title entry.

The attribution of authorship is a first principle of American catalogers. But why this tireless search? A second principle, even more fundamental, which necessitates the search, emerges. The book in hand is considered not as a single item but as a representative of a literary unit. It is the province of the catalog to assemble these literary units, issued in various forms, under a single caption. Pope's translation of Homer's *Odyssey* does not stand by itself. It is a version of the original Greek. The *Odyssey* in all its forms is the literary unit, and all forms of this unit are assembled under HOMER. The name DHAMMAPADA brings all versions of this specific work together, although an English translation may be disguised by some such title as "Buddhists hymns" or "Path of virtue." The attribution of authorship, or the substitution of a conventional form in lieu of author, is the quickest and surest way to assemble these units. These principles are incorporated in the Anglo-American code and apply to all classes of literature.

The identification of the literary unit and the attribution of authorship in establishing the form of entry is so thoroughly ingrained in our catalogers, it may be a surprise to many to be told that these principles, in the long history of cataloging, are something very new and that they have not yet attained universal

---

Reprinted by permission of The University of Chicago Press from *Library Quarterly* 6 (July 1936): 270-90.

acceptance. The older working principle upon which all European rules have developed is that the catalog is a ready finding list for the particular book wanted, irrespective of its relation to any other book. To serve this finding list purpose, *title* rather than *authorship* is emphasized, as furnishing the more convenient entry for all books where a personal author is not in evidence. This principle is implied in the present British Museum *Rules.* "The choice of heading for a main entry is, as a rule, based on the information supplied in print in a perfect copy of the book itself and *on that only*," and, as an application of this principle, we have the further ruling that even if the name of the anonymous writer is known to the cataloger, it may never be used as the entry (except for well-known classics), and may not even be supplied in brackets in the title without the consent of the author unless it is currently known through printed bibliographies. The European printed catalogs are not called "author catalogs," but more correctly "general catalogs," e.g., *"British Museum general catalogue of printed books, Catalogue général des livres imprimés de la Bibliothèque Nationale.*

Dziatzko in his *Instruction* for the arrangement of titles in a card catalog, which is the basis of the German rules (as well as some of our own), states explicitly that the theory of the use of the catalog is, in general; that a definite work is wanted and that this is remembered by its own peculiar sequence of important words in the title. Authorship is a matter of secondary concern.

The history of library catalogs throws much light upon our cataloging rules. Each catalog was compiled for its own collection. When such a collection grew formidable, changing groups of catalogers began to need some guide in making current work conform with that of their predecessors, and the usefulness of printed catalogs demanded consistency. Then rules of instruction were drawn up, based not upon theory, but upon practices already fixed by usage. Not until the possibility of co-operation in the work of making catalogs dawned upon Charles Jewett in the middle of the last century was any attempt made to compare the practices of different libraries and to formulate general rules applicable to all. The co-operative idea took root in America. Valiant struggles with the difficulties involved in systematizing and co-ordinating rules followed which has resulted in bringing to light a few principles[3] which have been accepted as fundamental to American practice.

In the history of European libraries catalogs of books have served various needs. In studying the purposes for which they were made we can sift the different factors in the entries and can note the growing differentiation of author, subject, and title elements.

The first purpose served by the catalog was purely that of an inventory list. Books were valuable property to be accounted for to an overlord together with other possessions. Thus the early catalogs listed the items one by one as they were stored in presses or monastic rooms with no reference to any arrangement but storage. The catalog as a bibliographical tool was unknown and unnecessary.

Later, in the medieval monastic lists, we occasionally find some attempt at a systematic arrangement by authors. Here we see a new purpose emerging. The list is coming to be used not only as a register of property but as a finding list arranged for ready access to the books. It is becoming a bibliography, answering, without loss of time, the question, "what books by certain authors does this library own?" This first bibliographical function of the catalog is served by the alphabetical author list. Books, in the Western world, are primarily associated with the man responsible for their creation. This is sound psychology from which there has been no important deviation. Where the author is an individual and the authorship is known, the personal entry under author, from the very beginning of European cataloging practice, has taken precedence over title or any other entry form. The form of entry for works without personal authors in evidence is still a matter upon which there is no general agreement in practice.

A convenient example of a medieval monastic catalog arranged alphabetically under authors is the catalog of the library of Corvey given in Volume I of Edward Edwards' *Memoirs of libraries.* In this author catalog we find the problems that have beset catalogers from the eleventh century to this very day and the clues to their solution.

One factor that has had considerable bearing upon our cataloging practice is the fact that the medieval cataloger was dealing with manuscripts and that he himself often supplied the captions for the listing of these books. These captions consisted in some concise phrase or sequence of words descriptive of the contents of the manuscript. If the author's name was obvious, this furnished the first word of the caption, e.g., ARISTOTELIS KATEGORIAE. But all the manuscripts did not contain the names of the authors.

Thus bibliographical lists from the beginning have dealt with two classes of literature—books whose authorship is known; and the *anonymi*,[4] all books where no personal author is in evidence. The entries for the *anonymi*, like the entries for the manuscripts with known authors, are succinct and easily remembered phrases descriptive of the contents of the manuscripts themselves. CANONUM CORPUS, DE SITU JERUSALEM, EXPOSITIO CUJUSDAM IN EVANGELIO, GLOSARII SEPTEM, GRAMMATICA, MARTINI EPISCOPI VITA ET TRANSITUS, REHTORICA [RHETORICA] ARTIS, QUESTIONES IN GENESI, REGULAE QUATUOR, TRIPARTITA HISTORIA, are typical examples. Even in the eleventh century these *anonymi* proved too wearisome for the patient cataloger. At the end of the list he lumps the remainder in a single entry: VIGINTI ET QUATUOR LIBRI SINE TITULIS.

These headings, fitted into the alphabetical list of authors, give us clues to the extensive rulings of our modern practice, all of which may be traced to an elaboration of types found in this Corvey catalog. The types are three:

1. Form entries—GLOSARII SEPTUM
This is a prelude to such British Museum entries as DICTIONARIES, LITURGIES, PERIODICALS, ACADEMIES.

2. Subject entries—GRAMMATICA; MARTINI EPISCOPI VITA ET TRANSITUS
This sets the example for a whole series of entry under the important subject word in the title, which includes persons and places.

3. Catchword entry—TRIPARTITA HISTORIA; QUESTIONES IN GENESI
This is especially developed in the German catalogs where entry is under important noun or phrase, and this method is covered by a number of British Museum rules.

A search through the early printed catalogs gives us no new principles, but the treatment of the *anonymi* shows a progressive development in both the uses and the structure of the catalog.

With the advent of printing and the greatly increased size of library collections the ready finding of a book became a problem. The listing by authors is satisfactory as far as it goes, but it is no help for the *anonymi.* The "real catalogs" of systematic subject lists now emerge and give rise to extensive debate. If a library can afford but one catalog, is it better to provide an author list, to serve the man who knows what he wants, or a list of books by subject for some topical browser who is on the scent of all books in his own line that he does not already know?

The straight author list was no help in finding the *anonymi* and was rejected unless combined in some way with subject and title entries. The subject lists developed in three forms: (1) the straight systematic catalog (real catalog)—a classed subject catalog with author index; (2) the alphabetical list of subject captions with an author index (alphabetical real catalog); and (3) subject captions arranged alphabetically and combined with author and title entry.

It is the third type[5] alone which concerns us—the alphabetical subject captions combined with author and title entry. These early alphabetical subject captions are not true subject headings but subject catchword headings taken from the important subject word in the title of the book. Synonymous terms such as ANGLETERRE and ANGLIA, ABYSSINIA and ETHIOPIA occur. In one catalog ALCHEMIA has a good "see" cross-reference from both CHEMICA and CHYMIA, but under ALCHEMIA only *anonymi* are included. Bede's ecclesiastical history is not found under ANGLIA. An entry under ALLIANCES is a pure title first-word entry. These subject captions make no pretense of being either systematic or comprehensive. They supplement the author list and are intended to serve the double purpose of caring for the *anonymi* and, at the same time, partially serving the reader who wishes topical material. These subject captions are catch phrases taken from the titles of the books and, as far as they are substitutes for author headings, they become an integral part of the author catalog and concern author rules.

Although in these early catalogs these subject captions perform the double purpose of both subject entry and substitute for author entry we must not confuse these two quite distinct functions. The author entry is designed to facilitate the finding of a particular book; the true subject entry groups topical material. The early alphabetical subject captions never attained complete efficiency in this second function. The classed catalog was far superior for subject reference. For this reason the second type[6]—the alphabetical subject catalog with author index— has not persisted. The author index proved inadequate for author entries, while the function of the alphabetical subject captions was still confused and the entries too haphazard for satisfactory subject reference.

The third type—author entries in combination with subject and title entries for the *anonymi*—is the true predecessor of our author catalogs. In its dictionary form only a practical consideration prevented its direct development into our modern dictionary catalog. It has both the subject and title elements in embryo, but the labor and expense of duplicating subject entries necessary for the efficient subject catalog in this form was prohibitive and its usefulness for subject reference became gradually negligible. As a matter of economy it was the practice to make a single entry serve as many purposes as possible and nothing was better calculated to do this than these catch-title, subject-word, and form entries after the fashion of the Corvey list. This developed a type of catalog of maximum usefulness, not too costly to print, which became the model of our English general catalogs.

With the multiplication of books more careful cataloging became necessary. Not only the ready finding of books by author and subject was demanded but a distinction had to be made between authors of the same name. Authors known under various different forms of name must be brought together under a single form. The book published without personal author became an increasingly perplexing problem. The printing process, which had introduced uniform title pages, made imprint and collation a matter of importance.

Be it noted in passing how meager are the references to the catalog in the early treatises[7] on librarianship. The librarian is an erudite scholar who knows and loves his books, who is interested in acquiring them and solicitous in guarding them, but catalogs do not seem to worry him. It is taken for granted that the superior intelligence of a librarian will be equal to transcribing the *titles,* and their arrangement is more or less a matter of individual judgment. We find, however, that no early librarian who had time to write upon his profession had ever been burdened by the labor of compiling a printed catalog. If he had been responsible for such a labor, he would not have dismissed the catalog with a mere sentence or so.

Many excellent catalogs were produced in the seventeenth century. As a rule the Preface gives a brief statement of the method of entry. Of these, the Bodleian catalog of 1674[8] may be singled out as important because the rules set the practice followed by all British libraries, anticipating the British Museum rules by nearly two centuries, and are, as far as I know, the first considerable body of cataloging rules ever drawn up.

The Bodleian at that date was the most important library in England and one of the great libraries of the world. It had at its head a brilliant scholar, Sir Thomas Hyde, and the Preface to the catalog for which he was responsible goes straight to the heart of the cataloger of today.

With wit and acumen he sets forth in the Preface the difficulties of compiling a catalog. This one, which he estimated would take two years to see through, took nine years, in which, however weary, he labored steadfastly that he might bring the work to the most desirable conclusion. He expected little thanks, for, he continues, they say "What can be more easy, having looked at the title-pages than to write down the titles?" But these inexperienced people, who think making an index of their own few private books a pleasant task of a week or two, have no conception of the difficulties that arise or realize how carefully each book must be examined when the library numbers myriads of volumes. In the colossal labor, which exhausts both body and soul, of making into a alphabetical catalog a multitude of books gathered from every corner of the earth there are many intricate and difficult problems that torture the mind.[9]

After thus forcefully calling the reader's attention to the difficulties of the task, he proceeds to analyze these difficulties and to state clearly his working rules. These cover imprint, collation, form of author's name, and, what interests us particularly in this paper, rules for main entry.

These rules for main entry in 1674 may be summarized as follows:

Personal authors:
> If author is given in book, enter under surname, choosing one form if he is known under several names. For the sake of uniformity, even if author is always known by his given name, use surname, although it may inconvenience the reader.

> If author's name is not given, enter under assumed name (why one should
> want to use it he can't see!) or initials, but always ferret out name of
> author and make cross-reference.
> Enter translations under original author.

Anonymi:
> Compilations:
>> Enter under such words as LEXICA, CONCORDANTIA, JUS, CONCILIA,
>> those books which are likely to be thumbed to pieces by use, but
>> enter others (not in demand) under place or editor.
> Other anonymous books are to be entered under person referred to or under
> a subject word.

Thomas Hyde, it seems to me formulates the first principle of modern cataloging—that the cataloger should recognize and assemble literary units under a single caption.[10] He makes clear that an author known under several names is to be entered under a single selected form, that translations should be entered under the author of the original work, and that where a pseudonym is used, no pains should be spared to identify the author and at least to make a cross-reference from him.

The first high-water mark in modern English and American cataloging is the formulation of the British Museum rules in 1841. Like all preceding rules they were printed as a preface to the catalog itself, but, unlike earlier rules, they were drawn up by a group of men, were formally authorized by the trustees of the Museum, and were issued later independently as *Rules.*

The British Museum had issued two previous catalogs (in Latin), and now, under Panizzi, proposed a monumental catalog in English of the greatly increased collection. Inconsistencies and inadequacies of the earlier editions were noted, and, for the guidance of the staff who were to prepare the new edition, Panizzi sought the advice of the distinguished librarians of the Kingdom. With their help he drew up a body of rules generally spoken of as "the famous 91 rules." Incidentally, the project of the printed catalog fell through after the issue of the first volume, but the rules themselves are a most important contribution to library science, forming the basis of our present practice. It is worth while to examine these in detail.

Rule I and Rule X are forward-looking innovations—Rule I directing that entries be made on slips of uniform size, a practice that was the forerunner of our card catalogs, while Rule X concerns the use of the vernacular in the authors' form of name. It had been the practice to enter all names in Latin.

The rules concerning entry forms divide themselves into two main groups: (1) *personal authors*, with name printed on title-page or in book; (2) *anonymous works,* which include all works not having personal authors in evidence on the title-page or in any other part of the work.

I. Personal authors:
> Rule II defines and limits personal author entries, directing that entry is to be
> made under surname of the author when it appears printed in the title
> or any other part of the book. Rules II-VIII, X-XVII relate to the form
> of author's name.

Pseudonyms and assumed names are to be treated as real names and entry
made under them (Rules XLI-XLII).

Translations are to be entered under original author (Rule LI).

Commentaries unaccompanied by text are to be entered under commentator; accompanied by complete text, under author of the text (Rules
LI, LIII).

2. Anonymous works:

The remaining rules (except those covering transcription, collation, and
imprint) relate to anonymous works.

Rule IX is a most important ruling laying the foundation for our corporate
entries. It is here quoted verbatim:

Any act, resolution, or other document purporting to be agreed upon,
authorized or issued by assemblies, boards or corporate bodies
(with the exception of academies, universities, learned societies
and religious orders....) to be entered in distinct alphabetical
series under the name of the country or place from which they
derive their denomination, or for want of such denomination
under the name of the place from whence their acts are issued.

Here we see the English practice of referring all acts of governing bodies,
conventions, and local corporate bodies to the country or place from which they
emanate and the derivation of our whole series rules under place name. Rule
XLVII is a further elaboration concerning laws, edicts, and public acts.

Another series of important rulings refers to the various types of works of
corporate authorship which are to be entered under form headings:

Academies, universities, and learned societies excluded from Rule IX call for
a lengthy rule (LXXX). These are to be entered under the word ACADEMIES, then
grouped by the four main country divisions—Europe, Asia, Africa, America. Under
these the arrangement is to be under political division—France, Germany, etc.—
and under political divisions by name of town where institution or society is
located; and last of all, subordinated to place, is the name of the society. Volume I
of the catalog of 1841 contains this large classed group, ACADEMIES. In the catalog
of 1881-1900, which devotes nearly a whole volume to the form heading
ACADEMIES, the four large groups and the political divisions are dropped, and the
entry is under place. In the new catalog just appearing, the form heading itself is
discarded, and the entry is directly under place.

Other form headings set up are PERIODICAL PUBLICATIONS, EPHEMERIDES,
CATALOGUES, LITURGIES. Dictionaries and encyclopedias are entered under these
words if they are used in the title. A special rule (LXXIX) provides for the entry
under BIBLE—the first rule formulated for the type of literature now known as
anonymous classics.

A miscellaneous remnant of *anonymi* both of personal and collective authorship (no distinction in treatment is accorded these two types) are not covered by
the above rules and come in for special rulings:

Criminal trials are entered under defendant (Rule XXXVII).
Trials relating to vessels, under vessel (Rule XXXVII).

If a person is referred to in the title, the entry is under the person's name (Rule XXXIII).

If no person is mentioned then entry, if not covered by rule IX, is under any place name on the title-page (Rule XXXIV).

If no person or place is given, then entry is under *first substantive* (Rules XXXVIII and XXXVI).

If no substantive, in title, then entry is under first word. Nouns are to be substituted for derivative adjectives as entry word, and modifying adjectives may be combined (Rules XXXVIII and XXXVI).

These, in brief, are the main provisions of the famous "91 rules." It will be seen how much they owe to Thomas Hyde. Author entries, entry under pseudonym, form entries, and subject entries follow the precedent set by him. The significant forward step lies in separating from the general group, *anonymi,* publications of governments, corporate bodies, and societies for special rulings, and the use of corporate names for the latter even though submerged under a mountain of form and place captions. The idea of treating literary units under a single caption is extended to the word BIBLE to collect editions of that classic, and in large measure Rule IX and Rule LXXX assemble works of corporate bodies. Rulings for *anonymi* not specially provided for call for catch-title, first-noun, or subject-word entries.

The subsequent issues of British Museum *Rules* have deviated little in principle, and are for the most part elaborations and expansions. A few more form headings have been introduced, and several important tendencies in the direction of authorship entry are noted—one, the ruling in the 1906 edition permitting the entry of well-known classics under the author, even though the author's name is omitted from the title-page, and now in the new edition just appearing, works formerly subordinated under ACADEMIES are entered directly under place.

While Panizzi was building up the British Museum collection and Edward Edwards and other scholarly librarians were active in England, American libraries were becoming important factors commanding scholarly and able men to administer them. Among this early group of American librarians, Charles Coffin Jewett stands out conspicuously as a leader and organizer of library interests. Appointed librarian of Brown University in 1841, he rearranged the library and printed a catalog which attracted much attention. After spending several years in the study of European libraries, in 1848 he became librarian of the Smithsonian Institution, and while the head of this national library he had a great idea and proposed a scheme for printing a union catalog for American libraries. His scheme for the union catalog, though enthusiastically supported by able men, was never carried out, but the plan as developed necessitated the formulation of rules to guide the various libraries which were to contribute copy. These were first issued in the Smithsonian report of 1852, as part of his paper "On the construction of catalogues of libraries," which was reissued in 1853 in a second enlarged edition.

Jewett's rules, which he acknowledges as mainly drawn verbatim from Panizzi's "91 rules," owe much of their merit to Panizzi, but in their deviation introduced two new principles which are of the greatest importance in the development of future codes.

Jewett's Rule XXII is a sweeping innovation extending the principle of authorship entry to all corporate bodies. It must be quoted in full.

Academies, institutes, associations, universities, colleges, literary, scientific, economical, eleemosynary and religious societies; national and municipal governments, assemblies, conventions, boards, corporations and other bodies of men under what ever name and of what ever character issuing publications, whether as separate works or in a continuous series under a general title, are to be considered and treated as the authors of all works issued by them and in their name alone. *The heading is to be the name of the body, the principal word to be the first word not an article.* A cross-reference to be made from any important substantive or adjective to the principal word.

This drastic rule is supplied with a note which explains that government publications issued by committees and departments are to have as heading the name of the chief (body) not subordinate body and as an example gives UNITED STATES. Significantly, it regards United States as an author and not as the place mentioned on the title-page.

The second innovation (Rule XXIX), borrowed from the French, which has set American practice, prescribes that the various types of catch-title and subject-word entry be discarded, and that anonymous works be entered under the *first word of the title.* This rule has now for many years been the standard American practice.

After leaving the Smithsonian, Jewett entered the Boston Public Library, being appointed chief librarian in 1858. He took his rules with him, and these were issued by the Boston Public Library and presumably were adopted there. In 1858 Charles Ammi Cutter, a young man of twenty-one, entered the Harvard Divinity School in the double capacity of student and librarian. He soon gave up preaching and became an assistant in the Harvard Library. In 1868 he was elected librarian of the Boston Athenaeum, and between 1874 and 1882 he issued a formidable five-volume catalog of that institution. Cutter, it will be seen, had the opportunity of coming into close personal touch with Jewett and, in his own work, of testing out the rules Jewett had formulated. In 1876, twenty-four years after Jewett's codification, Cutter issued the first edition of his *Rules for a printed dictionary catalogue* as a special report of the Bureau of Education. This he modestly calls a first attempt to set forth rules in a systematic way and to investigate what might be called the first principles of cataloging. It is with his author entries alone that we are concerned.

What Jewett embodied in his Rule XXII, Cutter, in his first direction, restates in the form of a general law, specifically extending the authorship principle to corporate bodies: "Make the author entry under the *name of the author, whether personal or corporate, or some substitute for it.*" He amplifies this principle under the division "Corporate" in his rule: "Bodies of men are to be considered authors of works published in their name or authority." Out of his experience in applying this innovation of Jewett's he sees the difficulties that lie in the name. Place name and corporate name vie in importance. He weighs their claims and suggests solutions and alternate plans. Under the section "Substitutes" for author entry, Cutter extends his principle of authorship entry to works published under pseudonyms and initials and to collections brought together by a personal or corporate editor.

This reduces the class *anonymi* to modern works where personal authorship is unknown, to the anonymous classics, and to works of multiple authorship—

periodicals, almanacs, etc. For these classes Cutter has a section "Title entry," a caption which has persisted and is repeated in our present code.

In dealing with anonymous classics Cutter makes an original and vital contribution to the authorship principle. He regards this species of literature as a class by itself. He sees that it is the function of the catalog to assemble these classics and consider as a unit of literature, under a single heading, all texts derived from the same source, however the individual titles may read. The entry form should go back to the original source and for a classic of unknown authorship he suggests the Latin form by which it was originally known; or, for a medieval legend, the name of the hero by which it is known, giving as examples, SEPTEM SAPIENTES and SIR GAWAIN. These entries are neither catch-title or subject-word entries but entry under a fixed conventional name as substitute for author.

This idea that the literary unit rather than the individual book should determine the entry word has been long in gaining acceptance. Thomas Hyde accepted it for translations. It spread gradually in the British Museum rules which made special provisions for BIBLE and the IMITATIO CHRISTI. But Cutter ventures to apply it wholesale to the whole group of anonymous classics. The English practice had been feeling its way toward assembling units of corporate authorship through cumbersome form and place headings. Jewett seizes upon the idea and with one bold stroke frees these corporate units by his rule for direct entry under corporate authorship names. Cutter goes farther. Authorship forms, personal, corporate, or conventional name as substitute for author, are fundamental to his author rules. These authorship forms assemble literary units.

We find in Cutter, fixed for all time, I believe, the two fundamental principles of the modern author catalog:

1.   The author catalog is more than a finding list of separate and particular books. It deals with literary units and its function is to assemble under a convenient heading all issues or forms of the same literary unit.

2.   The most satisfactory method of doing this is through the attribution of authorship, using as heading the name of the person, or corporate body responsible for the work, or using as a substitute for author heading, a conventional name not derived from the title-page but from the literary source of the book or document.

The cataloger must identify the literary unit and provide the unit, not the single book, with an entry name; and this name goes back to the source of its authorship.

In the evolution of catalogs we can clearly distinguish three stages corresponding to the purposes for which they were made. The first purpose was to account for property. The catalog is an inventory list. This function has now been completely taken over by a supplementary list, the shelf-list. In the second stage the purpose is to provide a finding-list for particular books. In serving this function the author catalog is still a most useful instrument. If a personal author is in evidence, this is usually the most important memory cue. In the case of *anonymi* this convenient personal aid to the memory is wanting, but the finding-list function is amply provided for by secondary entries under editor, title, catch title, or subject. A third purpose,[11] that of assembling literary units, has come to the front as important, and our term "main entry" recognizes this as a primary function. In this third stage our catalogs are highly developed instruments. Author, subject, and title entry are now clearly differentiated. Authorship determines the main entry. We have relegated the finding-list function to "secondary entries," where the main entry is inadequate for quickly "finding" the individual book.

We have traced the gradual extension of the authorship idea, in our English and American rules, from personal authors to corporate bodies and anonymous classics. It seems to the writer that the final step which will extend it to cover the chief remaining group–works of composite authorship–is a short and easy one. This type of literature–periodicals, dictionaries, and all works of multiple authorship known by their titles only–are compilations of groups of men associated for the specific purpose of producing a particular unit of literature. The group itself is only known by the literary work which it produces; for example, we speak of the editors of the *Atlantic monthly* or of the *Encyclopedia Britannica.* The literary work itself is the entity, and its name, in the word-by-word order the publishers have given it, is its true baptismal name. This name itself is entitled to rank, in its own right, as a substitute authorship entry. This leaves only works of personal authorship whose authors remain unknown (and these too, until their parentage is revealed, are orphaned units) alone and on their own, and the only name they can claim is the name given them on the title-page. Perhaps, as a matter of charity, we might stretch the idea of authorship entry enough to bring these in–the last lambs outside the authorship fold. If the entry under title for these two groups may be considered as substitute for author entry, as I think it may be, all main entries may be considered authorship entries and all come under Cutter's general law: "Make the author entry under the name of the author, whether personal or corporate, or some substitute for it."

Since Cutter's first edition of *Rules* there has been no further development in principles, though an enormous amout of work has been done in amplifying, codifying, and clarifying rules, which has contributed to a needed uniformity in practice.

Perkins drew up an amplification of Jewett's rules in 1869, previous to Cutter's, which he withdrew on their appearance, but later issued the San Francisco rules, a modification of Cutter used in that public library. In 1890 Linderfeld translated the portion of the important German codification, Dziatzko's *Instruction,* relating to personal authors, supplementing this with a comparative study of other rules. In 1883 a committee of the American Library Association, appointed in 1877, issued its "Condensed rules for an author and title catalogue,"[12] which were based on Cutter and to which are appended the seven cases in which the English rules drawn up by the Library Association of the United Kingdom differ from them. Dewey's *Library school rules,* issued in 1888 (and later, in many editions), amplifies these and adds illustrations. The American Library Association "Condensed rules" of 1883 goes back to Jewett in a sweeping ruling entering all corporate publications directly under the name of the body issuing them. Dewey differs, preferring Cutter's alternate way of entering local and municipal societies under place. In 1908 the present American Library Association code was issued, strictly in line with the authorship principles laid down by Cutter. Mr. Hanson, the American editor-in-chief, brought to this code his experience in applying Cutter's rules to the reorganization of the Library of Congress catalog then under his direction. To him is attributed the clear-cut distinction between societies and institutions and the limitation of place name as entry to local institutions. Cutter struggled with this problem, but it was left to the 1908 code to analyze and simplify Cutter's special rulings. This code represents a culmination of the friendly interchange of ideas between English and American librarians. It is the result of the joint deliberations of two separate committees—one American, the other English—working in collaboration and is the first step toward the future goal of an international code. It has been adopted by many libraries in England, where it is known as the Anglo-American code.

Since 1908 the idea of co-operative cataloging, growing out of the general use of Library of Congress printed cards, has created a great demand for more definitions and much amplification of the 1908 code. The Library of Congress has met this demand in part by its issue of "Supplementary rules" on cards, but a mass of suggestions and questions has accumulated. In 1932 a new committee was appointed and now has before it the task of supplementing and revising the code of 1908.

If we accept these two general principles as already fixed in the Anglo-American code—(1) that the catalog seeks to identify and assemble literary units; and (2) that authorship determines the entry form—what bearing does it have upon the work before the present committee on the revision of the code? In the first place, as the 1908 code was formed upon these principles (although this was not specifically stated), there will be few fundamental changes in the present rules. But in the changes that are made the conciliatory policy of "establishing headings which are most likely to be looked for in our English and American libraries"[13] will have less weight. The Library of Congress is effectually weaning us from this earlier practice.[14] Who but a cataloger would look for Tagore under "Ravindranatha Thakura"?

The form of name—personal, corporate, or substitute for author—under which the unit of literature is assembled will be determined by the best international or English usage, and will not be some guess at the catchword form which the reader would naturally expect. Thomas Hyde's principle, that the consistency of the catalog should take precedence over the convenience of the reader in looking for a particular book, is a sound doctrine. The "ease of cataloguer"[15] is not in question. This serves the "ease of the reader" best in the long run.

Then, as far as possible, all forms which one cannot correctly consider literary agents, responsible for the production or distribution of the literature under consideration, must finally go. We must eliminate as author entries such headings as CONGREGATIONALISTS, BAPTISTS, etc., which are subject forms and do not exist as corporate bodies. We cannot use, for example, MORMONS, LITURGY AND RITUAL as an author entry. Will it be possible to use as author, without subhead, the name of a government or corporate body with extensive administration departments—UNITED STATES, for instance? Can the United States, except through some department or executive office, issue any literature? What standing have our useful form subheads, LAWS, TREATIES, LITURGY AND RITUAL?

The whole series of rules regarding entry under place is open to question. Place, under which it is our useful practice to enter local institutions, in many cases forms no part of their legal name. Shall we go back to Jewett and the "Condensed rules" of 1883? The use of corporate name in its legal form is increasing. The present revisers will probably make few changes, but in future rules, place name, if not a part of the corporate title, will probably become less important.

Shall we regard the entry for diplomatic conferences as entry under place name, as the present rule implies? Is the entry VIENNA, CONGRESS OF, for example, an entry under place of meeting? Is it not, rather, an entry, in inverted form, under the name of the congress—a true authorship entry directly under name? With no change in our practice the wording of this rule might be revised.

Shall we continue to enter civil actions and ships under subject forms? Is the name of the ship or the name of the defendant, in truth, the responsible author? If they are author forms, do they merit special rules? It is interesting to note that these two minor rules have been repeated verbatim from the "91 rules" in every code down to date—not, I think, because they are very important, but because they have been difficult to bring in under other rulings.

Cutter has appended to his rules a useful caption, "Economies," and although we have dropped that heading from our code we might revive the idea to cover all exceptions in practice which we can not yet conveniently bring strictly under Cutter's general law. There are many holdovers in common usage in our catalogs which a code of rules must take into consideration. For practical reasons catalogs of individual libraries can no more cut free all at once from former practices than could the British Museum catalog adopt the Anglo-American code. But it will be a distinct step in advance if we detect these holdovers, and where they have proved inconvenient and are in question, we may suggest new rules which are more consistent with the authorship principle.

The unit card contributes much to the possibility of perfecting the rules. The principle of authorship entry relates only to main entry. With the availability of printed cards the importance of this entry in a finding-list function is reduced to a minimum. Added cards with catchword, subject, or even form headings serve the purpose of entries designed to facilitate the ready finding of the individual book. Nothing is lost, and increased bibliographical service is rendered, by the new emphasis upon the necessity of assembling literary units and the importance of authorship forms for the main entry.

The rapid development of co-operative cataloging, for which many libraries contribute copy, has created a demand for a multiplicity of minute rulings to aid in producing uniform work. The writer believes the very formidable extent of this demand makes necessary a most careful analysis of all rules to discover basic principles which, if applied consistently, will simplify the problems and eliminate many special rulings. Heaven forbid an encyclopedic work of pedantic distinctions and specific directions for every possible vagary. The revisers themselves, indeed, should be cognizant of every possible contingency that can arise, but they should seek to formulate simple and clear definitions and rulings that will cover the main questions which practical catalogers are raising. If the revisers' work is structurally sound, the possible slight variations of intelligent catalogers in applying rules to details will not be a serious impediment to co-operative cataloging. No scholar will carp over the form of a note if the substance is correct and the English is clear.

As stated in the beginning, this paper is limited to tracing the authorship principle formulated in the rules of the Anglo-American code. The divergence of European, especially German, practice in favor of the title forms and the growing influence of the Anglo-American code in European practice should certainly be taken into consideration by the new revisers. Its importance merits distinct treatment, which no one is more able to give than Mr. Hanson himself, and such a comparative study of European practice should supplement this paper.

Notes

1.   J. C. M. Hanson, "Corporate authorship versus title entry," *Library quarterly,* V (October, 1935), 457-66.

2.   The extension of these principles outside the American and British libraries adopting this code and the influence of the Anglo-American code upon the recent Vatican, Norwegian, and other codes is outside the scope of the present paper.

3.   These principles are three: (1) the recognition of the literary unit; (2) the attribution of authorship for preferred main entry; and (3) the entry for titles under the first word not an article. The first principle had in part been recognized quite early, and its importance is accountable for the growing tendency in European practice to adopt authorship forms. The direct entry under first word of title is borrowed from the French. It was used by Barbier in his *Dictionnaire des ouvrages anonymes et pseudonymes* (1806-9), who defends this practice in the Preface. There are other principles, such as the use of the vernacular, but these three have been promoted particularly in America.

4.   Both terms, *anonymi* and *annonyma scripta,* are found; the masculine ending emphasizing the absence of author; the neuter, the type of literature.

5.   Examples of this type are numerous and include Hyde's catalog of the Bodleian Library, all the issues of the British Museum *Catalogue* to date, and other English catalogs. The excellent catalog of the Barberini Library, *Index Bibliothecae qua Franciscus Barberinus ... reddidit* (Romae, 1681), is of this type. This catalog contains one real subject heading VITA VARIA, under which duplicate entries of lives listed also under BIOGRAPHEE, are entered. The new edition of the British Museum *General catalogue* now in press contains three columns of subject-word entries under ARITHMETIC, all substitutes for author entry for anonymous works.

6.   Martin Lipen's *Bibliotheca realis theologica omnium materiarum rerum et titularum* (1685), is a most excellent and comprehensive bibliography arranged by this method. I know of no modern examples.

7.   Gabriel Naudé, *Advis pour dresser une bibliothèque...*(1644), as an example, devotes a single paragraph to the catalog.

8.   *Catalogus impressorum librorum Bibliothecae Bodlejanae in Academia Oxoniensi. Curä & operä Thomae Hyde* (1674).

9.   A free abridgement of a translation made by Miss Mary McClure, Columbia University Library.

10.   In European practice this principle has not been developed greatly beyond Thomas Hyde, but is gaining recognition. The various continental rules merit separate treatment.

11.   Does the growing bibliographical demand that books of the same authorship source be brought together under a single caption justify the expensive scholarship which must be brought to this task, or shall our great catalogs abandon this principle and go back to the finding-list stage? There can be but one answer. It is not for us to stay the normal advance of the authorship idea.

12.   Reported in the *Library journal*, VIII (1883), 251-54, 263-64.

13.   This statement is made in the Preface of the 1908 code as a justification of rules for corporate entry.

14.   This brings up the question of two editions—one for scholarly collections, taking cognizance of international usage; another for popular use in small libraries.

15.   Preface to the 1908 *Rules*: "The convenience of the public is always to be set before the ease of the cataloguer."

The Crisis in Cataloging

Andrew D. Osborn

Editor's Introduction

During the late 1930s, it had become obvious that the processing operations of the Library of Congress (LC) were undergoing a grave crisis: arrearages were increasing and cataloging production was declining. This was of consequence because LC had become the de facto national center for the production of cataloging copy. By the time Archibald MacLeish was appointed Librarian of Congress in 1940, the moment had arrived to resolve the problem. Accordingly, MacLeish appointed a committee of three, one of whom was Andrew D. Osborn, a philosopher turned librarian, to investigate the status of LC cataloging operations and to suggest means for their possible reorganization. At the same time, the preliminary American second edition of the 1908 cataloging rules was in preparation, but because these rules represented more a compilation and extension of existing practices than a thorough examination of cataloging procedures, it was obvious that even in the revised form they would not prevent arrearages from continuing to mount or costs from continuing to escalate, and cataloging would reach libraries outside LC at increasingly slow rates.

The conclusions of the LC committee were presented in a series of reports, some parts of which are still under a security classification. These reports pointed to several failures in cataloging administration, not the least of which pertained to the contents of the cataloging rules then in force. Certainly, as key members of the Association of Research Libraries became aware of the general conclusions of the LC investigation, and themselves became familiar with the contents of the preliminary code, they became convinced that the new code had to be vetoed. But that message had to reach the public. In a talk at Harvard titled "What the Library Administrator Needs to Know about Cataloging: The Crisis in Cataloging," Osborn presented his thoughts,* which were printed in a pamphlet and later circulated widely through the medium of the October 1941 issue of *Library Quarterly* as "The Crisis in Cataloging." The message of "The Crisis" is far broader than that of the LC reports; the sterotypes presented by Osborn seem valid even today. That this should be the case is perhaps related to the conflicting demands placed on library catalogs.

The recent tendency of AACR2 to accumulate a group of interpretations more voluminous than the code itself, along with manuals for special types of materials, is evidence that the legalistic theory of cataloging is dominant again. The reason for this may be the requirement for uniformity in a network system.

As one examines many proposals for rule revision, one is impressed by the dominance of the perfectionistic school. Details are to be added ad infinitum, details whose addition has prevented the acceptance of a uniformly satisfactory definition of a standard level of cataloging.

MC

Further Reading

Carpenter, Michael. *Corporate Authorship: Its Role in Library Cataloging,* 23-26. Westport, Conn.: Greenwood Press, 1981.

Provides details on the milieu of the "crisis."

Personal communication from Andrew D. Osborn to Michael Carpenter, 18 November 1984.

The Crisis in Cataloging

A wise German librarian has linked the library administrator and the cataloger as working for the common aim of economy in work and cost coupled with better utilization of a library's resources. This aim, he thinks, is expressed in various kinds of co-operative work, of pooling interests, and of setting standards. It is to be developed prudently, he says, with the objectives setting limitations in such a way that more values will not be destroyed than are created.[1]

This ideal he set out in a chapter entitled "Tasks for the future." There was a time, and not so very far back, when the library administrator and the cataloger worked side by side. In the more immediate past, however, the two have become separated, so that their closer collaboration does need to be set down as a task for the future, the immediate future at that. Many new problems of administration have served to busy the administrator, and most catalogers have had more work than enough, with the result that administrators have come to know less and less of cataloging, and catalogers have come to know les and les about general library administration. The situation now is that the administrator will be forced to pay more attention to cataloging because it has become a major problem field. Neither the administrator alone nor the cataloger alone can solve the many problems. Collaboration is essential, and to this end administrators must know more of cataloging and catalogers must know more of administration.

This is not to say that administrators must be catalogers, although it is true that there is a great need for catalogers who are administrators. The administrator does need to know enough of cataloging from the inside to be able to control the destiny of his catalog department wisely. Thus it would appear that, if the internship is to be looked on as a possible element in the training of a library administrator, then one excellent way of exploiting the internship would be to have the prospective administrator spend a year in a good catalog department. Another way for prospective administrators to study the problems to be found in a catalog department is to take the second-year course in cataloging in library schools where that

Reprinted by permission of Andrew D. Osborn and The University of Chicago Press from *Library Quarterly* 11 (October 1941): 393-411.

course is treated as a seminar devoted to problems of catalog department administration and not merely as an advanced course in cataloging techniques, as, for example, the cataloging of rare books. Library schools should be encouraged to plan such a course with administration uppermost in mind, and administrators should be urged to take it.

It seems a little odd to be saying such things when as far back as 1915 Dr. Bishop put the matter in classic form in his address to the Albany Library School entitled *Cataloging as an asset.* "The cataloger," he said, "must be an administrator if he is to meet the needs of the future: and the administrator can not afford to be ignorant of these problems in cataloging, which must be solved."[2] And again: "If you are to administer libraries, you must know libraries, you must be able to work your machine, you must have practical knowledge of its parts. Nothing in the craft should be foreign to you, least of all the art of cataloging."[3]

Cataloging is an art, and as an art it is technical. Its basic rules are actually few and simple, and, in so far as the rules are kept few and simple, it is a delightful art to practice. That is admittedly the romanticist point of view. A period of romanticism tends to be followed by a period of classicism with its subservience to rules, and this is what has been happening to cataloging. More and more rules and definitions are being worked out constantly, until at the present time it begins to appear that classicism is taking full control. Thus it is that cataloging has become elaborate, highly technical, a skill too often existing in and for itself. This is the kind of cataloging that the administrator finds himself out of touch with, at a loss to comprehend, and without sufficient depth of understanding to guide it to safer and surer paths. Cataloging does not need to call for so much sheer craftsmanship. In point of fact, the less the cataloger is a craftsman pure and simple, the more room there is for him to be just an excellent librarian.

Much of library science and library administration is not at all scientific. Over a period of years good administrators have developed a body of sound practice, and this it is that can be called library science. Perhaps there has been a minimum of theory and a maximum of common sense in developing this body of sound practice, and it may be that there are certain losses in minimizing the role of theory.

The Legalist Theory of Cataloging

Actually there are a number of theories of cataloging more or less vaguely in application today. The principal ones might be characterized as the legalistic, the perfectionistic, the bibliographic, and the pragmatic.

The dominant one is probably the legalistic. According to it, there must be rules and definitions to govern every point that arises; there must be an authority to settle questions at issue. So the reviser sits in judgment on the cataloger, and the head cataloger is in the supreme court for his particular library. Many of the decisions handed down are purely arbitrary, partly because many of the points at issue are simply a matter of taste or judgment.

On the face of it, this seems too arbitrary to be true, but it is precisely the way things are done. Here are a few examples from everyday practice. The cataloger says in the collation that the book contains a portrait. The reviser changes the collation because she says it is not a portrait, the reason being that it is not the picture of anyone named or determinable; or it is the picture of the author's wife standing in front of the great pyramid, and so the reviser rules that it is to be taken as a picture of the pyramid instead of as a portrait; or it is the picture of a native in a book on ethnology, the native being taken as an object of study rather than as an individual, apparently; or a hundred and one other nice distinctions. Here is another case in point. Thomas Thompson writes a book of short stories entitled *Lancashire lather*. The setting is a barber's shop, and the frontispiece depicts a barber. The cataloger enters in the collation *front. (port.)*. There is no question but that it is the portrait of a real person attired as a barber; but it might be an actor dressed up to represent a barber; at any rate, it does not say "Tom Smith," who could be verified as this particular Lancashire barber. Accordingly the reviser, with much justification, changes the collation from *front. (port.)* to mere *front*.

It requires definite skill to determine when a portrait is not a portrait. The cataloger must pass on caricatures, likenesses on coins and medals, effigies from tombs, pictures of mummies, spirit photographs, and a host of other difficult situations. And then, of course, there is the group portrait to add to the problem. How many people are needed to make a group? Here is the autobiography of a distinguished English lawyer. The frontispiece shows him in his wig and gown attended by various flunkies in front and behind. Since it is a picture of three or four people, the cataloger enters in the collation *front. (group port.)*. The reviser changes the collation to *front. (port.)* on the ground that the flunkies do not count and that the intention is to provide merely a portrait of the author in an appropriate setting.

This kind of procedure is part and parcel of the daily conduct of catalog departments. Examples could be multiplied to show that there is the greatest of confusion in catalogers' minds as to what a facsimile, a map, or many other seemingly innocent thing might be when they begin to take on some of their varied forms. The cataloger takes time debating the question; the reviser takes still more time; and the head cataloger may be called on for a final decision. Debate, discussion, and decision eat up a surprising amount of time. Hence the demand in some quarters for a cataloging code that will define or rule on all debatable points.

Some catalogers are so impressed by this legalistic theory of cataloging that they are ready to maintain that a fully developed body of definitions, rules, decisions, and precedents will result in decreasing the cost of cataloging. The argument is that if everything has been covered in the code of laws then there will be no more debates, no more wasted time. If there are "57 varieties" of facsimile, they must all be differentiated. Some kinds would be called facsimiles on the catalog card and others would not. It would not matter if the word *facsim.* in the collation stood ambiguously for any of the valid kinds of facsimile. The decisions are not concerned with that kind of knowledge. The decision is simply to determine whether in this particular instance the general term *facsim.* has been used legitimately or not in the collation.

Thus the classical tendency in cataloging tends to push on to the final phase of classicism—the phase that leads to decline, the valuing of rules and definitions for their own sake. In this way cataloging can become an end in itself, and the cataloger can become a craftsman instead of a librarian. Such cataloging does not ask whether the close definition of a facsimile results in economy of work and cost coupled with better utilization of the library's resources. The systematic determination of out-of-the-way, unusual, or exceptional points, the attempt to rationalize vague, ambiguous, and highly diverse concepts—these result in a theory and practice of cataloging neither economical nor particularly effective.

The weakest point in the legalistic theory is its treatment of matters that must be left indefinite. The proposed revision of the A.L.A. cataloging code has been worked out from a legalistic point of view. Where it has failed most signally, in the light of its own theory, is in the rules that result in a choice of entry. In the old code such rules (e.g., in the treatment of collections under editor or under title and in the treatment of government and other publications under personal or corporate name) led to great difficulty. They were probably the hardest rules in the whole code to apply. The proposed revision has not improved the situation in the slightest, simply because matters of taste and judgment are too intangible to operate well in cataloging or other codes.

A second serious defect in a legalistic approach to cataloging is that, once it is decided to formulate rules and decisions for all points, the process must go on indefinitely. When in the future a point arises not covered in the past, the cataloger cannot use judgment to settle the matter but must set a complicated decision-giving apparatus in motion. Time and attention must be given to settling an infinite variety of small details such as the scholastics of the Middle Ages might have delighted in debating.

A final weakness worth emphasizing is that codification tends to obscure reasons and principles. Much of the original meaning and intention has been lost from the 1908 code. As a result the approach to cataloging becomes less and less a matter of comprehending and principles and more and more a matter of the mere learning of arbitrary rules and definitions. Thus elements of cataloging practice that were introduced for historical reasons come to be accepted and perpetuated without any understanding of why the rule was made. For example, there was sound reason for introducing the cataloging form known as hanging indention. That reason no longer exists, yet the form carries on and receives new emphasis in the proposed new code. Survivals of this kind tend to make the teaching and practice of cataloging mere techniques.

Since the proposed revision of the A.L.A. cataloging code has the weaknesses of the legalistic point of view, it is accordingly to be deprecated strongly. The dignity of cataloging as an art calling for the display of intelligence and sound judgment is something that stands in sharp contrast to a tendency that would so define and regulate that catalogers would need little more enterprise than good clerks.

Perfectionism

Since the legalistic approach to cataloging is the principal danger to be watched at present, there is little need to discuss the perfectionistic or bibliographic approaches in detail.

The perfectionist cataloger is guided by the compelling desire to catalog a book in all respects so well that the job will be done once and for all. In 1935 the Library of Congress promulgated a definition of cataloging along such lines. Every detail on the catalog card is verified according to some authority, nothing has been omitted, and all users of the library now and in the future must be satisfied with the product.

The error behind the perfectionist theory is that so far no cataloger has succeeded in doing work that would last indefinitely. Invariably one generation of catalogers does over the work of its predecessors. This fact is clear from the history of older libraries. The library of Harvard University has had a dozen or more catalogs since 1764.

Obviously there is much to be said for a theory of cataloging which will not be rapidly outmoded. Ways and means must be found to make cataloging products endure. Yet recataloging proceeds apace in many a library, while classification, subject headings, and other details are constantly subject to change with the lapse of time. Tastes and needs change continually, and with them go the elements in cataloging that are based on taste or the needs of the time.

The perfectionist cataloger has been overwhelmed by the enormous masses of material constantly flowing into twentieth-century libraries. As a result many libraries have accumulated considerable arrearages of cataloging, material has sometimes been temporarily processed, records may be made inadequately or temporarily with the expectation that the work will be done over more fully at a later date, and all the time the cost of cataloging increases. Perhaps even more disconcerting is the fact that if there were time and opportunity, owing to less pressure from the current work, much good work could be done polishing up what has been accomplished in the past and planning for the future.

So the judgment on perfectionism must be that, although efficient technical work is to be desired in cataloging, perfectionism is not necessary to such work. The time element is the great foe of perfectionism. Catalogs cannot be created at one stroke; they contain many inconsistencies and imperfections. Many of these inconsistencies and imperfections hurt no one but the perfectionist.

Bibliographical Cataloging

The relationship between cataloging and bibliography has been a difficult one to define. The two have many points of contact and many elements in common. Their history has been intertwined in many respects.

The bibliographical theory of cataloging attempts to make cataloging into a branch of descriptive bibliography. The collation and the bibliographical notes are much affected. They become detailed to a degree. This detail is right and proper in its own place; it does harm when it is applied to everyday cataloging. For example, much processed material is being produced and cataloged today. How much of it needs to be collated in the detailed way that the printed book is? It is not at all uncommon, when bibliographical details are overemphasized, for the collation to become a meaningless conglomeration of terms which puzzle even the most experienced cataloger.

Descriptive notes, such as "Head and tail pieces," "Title vignette," "Illustrated lining papers," tend to fill up the catalog card without serving any real library or bibliographic function. Some of these formal descriptive notes are fortunately passing into disuse, and more could do so without loss. Examples of notes that are drifting from use are "Plates printed on both sides," "Title in red and black," and "Reprinted in part from various periodicals," the latter being for a volume of poems.

Kaiser's criterion of cataloging reads: the minimum of cost and effort in conformity with the best use of the library. It is from the practical point of view that the problem of bibliographic cataloging must be approached. The card catalog is at best a barrier between the reader and the book. "To the books themselves!" must be the motto for as much as possible.

The ordinary book and the rare book commonly need little bibliographic description; the one because it is ordinary, the other because there are printed bibliographies to provide much of the description. It is an intermediate type of book, the one that belongs in a local collection or a highly developed special collection, that may call for more detailed work from time to time. Such books are not treated as ordinary holdings and are not so likely to be listed in readily available and well-known bibliographies.

The Pragmatic Theory

Many libraries have for long been conducting their cataloging along purely practical lines. Rules hold and decisions are made only to the extent that seems desirable from a practical point of view. As a consequence nothing is pushed to an extreme, and hence the rules and definitions have no opportunity to become ends in themselves.

The quality of cataloging in such libraries is satisfactory, because it has been developed with the practical needs of the library constantly in mind. The legalistic cataloger would not approve of its standards because they have not been defined to any very great extent; the perfectionist cataloger would dislike the omissions and the failure to check with enough authorities; while the bibliographical cataloger would think the job only half-done.

It is difficult to systematize cataloging according to the pragmatic theory. In the first place, standards and practices need to be set for a number of types of library. Where the legalistic code is likely to set one standard, ignoring the needs of certain types of libraries, or leading to a degree of standardization whether wisely or not, the pragmatic emphasizes the differing needs of various types of library. The school library, the special library, the popular public library, the reference library, the college library, and the university library—all these have differing requirements, and to standardize their cataloging would result in much harm. There have been standardizing tendencies: the A.L.A. cataloging code, the use of Library of Congress cards, the development of union catalogs, and the teaching of cataloging in library schools. Some but not all of this standardization has been good. For example, all types of libraries can and do use Library of Congress cards— not necessarily all available Library of Congress cards, but still some; yet this does not mean that such libraries should adopt any more Library of Congress standards than are right and proper for their particular type of institution.

The forgotten man of cataloging is the college library. The last annual report of the Library of Congress showed that the principal user of Library of Congress cards is the college library. One-half the cards sold by the Card Division go to college libraries. But the A.L.A. cataloging code of 1908 was made without regard to college libraries. It was made for "larger libraries of a scholarly character,"[4] and there was not a single representative of the college library on the editorial committee. The college library has found it expedient to use Library of Congress cards and to follow the A.L.A. cataloging code. There are many college libraries but relatively few large, scholarly libraries. More attention should be paid to the needs of these many libraries, and they should more frequently express their requirements.

The A.L.A. *List of subject headings* presents an interesting study from this point of view. It was one of the very few tools worked out for the medium-sized library. The effectiveness of that list and the satisfaction which everyone who used it had for it seem to indicate that the medium-sized library may have an important stabilizing role in cataloging practice. The A.L.A. *List of subject headings* is dead and should never be brought back to life, but its significance should not be forgotten. Perhaps more tools should be worked out with the interests of the medium-sized library at heart; perhaps this type of library should be willing to take on more responsibility and leadership in cataloging councils.

Rules specially worked out for large scholarly libraries did not result in plain sailing for those libraries. The biggest of them—the Library of Congress—steadily lost ground, acquiring annually some thirty thousand more books than could be cataloged on this basis. When the cumulative effect began to be felt, the Library of Congress had amassed several million uncataloged books. The cataloging system had plainly broken down. At present the old rules need simplification, not amplification, if the Library of Congress is to carry on. In other words, a practical set of cataloging rules must be drawn up for such a library. The day of the legalistic, perfectionistic, or bibliographic cataloger is over; the day of the pragmatic cataloger has begun.

If this is true for the Library of Congress, it must apply likewise to the other large scholarly libraries of the country. No regular library need calls for more detailed cataloging than that done at the Library of Congress. Other libraries, then, should simplify their cataloging and should adopt the practical point of view. Consequently, the new cataloging code ought to be drawn up from that standpoint.

Generalizing, and passing over many minor matters, a pragmatic approach to cataloging and to the catalog code would result in the following developments:

1.   All cataloging practices would be meaningful, so that libraries where certain factors were present or absent would know whether they needed to adopt a given practice. For example, hanging indention would not be prescribed unless it was clearly understood for what use hanging indention is intended. It would be the function of the catalog code to make known such reasons or lack of reasons, so that libraries could determine whether to follow the particular rule or not.

2.   Three distinct and approved grades of cataloging would be followed in the code and in many libraries. These would be standard, simplified, and detailed cataloging. The classes of books which would be treated according to these methods should be specified. Standard cataloging would be less detailed in many respects than the 1908 code or the Library of Congress formerly required.

3.   In addition, self-cataloging methods must be put in good standing and exploited. This would apply in some measure to city directories, college catalogs, documents, large duplicate sets on open shelves, pamphlets and other ephemeral material arranged by subject, special collections of recreational reading, telephone books, and items in vertical files. Some or all of these practices are being used in one way or another; their use should increase.

4. Rules for cataloging would be relatively few and simple, partly because they would not attempt to cover exceptional and unusual cases. Revisions of the catalog code would thereafter result in slight change, so that whole classes of material would not have to be recatalogued.

5. The quality of the work would be high for anything regarded as essential. Nonessentials would be given little attention or passed over.

6. Catalogers would be trained to use their judgment, not to expect a rule or a precedent to guide them at all turns. It is hard to do intelligent work if that work has to be all by rule of thumb. If catalogers are called on to use judgment, the work will again become more interesting.

7. Unwritten rules and practices would be subject to the same pragmatic scrutiny. Some catalogers, for example, think that the sequence of subject headings in the tracing should follow certain requirements. Attention to such detail is completely valueless except where printed or mimeographed cards are concerned, and even there its value is doubtful.

8. The interpretation of any point will follow practical lines. If certain illustrations were intentionally included in a book as portraits, whether they are caricatures, representations on coins, or effigies on tombs, they can be recorded in the collation as portraits. This is the natural thing to do. Much artificiality has resulted from ignoring natural and obvious methods of procedure.

9. The cataloging of serial documents and nondocuments should be reviewed to see to what extent this class of material needs cataloging. Should superior indexes be provided instead for government publications? Should the *Union list of serials* serve as the catalog for such serials as it covers?

Organization of the Catalog Department

Catalogers and library administrators are thus faced with many and difficult cataloging problems of a technical nature. Organizational questions are equally pressing however. Far too little attention has been given in library literature to the organization of catalog departments, while in actual practice physical conditions have controlled matters to an undesirable extent.

Large or small divisions and sections are followed in some libraries. In others small groups of catalogers are under the control of revisers. Again the work may be done by units consisting of an experienced and a junior cataloger. Some catalogers do their own typing, ordering Library of Congress cards, or filing, while in other libraries special people are set aside to do such work. Some libraries are organized to catalog for others, as is the case with school libraries in Chicago and Los Angeles or with departmental and branch libraries. These are some of the many organizational patterns in use today.

Many catalog departments pay too little attention to the flow of material and hence tend to be organized less advantageously. The catalog department of any size will have to be streamlined in the future. Material that can move rapidly should be segregated from other books that move at an average or at a slow rate. Fiction, second copies, other editions, books to be stored directly in deposit libraries—these and others can be treated with considerable rapidity. Rare books and difficult cataloging of one kind or another may move very slowly. If the various types go along together, there are two dangers. One is that the slower books will obstruct the general flow, and the other is that if a cataloger pays special attention to getting the faster books along the others may be slighted either through setting them aside to be done when time permits or through treating them in the same way that an easy book might be treated.

Many popular libraries have for years streamlined their cataloging departments. It is not difficult to do if the types of cataloging are easily determinable, as, for instance, if second copies in considerable number keep coming into the catalog department as intentionally purchased duplicates. It is in the larger catalog departments where there may be many gifts and exchanges as well as purchased books that streamlining has been slow in developing. This may be partly due to the fact that such a department would need more central administration to take care of the decisions involved and to direct the flow of work.

It has commonly been stated that the three essential departments of a library are reference, circulation, and cataloging. In some school, branch, and departmental libraries the catalog department has been eliminated. More catalog departments ought to disappear in the near future. Cataloging can and should be supplied as a service in many libraries. It is possible that the development of regional deposit libraries will provide the means and the accommodation for regional cataloging centers. Neighboring libraries of a common type can at least share the work or concentrate it in one particular place.

This question is related to the further one regarding the future of official catalogs. Large libraries are finding official catalogs an increasing burden. It may cost the very large library ten thousand dollars a year to maintain such a catalog. If the building were designed so that all users of the library were conveniently brought together, then an official catalog would be unnecessary, providing the pressure on the public catalog were not too great. Money is better expended on service than on duplicating records. If library buildings can be designed so that an official catalog becomes unnecessary, the organization of a catalog department will be a simpler thing to control. As official catalogs have grown it has become increasingly hard to operate catalog departments efficiently. A layout that was close to ideal in the beginning may in the course of time result in situations far from ideal, owing to the growth of the official catalog as well as of the staff and its duties.

Mention of service, which is a basic factor in library work, brings up the need for considering the concentration of trained librarians who are working behind the scenes in catalog departments, while at the same time student assistants, untrained help, or insufficient professional help may be working with the readers. This is a major problem of organization, namely, how to make that concentration of trained people more generally useful throughout the library.

The Situation as regards Classification

The many problems confronting catalogers and library administrators are not confined to cataloging proper; they are both significant and numerous in the field of classification. The complicating factor in classification is that the theoretical literature on the subject is in a state of confusion. This is in no small measure due to the emphasis that certain writers place on the classification of knowledge and on bibliographic classification. German philosophers and scientists delighted in drawing up schemes for the classification of knowledge all through the nineteenth century. Such schemes had some slight value but were too much on the order of intellectual pastimes. As a practical matter library classification is far removed from any such schemes.

Bibliographic classification has been worked out and successfully applied in such an undertaking as the enormous card bibliography developed by the Brussels Institute for Documentation. Miss Mann successfully applied bibliographic classification in the classified catalog at the Engineering Societies Library in New York. On the books, however, she used relatively simple Dewey numbers. This example of the Engineering Societies Library shows clearly the difference between the two types of classification. Bibliographic classification is unsuited to the classification of books in workaday libraries; that classification must be governed by practical requirements.

In its application classification calls for a high degree of good judgment. Classification can be a game. It is good fun to build up long numbers, to put books in precise but out-of-the-way classes, to debate academic niceties. Such classification hurts a library. The classifier with good judgment will not waste time arguing which alternative is the better; the case will be decided pragmatically, according to the wording of the title, for example. There must be the realization that some books have one precise class, while fully as many again could go equally well in one of a number of classes.

Reclassification raises problems of two kinds. The daily question of reclassifying an odd book or two is one, while the reclassification of a whole library is another. As regards the former, it requires constant administrative pressure to prevent much reclassification. Relocation is, of course, a separate matter, as the relocation of a book from the reference room to the stacks. Much reclassification is purely academic in nature. A cataloger or a professor thinks that a book would be better in some other class. This kind of reclassification must be resisted as much as possible, and all the more so if the book concerned shows every evidence of not having been used in many a year.

Decisions to reclassify a whole library should be arrived at only after clearly realizing that the old classification scheme was ineffective to a high degree. Many libraries are using poor classification schemes, usually homemade ones. As long as those schemes work there is no real reason why they should be given up. Classification schemes age very rapidly. Both Dewey and the Library of Congress scheme have suffered the ravages of time. That situation will be aggravated with the further passage of time. Total reclassification of a library is terribly expensive. Partial reclassification may be a desirable compromise. Less used books may be left according to the old scheme, so that the new classification will represent a live collection of books; or some main classes which are unsatisfactory can be changed, leaving unchanged those that were satisfactory.

Suitability of a particular scheme to the type of library is a matter of importance. Modification of a standard scheme may be a solution. At the least, great caution is necessary before reclassifying a whole library. Some libraries have made serious mistakes by adopting the Library of Congress classification; it is not true that it is necessarily the best scheme for a college library. Perhaps the situation as regards classification and reclassification can be summarized by saying that the golden age of classification is over.

The Situation as regards Subject Heading

If it is necessary to say that the literature on classification is in a state of confusion, it is equally necessary to say that the literature on subject heading is almost nonexistent. At most, it would be only a slight exaggeration to say that Cutter's *Rules for a dictionary catalog,* the fourth and final edition of which appeared in 1904, provides the latest word on the theory and practice of subject heading. Cutter's work was that of the pioneer. He saw a new day dawning with the printing of Library of Congress cards, but neither he nor anyone else has been a guide through this era of printed cards.

Even the best of cataloging instructors admit they do not know how to teach subject heading properly. The theory, practice, and needs are all ill defined. For such reasons it is better to say less rather than more about subject headings here.

In part the trouble springs from the use of words, since words can be local, obsolescent, or technical, or they can stand for vague, ambiguous, or emergent concepts, or they can even be lacking for some ideas or relations of ideas. In part the trouble comes from trying to make a science of subject heading when it is necessarily an art. Some subject heading has no other dignity than the mere expression of opinion; much of it has to be based on judgment, in which experience counts greatly; some has to be precise. In part the trouble comes from differentiating insufficiently between the needs of different types of libraries. Here the compelling dictionary-catalog idea has been a handicap.

The principle of the dictionary catalog is to provide a record that will make for a maximum of self-help on the part of readers. This means that the catalog must be adapted to the needs of varying institutions. It also means that the maximum of self-help can be obtained only as long as the catalog does not become too complex. Many dictionary catalogs are becoming too complex and are accordingly defeating the ends for which they were created. That is why there are signs of the decline of the dictionary catalog, as would be indicated by the possibly unfortunate trend toward a divided author and subject catalog and by the search for substitutes for the dictionary catalog.

What the Library Administrator Needs to Know

These, then, are the things the library administrator needs to know about cataloging and these are the pressing problems which confront cataloger and administrator alike. It is not that the library administrator needs to be a technician, though some knowledge of cataloging technique is desirable. It is rather that he must know the nature of present-day cataloging problems if he would be in a position to help in their solution and to supply a certain amount of leadership and direction.

A crisis has been reached in cataloging history. The system that shaped up about the year 1900 showed ominous signs of falling apart in 1940. In the Library of Congress the system actually broke down, and what happens in that library as far as cataloging is concerned affects libraries throughout the country while the Library of Congress holds the key position that it does.

Excellent work was done between 1900 and 1940. Praise and appreciation can properly be expressed for the accomplishments of those four decades. Perhaps at the same time there is a certain satisfaction in realizing that the giants of those days did not solve all the problems, leaving little if anything for their successors to accomplish. This problem field known as cataloging is still a challenge to clear thinking and sound judgment.

The foremost problem confronting library administrators has been set down as the cost of cataloging. Elements contributing to that problem are questions as to what theory of cataloging to follow, how to work out a satisfactory cataloging code, how best to organize a catalog department, what classification scheme should be used, and how it should be applied. These and many other questions of greater or less significance are what the library administrator must know about and be prepared to tackle in collaboration with catalogers.

Cataloging policies and practices are about to be set for another generation. Whether the people of the 1980's will say librarians and catalogers of today had as much understanding and ability as can now be attested for the people of the early 1900's depends on the success of the deliberations of the 1940's.

It is important to say that the awareness of these problems is not to be taken as one generation criticizing another. I have cataloged through twenty of the forty years that made up the era which I believe has now come to an end. In 1920 there was enough remaining of the original inspiration to make itself felt and appreciated. Nevertheless, there were clear signs that the picture was rapidly changing. Pressure of work was in no small measure responsible, resulting as it inevitably did in systematization and standardization to an unwelcome degree.

Those of us who see ourselves bridging the two eras have an added responsibility. We know and respect what was good in the past. We honor the traditions in which to greater or less extent we participated. And for such reasons our leadership in charting new courses should and can be so much the wiser.

Notes

1.   Rudolf Kaiser, in Fritz Milkau, *Handbuch der Bibliothekswissenschaft,* II (Leipzig, 1933), 318.

2.   W. W. Bishop, *Cataloging as an asset: an address to the New York State Library School, May 1, 1915* (Baltimore, 1916), p. 8.

3.   *Ibid.,* p. 22.

4.   *Catalog rules* (Chicago: American Library Association, 1908), p. viii.

Principles of Descriptive Cataloging

Seymour Lubetzky

Editor's Introduction

Aside from Osborn's plea that the catalog not be the repository of a "perfectionistic" bibliography, there is no discussion of the objectives of the descriptive portion of catalog records in the material reprinted earlier in this volume. Yet overly lengthy or detailed catalog records can hinder both a cataloging department, trying to ensure that it has no arrearage, and also a user, wandering through a maze of what seem to be tendentious notations on a card. Panizzi claims that sufficient detail should be present to permit the identification of a desired edition; he also allows for difference in detail among the catalogs of libraries of various sizes. In the context of a manuscript catalog his position is understandable. In the case of a nationally produced catalog record, however, differences become hindrances to the effective use of cataloging copy.

A cataloging code intended for national use presents another difficulty: rules for description without aim or focus tend to proliferate, increasing the complexity of a catalog without increasing its usefulness. Such a proliferation of rules occurred during the first half of this century. In the early 1940s, the administrators at the Library of Congress attempted to stop the growth of arrearages, which were caused by the ever slower production of cataloging, by simplifying the rules for description.

The LC administration decided that the best way to simplify the rules of a cataloging code was to provide principles for a new code. This entailed agreement on the functions of catalogs and the cataloging rules used to build them. The following selection, originally Appendix A of the *Studies of Descriptive Cataloging,* was written by Seymour Lubetzky. The points enunciated herein became the guiding principles for the rules used in various forms of LC cataloging from 1949 to 1973. It was at this later date that the kind of rule found in the various editions of the International Standard Bibliographical Description (ISBD) became the standard for American cataloging practice. Rules based on the ISBD have a focus substantially different from that found in the following selection; it is unclear whether the ISBD-based rules include the objectives set forth by Lubetzky as part of their own.

It is sometimes claimed that a fundamental difference in objectives for rules for description centers around whether a piece is to be described in its own terms first and only later related to other items represented in the catalog, or whether it is to be described first of all in relation to other items in the catalog. If this distinction has any meaning, the article reprinted here clearly espouses the second alternative.

MC

Principles of Descriptive Cataloging

This statement[1] undertakes to present the general principles which are to underlie the code of rules for the description of books in the Library of Congress. The basic aims sought in the preparation of our code are:

1.   To formulate principles and rules which will best serve the functions of descriptive cataloging.

2.   To design a catalog entry which will present an integrated and intelligible description of the book and indicate clearly its relation to other editions and issues of the book, and to other books recorded in the catalog.

We are also keeping in mind the possibility that the catalog entries prepared for printed cards may also be reproduced in a book catalog.

In pursuance of these aims, we are close to agreement on the following.

Contents of the Code. Our code will present a statement of the functions which it will undertake to serve, the principles which will be employed to serve these functions, and the rules which will detail the application of the principles in typical cases.

General Functions of Descriptive Cataloging. We are agreed that the general functions of descriptive cataloging are:

1.   To describe the significant features of the book which will serve (a) to distinguish it from other books and other editions of this book, and (b) characterize its contents, scope, and bibliographical relations;

2.   To present the data in an entry which will (a) fit well with the entries of other books and other editions of this book in the catalog, and (b) respond best to the interests of the majority of readers.

Reprinted by permission of Seymour Lubetzky and the Library of Congress from U.S. Library of Congress, Processing Department. *Studies of Descriptive Cataloging* (Washington, D.C., Library of Congress: 1946), 25-33.

The Title-Page. We are agreed on the importance of the title-page as "the face of the book" which serves both to identify and characterize it. We recognize also, however, that the title-page is often insufficient for these purposes; frequently contains unnecessary matter or details; and very often is arranged and otherwise affected by typographical design in a manner undesirable for the intelligbility of the entry and unsuitable for its integration in the catalog. Hence the need of supplementing the title-page in some cases, curtailing it in others, and rearranging or modifying it when necessary so as not to impair its identifying value and to produce the entry desired for the catalog.

Principles of Description. We are agreed, first of all, that the formulation of principles is necessary as a basis to give our code direction, coherence, and logical construction; and also, to provide the cataloger with general guidance in meeting the numerous cases which cannot be specifically provided for in the rules. We are also generally agreed on the formulation of these principles, but in their application we are still faced with some conflicting alternatives which require careful evaluation before final decision is reached.

The principles relate to the following aspects of book description: (1) the terms of description, (2) the extent of description, (3) the organization of the elements of description, (4) the integration of these elements, (5) the indication of sources, and (6) the style of capitalization, punctuation, and accents to be followed in the entry.

Terms of Description

The book is generally to be described in the words or the terms in which it is described by its author or publisher on the title-page or elsewhere in the book. Ambiguous or unintelligible statements are to be followed by explanations, and inaccurate statements by appropriate corrections. Where the original statements are covered by labels bearing different statements, the original statements are to be given here.

There is general acceptance of this principle, except in application to the collation statement. For example, if a work has been issued in five separate sections, with individual title-pages, and designated respectively as *Part I, Part II,* etc., or *Volume I, Volume II,* etc., it has not been our practice to follow always the given designations; but the five "parts" might be described in collation as *5 v.,* and the five "volumes" might be described as *5 nos.,* although in the following notes and contents the same units would be referred to by their given designations. This practice is defended on the ground that the collation is the cataloger's own statement and as such, need not agree with that of the publisher. It is also pointed out that the publisher's terminology is sometimes difficult to follow even in English books—*e.g.,* the terms *issue, edition, lesson, course, lecture, award, reader, meeting, session,* etc.—to say nothing of foreign languages. In addition, since the publishers do not follow a uniform terminology, and since the books themselves are not always designated as *volume, part,* or otherwise—but are sometimes simply numbered as I, II, etc.—and the cataloger must adopt a terminology of his own, the meaning of the collation statement will not be clear if the publisher's terminology is followed.

On the other hand, it is countered, the designation *Part, Volume,* etc., on the title-page is part of the bibliographical identifying label, and to ignore it in the description of the book is bibliographically as serious as to ignore any other identifying bibliographical element on the title-page. Also, it is pointed out, the reader referred to say, Part II cannot be expected to perform readily the necessary equation and conclude it is the cataloger's second volume. And finally, it is contended, to call the same thing by two different names in the same entry—*v.* in collation and *pt.* in the following notes—will contribute considerably more to the confusion of the catalog user than the description of similar units as *v.* in one entry and *pt.* in another. It is admitted that in certain cases—especially when the designation refers to the contents of the unit rather than its physical relation to the other units, as the above mentioned *meeting, session,* etc.—the given designations need not be followed and the units may be described uniformly as physical *volumes* in collation.

It is agreed, however, that the terminology in which the illustrations are described in the book is of no special bibliographical significance, and need not be followed in collation.

Extent of Description

The book is to be described as fully as necessary for the accepted functions, but witn an economy of data, words, and expression: no item should be transcribed from the title-page which will duplicate the information of another item, unimportant matter or detail should be curtailed, unnecessary words and phrases omitted, and standard abbreviations used whenever appropriate.

There is general agreement that economy is essential to enhance the intelligibility and effectiveness of the entry, and also to save the space of the crowded catalog and the time of the busy reader. In application of this principle, however, opinion is divided on several points:

Author Statement. The division of opinion regarding the transcription of the author statement from the title-page after the title stems from the question whether or not the author's name in the headings is to be regarded as an author statement. The case for our present practice maintains that the author's name given in the heading is intended only as a heading and has no relation to the author statement on the title-page, and the transcription of the latter after the title, therefore, does not constitute a repetition of the author statement. The opponents contend that this practice is uneconomical. They regard the author heading as part of the description of the book, and justify the transcription of the author statement from the title-page after the title only when the name in the statement differs in form (not in completeness, which can be shown in the heading by brackets, if desired) from that in the heading, or when the statement is construed as an inseparable part of the title, or when it may be necessary to bring out a relationship other than author, editor, compiler, etc., which cannot otherwise be shown.

Statement of Illustrations. It is agreed that the statement of illustrations given on the title-page need not be transcribed when it will only duplicate the information which is to be given in collation; for example, the statement "Illustrated with thirty-two plates, partly in color, and two folded maps in pocket" would only duplicate the collation statement "xxxii pl. (part col.) 2 fold. map (in pocket)." It is also agreed that when the statement of the title-page contains an important characterization of the illustrations not provided for in collation and not implied in the title of the book, it should be transcribed; for example, "Illustrated by wood-cuts, and by a map of India showing the localities of various art industries" (Catalogue of the Objects of Indian Art Exhibited in the South Kensington Museum, by H. H. Cole) ..

The disagreement concerns the common-variety statements which add little more than the number of illustrations; for example, "with one hundred and forty-two reproductions of famous paintings, in black and white" (Modern Master-pieces ... by Frank Rutter). Those who favor the transcription of such statements maintain that the number of illustrations is an important characterization, especially when the number is very large or very small. Those who favor their omission contend that if the number of illustrations is an important characterization, then we should give it in collation, and regardless of whether or not it is stated on the title-page (as we now do in the case of *1 illus.*); at least where these illustrations are numbered or listed in the book and their number is readily ascertainable—which is what we do in the case of plates. If it is not of sufficient importance to give the number of illustrations in collation even when it is readily avaialable, then they see no reason for transcribing the statement when, and only because, the number of illustrations is stated on the title-page.

Publisher Statement. There is fair agreement that the publisher statement need not be given in the imprint of publications which are entered under the names of their issuing societies or firms, or where the publisher is clearly indicated in the series note.

Collation Statement. The question of the collation statment—whether its principal function is to characterize the contents of the book by describing its significant physical features, or whether it is to account in detail for the completeness of the volume—continues in a stalemate condition. Those who favor detailed collation maintain that it eliminates the exercise of judgment on the part of the cataloger; insures uniformity of result; assists in the identification of an edition, issue, or copy, and in the detection of an imperfect copy; and obviates any confusion to the inquirer checking in the catalog a reference containing the pages not shown in the collation of the entry. Those who favor brief collation do not think that these ends justify the means; they point to the collation of works in more than one volume as an indication that detailed collation is unnecessary; and they regard detailed collation as a dissipation of cataloging energy on the production of a result which is unintelligible to many users of the catalog. Comments and advice on this question are especially needed.

Indication of Omissions. Another question connected with omissions in the transcription of the title-page is whether or not these omissions are to be indicated in the entry by ellipses. Those who favor such indication in the entry—except for the imprint where omissions have never been indicated—maintain that it facilitates the identification of a book in hand with that described in the catalog. Those who could abandon the use of the ellipses in the entry—except in the omission of a part of the title proper—see no reason why ellipses should be regarded as necessary in the transcription of the title-page before the imprint, when they have proved unnecessary in the imprint. They contend that the ellipses are unnecessary for identification, and their presence on the entry retards, rather than facilitates, the identification of a book by presenting more elements than necessary for comparison.

Organization of the Elements of Description

The bibliographical elements of the book are to be given on the entry in such order as will best respond to the normal approach of the reader and will be suited for integration of the entry with the entries of other books and editions in the catalog. For these purposes the following order has been selected: title, subtitle, author statement (where necessary), edition statement, place, publisher, and date of publication; followed by collation, series note, and supplementary notes.

There is fair agreement on this principle also, except with regard to the subtitle and author statement when they are given on the title-page before the title, or when they are supplied from elsewhere, *e.g.*

*An Almost-True Story
of Pirates and Indians
by Selden M. Loring*
MIGHTY MAGIC

Those who support present practice transcribe only *Mighty Magic* as the title of the book and give the subtitle and author statement in an at-head-of-title note. This form of presentation is defended on the ground that it shows the position of the subtitle and author statement on the title-page and thereby, again, facilitates the identification of a given book, especially for our acquisitions "searchers." It is also pointed out that the transposition of an author statement from a position before the title to one after the title will require the cataloger to supply a connective to show the relation of the title to the name, which is not always easy in the case of foreign languages and not always certain where the relation is not clear. Those who disapprove of the present practice do not believe that there is more reason for indicating the position of the subtitle and author statement on the title-page than there is for the series statement, edition statement, and the elements of the imprint. They contend that the separation of the subtitle from the title which it is designed to explain impairs materially the intelligibility of the entry, since in these cases the titles alone—*Mighty Magic; Rats in the Larder,* etc.—are ambiguous or misleading. And they go on to point out that the problem of supplying connectives to indicate the relation between a given title and the author statement is not a problem of transposition only, but one recurring daily with modern title-pages in various languages omitting these connectives, and met by the cataloger by supplying the vague [by], [par], [por el], or a more specific [tr. by], [ed. by], etc., and some times (in some Russian cases) by transcribing the title and author statement from the title-page as given, without undertaking to establish and phrase the missing connectives. They are, therefore, in favor of transcribing the above title-page (assuming the author statement to be necessary) as follows:

*Mighty magic [an almost-true story of
pirates and Indians, by Selden M. Loring]*

The brackets indicate that the statement after the title has been inserted at this place by the cataloger—in this case, from the head of the title. It might be preferable to use some other symbol than brackets, possibly a special symbol appropriate for the purpose.

Integration of Elements of Description

All information relating to a given bibliographical term should be integrated, except where the length or construction of a given statement makes its integration with the other data undesirable. In this case the statement may preferably be given in a note.

There is no disagreement on this principle. Its application means that if, for example, the imprint date is to be taken from the cover, we shall not give the story in two installments, by bracketing the date in the imprint and explaining its qualifying source in a note: Date from cover; but will give the complete story in the imprint; [cover: 1943], just as we now state: [pref. 1943]. Similarly, we shall not separate the publication date of the title-page from that of the cover by giving the former in the imprint and the latter in a note: Cover date: 1943; but will give the complete story together: 1942 [cover: 1943], just as we state: 1943 [c1936], or 1942 [i. e. 1944], where each date serves to qualify the other. Carrying the principle into collation, we shall not tell in collation *2 v.* and in a note: paged continuously; but state the matter together *2 v. (paged continuously).* Similarly, we shall not tell in collation *illus.* and explain in a note: Illustrations, p. 7-149; but will state the facts together: *illus. (p 7-149);* and so on. We are agreed that this principle will contribute to the coherence, intelligibility, and brevity of the entry.

One question yet to be decided concerns the place and language of such notes as *A novel, Poems, Essays, Short Stories, Burlesque on* ... etc., which the cataloger supplies to explain the contents of the book when the title is ambiguous or misleading. There seems to be agreement that these notes belong immediately after the titles which they are intended to explain. But this raises the question of the language in which these notes are to be given. Those who favor present practices— to give these as supplementary notes—justify it on the grounds of expediency; they maintain that words supplied in the "body of the entry" are to be given in the language of the title-page, and the present practice is therefore expedient for books in foreign languages.

Those who disapprove of present practice contend that these notes, removed from the statements which they are intended to explain, and easily overlooked, serve little to remedy the unintelligibility of the titles. They believe that most notes would offer little difficulty, but they also point to the practice of other national catalogs and suggest for consideration that these notes be given in the cataloger's vernacular.

Identification of Sources of Data

The sources of the data supplied by the cataloger in brackets in the main body of the entry need not be stated on its face, except when the data are supplied from: (a) *unusual or other than standard sources,* (b) *sources qualifying the meaning of the data (e. g., cover, preface, etc.) or* (c) *disputed sources.*

There is no disagreement on this principle either, save for the suggestion that the source of the title, when supplied, should always be given.

Capitalization, Punctuation, and Accents

If the title-page is capitalized, punctuated, or accented in accordance with the style of the text of the book, it should be transcribed in the style given. If the style is of a typographical character, the title-page should be capitalized, punctuated, and accented in accordance with the usage of the given language.

The alternative is unwilling to follow the capitalization of the title-page even if it is in the style of the text of the book, except in one case: when the title-page and the text of the book are all in lower case.

Notes

1. An earlier draft was read by Herman H. Henkle at the Conference of Eastern College Librarians, Columbia University, November 23, 1945.

The Cataloging of Publications of Corporate Authors

Mortimer Taube

The Cataloging of Publications of Corporate Authors: A Rejoinder

Seymour Lubetzky

Editor's Introduction

Since the invention of short-run printing processes such as mimeographing, multilithing and photocopying, the results of many scientific research projects have been disseminated in the form of technical reports. Technical reports have had the vast merit of publication at a rate much faster than that of conventional journals. Unlike conventional scientific serials, these reports are monographs, and thus require separate cataloging. Many library administrators have sought to handle technical report cataloging in a way more expedient than that prescribed in regular library cataloging codes.

Technical reports as a class have a number of characteristics setting them apart from books. Since they are printed by short-run techniques, they almost always use standard size duplicating paper (usually 8½ by 11 inch), and more importantly, do not appear in revised editions. Almost without exception, a corporate body is heavily involved in their preparation, so heavily that it is common to cite the report as a study performed by that body, even though there be a disclaimer of responsibility on the piece. They also usually appear in some sort of series sponsored by a corporate body, and are written in fulfillment of contractual obligations to another body, the funding agency.

The implications of the above characteristics for a library catalog can be enormous, provided that the catalog is devoted only to technical reports. The collative function of main entry, namely that of bringing the various editions of a work of an author together, is important only insofar as the works of an author should be brought together. In a catalog of technical reports, there are no editions of a work to be assembled; there are no works devoted solely to the exposition of the content of another work. Thus, as Mortimer Taube (1910-1955) noticed, the question of which corporate heading or personal author heading was important for a main entry is immaterial in a card catalog file. For policy reasons alone, Taube set up his catalog under corporate main entry. There is no reason why one could not have main entry under title and simply assemble all the other entry points by entries given in the tracings.

Although his catalog was set up on traditional catalog cards, the machinery Taube probably had in mind when arriving at his proposals was the punched card selector, the most advanced device then available for automating a catalog. A bibliographic description written on a punched card can be accessed through the keypunched codings standing for the various fields of a record. In this environment, there is no reason, or even ability, to make one entry more important than any other: the selector can locate all the reports for which entry has been made under the heading for a particular author, personal or corporate. The selected cards will contain readable descriptions of the materials coded under the heading. Clearly, there is no requirement for filing rules in this catalog, it being necessary to run the selector each time inquiry is made. Alternately, when not being processed through the selector, the cards can be filed by a particular field, such as that for title or corporate author, in order that some sort of access through the written records be possible.

But there has been no discussion yet on another characteristic of technical reports, the great involvement of corporate bodies in their preparation. Traditionally, the "establishment" of the correct form of a corporate body's name is one of the most expensive tasks in library cataloging. At the time Taube's article was written, there was an additional complication: corporate bodies were divided into societies and institutions. Societies were generally entered under their own names, while institutions (corporate bodies occupying a fixed location) were entered subordinately to the heading for the place where they were located. The vast majority of governmental bodies—in this case the majority of funding agencies—presented yet another complication. Since they are subdivisions of other bodies, the rules for the establishment of their names were necessarily complex. Taube attempts to deal with these complications in his article, which was published shortly after his resignation as Chief of the Science and Technology Project of the Library of Congress in 1950.

At the time Taube's article was written, the American library profession was coming to terms with the necessity to revise the rules for entry and headings, which had just been published in 1949. Lubetzky's *Cataloging Rules and Principles,* an analysis of the 1949 code, had not yet been published. However, he was requested to present the official Library of Congress reply to Taube, after several other attempts within LC had failed to be sufficiently analytical to warrant publication. Lubetzky presents an analysis of both the difficulties surrounding corporate names (especially the issue of subdivisions) and the appropriate amount of research that should be performed in the establishment of a corporate name.

The assumptions underlying the views expressed in these two articles are at the base of most disputes concerning the nature of library catalogs today. They are found in discussions of how headings are to be established, whether main entry should be employed, how subdivisions of corporate bodies should be treated, whether authorship has a role in determining entry points, how works about another work should be treated, and so forth. The debate presented here continues.

MC

Further Reading

Committee on Information Hang-Ups, Working Group for Updating COSATI. *Guidelines for Descriptive Cataloging of Reports: A Revision of COSATI Standard for Descriptive Cataloging of Government Scientific and Technical Reports.* Washington, D. C., March 1978. (PB 277 951).

The current version of the cataloging rules used by the National Technical Information Service. COSATI is an acronym for the defunct Committee on Scientific and Technical Information.

Lubetzky, Seymour. *Cataloging Rules and Principles: A Critique of the A. L. A. Rules for Entry and a Proposed Design for Their Revision.* Washington, D. C.: Library of Congress, 1953.

"The Corporate Complex," pages 16-35, discusses problems with the then current rules for formation of corporate headings, the same target as Taube's, but with somewhat different solutions.

The Cataloging of Publications of Corporate Authors

The preparation of an earlier draft of this paper was undertaken by the author as part of his regular duties as chief of the Science and Technology Project of the Library of Congress. The librarian of Congress saw in the Science and Technology Project not only an instrument for increasing the Library's service to the National Defense Establishment but an opportunity to develop new forms of documentation, that is to say, new forms of collecting, cataloging, indexing, organizing, and disseminating information.

With special reference to the topic of this paper, the Project was encouraged by Dr. Frederick Wagman, director of the Processing Department, and Miss Lucille Morsch, chief of the Descriptive Cataloging Division, to persist in the search for new techniques, in spite of the author's reluctance to venture into a field in which the defense of established practice is so passionate and so strong.

This is not to say that anyone other than the author is responsible for the arguments and conclusions in the paper. The draft submitted to the librarian represented the kind of self-criticism encouraged and fostered by the present administration of the Library; yet in its final form the paper must be regarded not as expressing the official views of any part of the Library administration but as representing only the views of the author in his private capacity.

Only a great viable institution would encourage in its employees, or even former employees, the kind of uninhibited criticism I have attempted; and Dr. Wagman has assured me that he intends to devise and institute experiments in order to determine whether or not the conclusions of the paper are indeed applicable, beyond the requirements of the special library, to the cataloging operations of the Library of Congress as a whole.

In the last analysis, what the Library of Congress does must be definitive for other libraries, since the distribution of printed cards constitutes an argument in favor of following Library of Congress practice which is stronger than any reasons that could be offered for divergences from its practice. Hence, the Library of Congress, as the citadel, must be captured if victory is to be won. But this means that, however cogent the conclusions reached in this paper, we are left with a series of unanswered questions. Should present catalogs be frozen and new ones started?

Reprinted by permission of The University of Chicago Press from *Library Quarterly* 20 (January 1950): 1-20.

Should recataloging be undertaken? Should entries according to the new rules be filed in with older entries?

Whatever the answers to these questions, I am certain of one thing: If we allow the weight of the past to stifle change and progress, however advantageous and justified, we shall indeed become the caricatures which form the stereotype of a librarian in the public mind.

Governments, Societies, and Institutions

As a major part of its work for the Office of Naval Research, the Science and Technology Project of the Library of Congress is required to conduct research and experimentation in methods of handling scientific information—a field that has come to be known as that of "scientific documentation." A general account of this field of activity, with some mention of current research and experimentation being carried on in the Science and Technology Project and in other organizations, is contained in a paper[1] presented before the 1948 autumn general meeting of the American Philosophical Society in Philadelphia. More specific accounts of the work of the Project have also appeared. A paper setting forth certain new developments in subject heading and in indexing was presented by Mr. C. D. Gull of the Project's staff before the science-technology group of the Special Libraries Association, in Washington, on June 11, 1948. Mr. Gull's paper has since been issued with some modifications as the Introduction to the *Science and Technology Project List of Subject Headings.*[2] A paper on our methods of producing catalog cards, bulletins, and indexes from one typed copy appeared in the July, 1948, issue of *College and Research Libraries.*[3] The present paper will describe an outstanding development in the simplification and rationalization of cataloging techniques resulting from the research and experimentation carried on in the Project.

In order to bring certain common problems of scientific documentation to the attention of the several government agencies concerned with them, the Project held a conference in September, 1947, devoted to the bibliographical control of government scientific and technical reports. The memorandum which formed the basis of this conference has also been published.[4] It is referred to here, since the topics set forth in the memorandum indicate those fields in which research and experimentation are being conducted under the Science and Technology Project. The balance of this paper will be concerned with the conclusions so far attained by the Project with reference to one of these topics: the problem of determining uniquely, for the purpose of identification, the catalog entry for government scientific and technical reports. The meaning and limitation of this topic are perhaps best expressed by the following statement from the memorandum:

> To catalog is to describe uniquely. The notation of unique description is difficult to explain and may differ according to different requirements. In general, a unique description enables one to recognize and identify the item or class of items so described and to differentiate it from other items or classes not covered or excluded by the description. Thus, a catalog of rare books or prints might attempt to describe exhaustively particular items so that each item can be identified and distinguished from all other items however similar.
>
> Ordinary library cataloging of books is concerned with classes of items, i.e., with identifying titles or editions, each one of which may have many copies. Hence,

a catalog card prepared for a book in the Library of Congress usually serves for copies of the same book in many different libraries. But even this ordinary library cataloging is called upon to identify uniquely one title out of millions or one edition out of hundreds, and it has been [thought] necessary to develop elaborate cataloging codes to regulate and guide such descriptions.

It has, therefore, seemed to many that the complexities of library cataloging were not germane to the problem of cataloging scientific and technical reports. In one sense, this supposition has been justified. Given a handful of reports with no problem of differentiated editions, it seemed unnecessary to concern oneself with the niceties and minutia of cataloging. Words on a cover or title page might be copied in the order given, or omitted if their importance to the description was not immediately manifest; or titles could be made up or supplied to fit an intra office filing system. Unfortunately, the number of reports multiplied, and once filed, could not be found or identified; citations could not be identified and verified and the product of research was lost in masses of undifferentiated paper.

Under these circumstances many agencies sought solutions in mechanical sorting and finding devices, only to realize that a machine can select or sort only those things properly cataloged, coded or described and hence, proper descriptions have become the first order of business.

There is required a code for cataloging scientific reports. Such a code should be detailed, as is required by the material to be cataloged—it need not and should not be more so.[5]

Although it may seem at first glance that descriptive cataloging, as contrasted with subject cataloging or indexing, is or should be a relatively simple and straightforward affair, there are certain problems not always apparent to those who lack firsthand experience with the difficulty of devising uniform entries from the haphazard information which appears on the title-pages of the various publications and reports requiring organization. An appreciation of this difficulty can be gained from the fact that almost all publishers of scientific books and journals find it necessary to issue rules for bibliographical citation to their contributors. But there is a more dramatic demonstration of the problem. Appendix I of the *Annual Report of the Library of Congress for 1946* offers a justification for the estimates for 1947 which the librarian presented to Congress. It contains a table showing the "estimate of man-years required to catalog fully 100,000 foreign language titles in one year."[6] According to this table, the ratio of descriptive catalogers to subject catalogers is between five and six to one. This means that, in terms of present practice in the Library of Congress, six times as much manpower is devoted to describing books (i.e., setting forth author, title, pagination, etc.) as is devoted to determining what the books are about by classifying them and indicating the proper subjects under which they are to be cataloged. It means, further, that descriptive cataloging is the great bottleneck in the Library's attempts to control its collections and that the cost of descriptive cataloging is one of the most serious problems facing library administrators whose libraries follow Library of Congress practice. This includes most of the major research libraries of the United States.

It is hoped that the seriousness of the problem has been demonstrated; at the same time, it must be emphasized that the solution cannot be found in a blind rejection of the complexities of descriptive cataloging. One of the largest cataloging and abstracting services in the country neglected to establish its descriptive cataloging on a reasoned basis and found itself requesting material already in its files, cataloging different copies of the same items several times, and breaking up series of reports by cataloging under different names reports by the same authors.

In the face of this situation the Science and Technology Project as one of its first activities instituted certain experiments in descriptive cataloging, having made a thorough search of the literature on the subject for the purpose of developing a type of descriptive cataloging which would be adequate to the needs of the Project and which would not be prohibitively expensive. It was hoped, further, that the rules of cataloging developed in the Project might be applicable beyond the Project and thus constitute a contribution to the problem of cataloging in general. We realized that it would be necessary to develop not only a more expeditious method of cataloging but one which would answer the needs of major research libraries, including the Library of Congress itself. It can be reported at this time that, although many problems remain unsolved, we have been successful to a degree far beyond our initial expectations. We have developed certain rules and techniques which radically reduce the cost of cataloging, and, what is more important, the product of our cataloging is believed to be more logical, more consistent, and easier to use than that resulting from the more elaborate A.L.A. catalog rules.

The ratio of descriptive-cataloging cost to subject-cataloging cost in the Library of Congress is, as we have already noted, between five and six to one. In the 1947 estimates the average time required to perform descriptive cataloging is given as two hours and twenty minutes per title, or three books per cataloger in a seven-hour day. Within the last two years there has been a real effort to lower costs and increase production, and the Library is gathering figures which will indicate how much has been accomplished. But it is unfortunately true that the savings are being made by lowering standards rather than by eliminating complexities and furbishings which have little relation to the bibliographical adequacy of the resultant product. In the Science and Technology Project three catalogers handle an average of sixty titles a day, or twenty titles per day per cataloger.[7] The difference in cost need not be labored here; it may be argued that the cost difference is not significant because the purposes of and conditions prevailing in the Science and Technology Project are quite different from those in the Descriptive Cataloging Division of the Library of Congress. But such a general disclaimer need not concern us if the balance of our claim can be made good, namely, that the cataloging techniques and rules developed in the Science and Technology Project can be applied *mutatis mutandis* to the general cataloging activity of the Library and that, if they are so applied, the resultant product will be bibliographically more consistent, more logical, and easier to use.

It is unfortunately true that a reasoned and logical explanation for present cataloging practice cannot be found. Miss Julia Pettee, one of the leading figures in American cataloging and a member of the committee which prepared the new edition of the A.L.A. code, has stated: "Since Cutter's first edition of *Rules* there has been no further development in principles, though an enormous amount of work has been done in amplifying, codifying and clarifying rules...."[8]

Further, Miss Pettee expresses the belief that the foundation for the present Anglo-American rules for the corporate entry can be found in Sir Anthony Panizzi's rules for the compilation of the 1841 catalog of the British Museum. Panizzi's Rule 9 states:

Any act, resolution or other document purporting to be agreed upon, authorized, or issued by assemblies, boards, or corporate bodies (with the exception of
academies, universities, learned societies, and religious orders, respecting which
special rules are to be followed) to be entered in distinct alphabetical series, under
the name of the country or place from which they derive their denomination,
or for want of such denominations, under the name of the place whence their
acts are issued.[9]

The publications of academies, universities, learned societies, etc., are also,
according to Panizzi's rule 80, to be "alphabetically entered according to the
English name of the country and town at which the sittings of the society are
held...."[10] But all publications of this sort are grouped by Panizzi under the general
heading "Academies," and entry under locality follows this general heading.

Now in the case of Panizzi, as with other rule-makers to be considered, it is
noteworthy that these rules are presented without justification or argument. We
can assume that Panizzi had what seemed to him excellent reasons for these rules,
and any cataloger could undoubtedly think of several based on his own experience.
But in the last analysis we can only guess at the considerations which seemed deter-
minative to Panizzi, since, ten years later, in this country, Jewett presented a rule
which without exception called for the entry of works by corporate authors under
the corporate name rather than under place:

Academies, institutes, associations, universities, colleges; literary, scientific,
economical, eleemosynary, or religious societies; national and municipal governments; assemblies, conventions, boards, corporations, or other bodies of men under
whatever name, and for whatever purpose, issuing publications whether of separate
works, or of continuous series, under a general title, are to be considered and
treated as the authors of all works issued by them, and in their name alone. The
heading is to be the name of the body, the principal word to be the first word,
not an article.[11]

There is a curious anomaly in these two rules in that, for publications of one
kind of corporate bodies (governments), even though the rules are opposite in
intention, they issue in identical entries. The reason is that certain proper names
are at the same time names of places and names of governments. Thus, Panizzi
enters a report by the Burgomaster of Antwerp under "Antwerp. Burgomaster...."
According to Jewett, such a report would also be entered as "Antwerp.
Burgomaster...," but in Jewett's entry "Antwerp" would not be considered as the
name of a place but as the name of a corporate body. This is made clear in the
explanation which Jewett appends to his Rule 21:

When committees or branches of a body issue publications the heading is to
be the name of the Chief, and not of the subordinate body. Thus under "United
States" would be placed all public documents issued at the expense of the United
States whether as regular Public Documents, or by particular Departments, Bureaus,
or Committees.[12]

Cutter seemingly reintroduces Panizzi's rule, although he is not always careful
to distinguish between a term used as the name of a place and the same term

used as the name of a government. He states as a general principle that "bodies of men are to considered as authors of works published in their name or by their authority." But his first rule under this principle is:

> Enter under places (countries or parts of countries, cities, towns, ecclesiastical, military, or judicial districts) the works published officially by their RULERS (kings, governors, mayors, prelates, generals commanding, courts, etc.). Refer from the name of the ruler.[13]

From this rule and from several others (e.g., 47, 48, 50), we would assume that Cutter followed Panizzi, but from still others (e.g., 58) he seems to be following Jewett.

It may be said that, if both rules lead to similar entries, there is no point in deciding between them, but the issue cannot be disposed of so easily; for when we come to the problem of subdivisions of government agencies, Cutter's recommendation for the treatment of subdivisions is only valid if we regard the "U.S." as the name of a place and not as the name of a corporate body. Cutter's Rule 49 tells that "reports by a subordinate office to a department go under the office making the report."[14] In the example which he gives we are told that reports of the Bureau of Insular Affairs are to be entered directly under "United States," i.e., "U.S. Bureau of Insular Affairs" and not "U.S. War Dept. Bureau of Insular Affairs." Now, if "U.S." is a place name, the omission of "War Dept." makes sense, since the rule then tells us to enter publications of the Bureau of Insular Affairs under the place. But if "U.S." is part of the name of the corporate body, what logic justifies us in leaving out one part of the name, i.e., "War Dept.," and retaining a more general part of the name, i.e., "U.S."? It seems clear, therefore, that most of the time Cutter regarded "U.S." as a place name and not as the name of a corporate body.

This confusion is still apparent in the American Library Association's Anglo-American *Catalog Rules*, both the 1908 and the 1941 (second) edition.[15] There is, on one hand, ample evidence that names like "U.S.," "France," etc. are regarded as names of governments and not of places, as in the entries "U.S. Navy Yard, Boston," or "U.S. Consulate, Antwerp." On the other hand, the 1908 and 1941 *Rules* follow Cutter in entering subordinate offices directly under "U.S.," as, for example, "U.S. National Cancer Institute" instead of "U.S. Federal Security Agency Public Health Service. National Institutes of Health. National Cancer Institute," a practice which could be logically defended only if "U.S." were interpreted as a place name.

A question must naturally intrude at this point: If it is permissible to drop the names "Federal Security Agency," "Public Health Service," and "National Institutes of Health," why can we not drop the name "U.S." and use only "National Cancer Institute"? To a question of this sort the average practicing cataloger would make either or both of the following answers: In the first place, it might be said that "U.S." is necessary to distinguish the National Cancer Institute in this country from one in England or in Canada, if there should be one. [This answer presupposes a plurality of institutes with the same name, and this may not be the case. But even if it is, we can make the distinction parenthetically as follows: "National Cancer Institute (U.S.)" and "National Cancer Institute (Gt. Britain)."

Aside from the superior logic of this form of entry,[16] it helps to eliminate the cluttering of entries under local or government names.] Second, it may be argued that the name "U.S." is necessary in order to bring together in the catalog all United States official publications. [Aside from the fact that it is not self-evidently clear why it is necessary to bring together all United States publications and not necessary to bring together all Federal Security Agency or Public Health Service publications, it is not generally realized that the 1941 *Rules,* as contrasted with those of 1908, introduced the principle that, if possible, official publications should not be entered under the name of the governments which issued them.]

The specific and basic rule covering official publications in the 1908 *Rules* is that "governments (states, provinces, municipalities, ecclesiastical, military, or judicial districts) are to be considered as authors of their official publication."[17] In the 1941 *Rules*, however, the specification undergoes a radical change. It begins the same way, but then it continues:

> Certain classes of institutions and other bodies created, maintained, controlled or owned by governments are, however, to be treated according to the rules governing these bodies as authors, e.g., colleges, universities, schools, libraries, museums, galleries, observatories, agricultural experiment stations, hospitals, asylums, prisons, theaters, chambers of commerce, botanical and zoological gardens, banks, business corporations, churches, societies, etc.[18]

The use of the phrase "certain classes" serves, either unintentionally or intentionally, to disguise the revolutionary implications of this specification; for, in effect, the specification tells us that, if any agency, institution, or body is covered by a particular rule in addition to the general rule for official bodies, it is to be treated in accordance with the particular rule and not in accordance with the general rule. For example, publications of the national library of France are entered not, in accordance with the rule governing official publications, as "France. Bibliothèque Nationale" but, in accordance with the rule covering libraries and similar institutions, as "Paris. Bibliothèque Nationale." It is interesting to note that the institution which houses the national library of Great Britain is entered not under "Gt. Britain" or even under "London" but under its name directly, i.e., "British Museum," whereas the Library of Congress, which should be entered under "Washington, D.C. Library of Congress," is treated as an exception to the rules governing libraries and is entered under "U.S. Library of Congress."

This specification in the 1941 *Rules*, although revolutionary in its implications, merely sanctified practices which had developed in the Library of Congress between 1908 and 1941. In 1908, governments were relatively simple affairs, but a catalog department which witnessed the growth of our own government under the impact of a world war and the New Deal and which saw in the event of socialization and even socialism the possibility that all the publications of a country would be official and hence require entry under the name of the country might naturally, if not reasonably, search for devices and reasons to eliminate the growing mass of catalog entries under "U.S." or "Soviet Union" or "France" or "England." And although their practice was not sanctified until the appearance of the 1941 *Rules*, the Library of Congress catalogers followed the general practice of not treating a publication as official if it could be treated under some other rules, as the publication of a college, library, botanical garden, museum, or similar institution.

The Library of Congress practice in this regard was first set forth in 1934 by James B. Childs, then chief of the Division of Documents, in a paper on "Author Entry for Government Publications."[19] The rules set forth in this paper were later incorporated almost word for word in the 1941 *Rules*. Dr. J. C. M. Hanson, the editor of the 1908 *Rules*, in commenting on the changes introduced by Mr. Childs, supports the interpretation we have given in the previous paragraph. Thus he says:

> ...He [Mr. Childs] calls attention to one feature to which few librarians have given much thought. It is the increasing number of institutions, commissions, and organizations of various kinds wholly or in part supported by government funds. To enter all of them under country would obviously lead to an almost intolerable congestion of divisions and subdivisions under the names of large countries. Moreover, it would place the entries where the average person could hardly be expected to look for them.[20]

But if entry under the name of a country or any other jurisdiction is not required to distinguish between institutions of the same name, if it is not used to bring together all official publications of a government, if it does tend to lead to an almost intolerable congestion of divisions and subdivisions under the names of large countries, and if it would place entries where the average person could hardly be expected to look for them, why not eliminate such entries altogether? The answer is that it is possible: We can eliminate the whole collection of special rules for government publications and treat all publications of government bodies under the general rules pertaining to institutions and societies. However, this simplification, drastic as it is in principle, does not carry us very far toward a simplified and more logical practice. Jewett's Rule 21 does not distinguish between societies and institutions, but the 1941 *Rules* do and, by so doing, succeed, as we shall see, in introducing a great many unnecessary complexities.

In the 1941 *Rules* the general rule for institutions (Rule 150) is as follows: "Enter an institution (using the latest name) under the name of the place in which it is located."[21] This rule is followed by one which states a general exception:

> Enter an institution of the United States or of the British empire whose name begins with a proper noun or a proper adjective under the first word of its name and refer from the place where it is located. Add the name of the place to the heading if it does not occur in the name of the institution unless the institution is so well known as to make the addition of the place unnecessary. For countries other than the United States and the British empire follow the general rule of entry under place.[22]

The entry "Paris. Bibliothèque Nationale" is in accord with Rule 150; the entry "British Museum" is in accord with Rule 151.

The 1941 *Rules*'s general rule for societies (103) is contrary to that for institutions and provides for entry under the name of the society: "Enter a society under the first word (not an article) of its latest corporate name, with reference from any other name by which it is known, and from the name of the place where its headquarters are established."[23] It will be seen that Rule 103 agrees with Rule 151, and thus we are left with only one major group of entries which are entered under place, namely those institutions whose names do not begin with a proper noun or adjective. Now, if we ask why this distinction is made between those institutions whose names do and those whose do not begin with a proper noun or adjective, the rules are silent. Presumably the rule-makers believed that institutions lacking proper names would have to be distinguished by place, although, as we have shown above, it is very easy to make any necessary distinctions parenthetically or after the entry, wherever several institutions have the same name. Thus, if there is a Bibliothèque Nationale in Paris and one in Brussels, we can indicate as much after the name, without requiring our catalogers to make a theoretical and tenuous distinction between institutions and societies.

We are fortunate in this instance, however, in having available to us a discussion of the reason for the distinctive treatment of institutions and societies prepared by Miss Clara Beetle, head of the Foreign Language Section of the Descriptive Cataloging Division of the Library of Congress. Professor J. Frédéric Finó has proposed a general rule which eliminates the arbitrary distinction between institutions and societies and provides for entry under the name of the society or institution. Miss Beetle opposed Professor Finó's proposal in a written statement, which he has reprinted in his *Encabezamientos de entes collectivos.* [24] In summing up her position, Miss Beetle says:

> The chief objections to entry of all organizations...directly under their names would be 1) the expense and inconvenience of change of entry for institutions especially in long established libraries; 2) confusion caused to librarians and readers accustomed to present forms; 3) absence of proof that the change would agree with the natural approach of new readers; 4) concentration of similar names in long files which would prove difficult to use; 5) new problems created in regard to entry of institutions practically unknown by their names.[25]

The first two objections need not concern us at this point, except to note that Miss Beetle should have left them out of her summation because, in beginning her argument, she says: "Disregarding the practical question of the expense of change and the delay in new work resulting from recataloging projects, we may consider [Professor Finó's] proposal from a theoretical standpoint." We can proceed immediately to Miss Beetle's third objection, namely, the "absence of proof that the change [having one rule for societies and institutions] would agree with the natural approach of new readers." It is an accepted principle of science, first enunciated by Ockham, that, all things being equal, the simpler explanation is the truer. The burden of proof is not on Professor Finó (who proposes to get along on one rule for corporate bodies, whether societies or institutions) but on Miss Beetle or anyone else who contends that the one rule is not enough and that two or more are needed. As for the reader, who ninety-nine times out of a hundred has not the vaguest idea of the difference between institutions and societies as defined by the A.L.A. *Rules*, surely it is more natural for him to look for the publications of all corporate bodies under their names, and that is how he would find them if we used one rule for both societies and institutions. The present rules call for entering publications of societies under the name of the society and for entering the publications of institutions not under their names but under the names of the *locations* of the institutions. Since even experienced catalogers have difficulty distinguishing between societies and institutions, it would not help a reader to be required to make such a distinction before he could look in a catalog for the publications of either societies or institutions.

In her fourth objection Miss Beetle tells us that the elimination of entry under place would result in a "concentration of similar names in long files which would prove difficult to use." This objection cannot be taken seriously, since it is universally conceded that the present concentration of entries in the catalog under place names constitutes the most difficult part of the catalog not only for the reader but for the trained reference assistant.

The fifth and final objection, namely, that "new problems [are] created in regard to entry of institutions practically unknown by their names," is an excellent example of the complications and inconsistencies occasioned by a set of rules which lack a theoretical basis. We have pointed out that, in the 1941 *Rules*, Rule 150 provides for entry of institutions under place and Rule 151, as a general exception, provides for the entry of institutions whose names begin with proper nouns or adjectives directly under their names. Now, Rule 153 makes an exception to the general exception and tells us that, when the official name of an institution is practically unknown, even though the official name begins with a proper name or adjective, it is to be entered under place.[26] It is this rule which forms the basis of Miss Beetle's fifth objection. But in the face of all the rules which tell us to disregard common practice and knowledge in the interests of a higher consistency, this rule is almost catastrophic in its implications for present practices. The whole structure of research which forms the intellectual basis of Library of Congress cataloging would be in danger of disintegrating (perhaps a consummation devoutly to be wished) if we were to follow a general rule to avoid entry under unknown names. Miss Pettee, writing in 1936 about the forthcoming (1941) edition of the A.L.A. *Rules*, says:

> In the changes that are made the conciliatory policy of establishing headings which are most likely to be looked for in our English and American libraries will have less weight. The Library of Congress is effectively weaning us from this earlier practice. Who but a cataloger would look for Tagore under Ravindranatha Thakura....[27]

In the face of this statement that both the A.L.A. *Rules* and Library of Congress practice allow little weight to the policy of using entries likely to be known to the reader, Miss Beetle's fifth objection, like the first four, has no force.

The conclusion seems clear that, if these five objections are all that can be mustered in favor of present complexities, Professor Finó's proposal, and our own, to enter all organizations under their names has nothing against it and every recommendation for it.

At this point, before going on to state a positive program, a recapitulation is in order. We began by pointing out the cost of cataloging, and we have attempted to show that this cost is occasioned in large measure by a set of rules which are needlessly complicated and inconsistent. An analysis of the development of the rules for official entries in Panizzi, Jewett, Cutter, Childs, and the A.L.A. *Rules* of 1908 and 1941 indicated that the publications of official bodies should be entered under the names of the bodies responsible for them and that the name of the country or government need not precede the name of the body in the entry. This implied that the publications of official bodies could be treated according to the general rules for corporate bodies and need not be made the subject of specific rules. The next step was to show that there was no need for the distinction between societies and institutions, and we were thus brought to the conclusion that one general rule or scheme of rules for the publications of corporate bodies, whether governments, societies, or institutions, is a practical objective.

Subdivisions under Corporate Bodies

Perhaps the most difficult problem that any rules of entry are called upon to solve is that of subdivision. We have already given some indication of the nature of this problem in our discussion of the entry for publications of the National Cancer Institute. But it is necessary, at this point, to consider the matter in full detail. In the explanatory note which Jewett appends to his rule for corporate bodies he says:

When committees or branches of a body issue publications, the heading is to be the name of the chief, and not of the subordinate body. Thus, under "United States" would be placed all public documents issued at the expense of the United States, whether as regular Public Documents, or by particular Departments, Bureaus, or Committees. Such titles, when they become numerous, may be subdivided, and conveniently arranged in the catalogue.[28]

Here Jewett seems undisturbed by the problem of subdivision, but twenty-five years later and long before the Library of Congress catalog contained, as it does now, 212 drawers of entries under "U.S.," Cutter perceived some of the problems of subdivision and tried to cope with them. His Rule 49 is quite simple and straightforward: "Reports by a subordinate office to a department go under the office making the report."[29] There seems no difficulty here, and Cutter's Rule 324 is likewise direct and seems to offer no difficulties: "In arranging [making the entry] government publications make all necessary divisions but avoid subdivision."[30] But in the explanation appended to this rule Cutter manages to introduce the serpent into the garden. "There are," he says, "certain divisions or sections which have no independent existence and should be subordinated, as *Division of Statistics* under several departments or bureaus, and the various divisions of the Library of Congress (as *Catalog division, Order division*)."[31] This seemingly innocent qualification might have justified Cutter in saying, "après moi le déluge," for by it he confronted American catalogers with the metaphysical problem of "independent existence," to be solved anew each time a cataloger had to deal with the division of a corporate body. One has only to examine the mass of inconsistencies among "U.S." entries in the Library of Congress to be convinced that the catalogers were no more successful in solving the metaphysical problem of independent existence than were most of the philosophers from Plato's day to our own. And the cream of the jest is that, even when successfully utilized, the criterion of "independent existence" has no bibliographical significance, and its results serve only to bewilder the users of the catalog.

The Library of Congress enters publications of its Legislative Reference Service under the heading "U.S. Library of Congress. Legislative Reference Service." On the other hand, it enters publications of the Copyright Office, which occupies an identical position in the Library's administrative structure, under

"U.S. Copyright Office." The justification for this difference is supposedly found in the fact that before 1870 the Copyright Office was independent of the Library. Before the user of the catalog can find the proper entry, not only has he to know what offices now have or do not have "independent existence," but he must be familiar with the administrative history of each office. And the cataloger must also gain this knowledge at considerable cost in time and money, before he can properly succeed in mystifying the poor untutored user of the catalog.

The 1908 edition of the *Rules* avoids the concept of independent existence concerning the subdivision of official agencies and substitutes the concept of "minor divisions and offices [which] are usually to be subordinated to the bureaus or departments of which they form a part."[32] But the cataloger is still confronted with the task of determining what is major and what is minor and, beyond that, how often is "usually"; for, in accordance with this rule, a minor division or office should in some cases not be subordinated to the bureau or department of which it forms a part. Manifestly, a rule which permits you to do something in two ways and gives no criterion to enable the user to select one way or the other is not very serviceable.

However, the 1908 rule for subdivisions under a university reintroduces the concept of independent existence:

> Enter the colleges of a British university and the professional schools which form an *integral* part of an American university under the name of the university with the name of the college or school as subheading.... Professional schools whose names begin with a proper noun or adjective may be entered under their own names particularly if they are situated at a distance from the university of which they form a part, have merely a nominal connection with it, or for other reasons are unlikely to be looked for under its name. Cases in point are some American schools which, originally independent, have later affiliated with or become departments of a university.[33]

We will not stop at this point to give examples of the kind of difficulties which resulted from this rule but will remark only that it is a good example of the intrusion into cataloging theory and practice of matters which are bibliographically irrelevant. In the 1941 *Rules,* to which we again turn, the rules concerning subdivision reach an apotheosis of meaningless confusion. The first part of Rule 72 repeats, in essence, Cutter's Rule 49 and the first part of the 1908 Rule 58: "Enter government bureaus or offices subordinate to an executive agency, ministry or secretariat directly under the name of the jurisdiction, not as a subheading under the department, ministry or secretariat."[34]

The second part of this rule, which states when subdivision should be used, reads as follows: "But divisions, regional offices and other units of departments, bureaus, commissions, etc., subordinate to these departments, bureaus, commissions, etc., are usually entered as subheadings to the departments, bureaus, commissions, etc."[35] We may note that the concepts of "independent existence" and "major and minor" have been eliminated and, further, that the first part of the rule mentions bureaus, offices, departments, ministries, and secretariats, whereas the second part of the rule mentions divisions, regional offices, other units, departments, bureaus, and commissions. Now we can safely assume that the decision as to what is subordinated to what does not depend on the use of words like "division," "department," "office," "commission," etc. If it did, the rule would be meaningless in relation to foreign agencies and would not be in accord with actual cataloging practice. But if we eliminate this merely verbal difference between the two parts of the rule and concern ourselves with their essential meaning, then the first part tells us only that some government offices are entered directly under the name of the jurisdiction and not under other offices to which they are subordinate, and the second part of the rule tells us that some government offices are *not* entered directly under the name of the jurisdiction but under other offices to which they are subordinate. But since the rule does not tell us when to do it one way and when the other, it is utterly useless as a rule of procedure. In these circumstances, we cannot even allege an inconsistency in the present method of cataloging publications of subordinate offices because, no matter how they are cataloged, it will be in accordance with the rule.

The 1941 *Rules* enlarge upon the 1908 *Rules* with respect to subdivision under institutions and give more emphasis to exceptions. Rule 158 tells us to "enter the various faculties, colleges, professional schools, laboratories, libraries, museums, observatories, hospitals, shops, etc., which form an integral part of a university or other institution under the larger institution with the name of the particular entity as subheading."[36] Among others, the following entries are given as instances exemplifying this rule: "Oxford. University. Balliol college" and "Wisconsin. University. Washburn observatory." But "exception may be made," the rule goes on to say, "in the case of an observatory which is much more likely to be looked for under its own name than under that of the place or of the institution of which it forms a part."[37] As one example of such exceptions, there is listed "Allegheny observatory," which is not to be subordinated under Allegheny, Pennsylvania, its location, or Western University of Pennsylvania, of which it is a part. We are not told *why* one would be more likely to look for one observatory under its name and for another under the university of which it is a part.

Exception (*b*) under Rule 158 in the 1941 *Rules* is identical with the exception under Rule 42 in the 1908 *Rules*. And as an example of a college which should be entered under its name rather than as a subdivision under the university of which it is a part, it gives "Barnard college."

Thus, even though the College of Physicians and Surgeons, for example, was founded and for years existed independently of Columbia University, its publications are entered under "Columbia university. College of physicians and surgeons." We will be told that "College" is not a proper name and that, therefore, the direct entry for Barnard is justified, whereas a direct entry for College of Physicians and Surgeons is not. But if the direct entry is right for Barnard, why not for Balliol? With this last rhetorical question we can turn to the more rewarding task of presenting the way in which the Science and Technology Project attempted to meet the problems and difficulties thus far set forth.

The Search for Consistent Rules

The manner in which the Science and Technology Project arrived at its rules of entry can be better understood if one considers first certain problems which were solved in connection with its subject-heading list. We wished to create a subject-heading list which would be consistent in principle and based on a minimum number of rules. We believed that consistency in accordance with a small number of rules would make the work easier for our subject catalogers, but our chief concern was for the users of our catalog. The same few rules used by the catalogers could also be explained to the users of the catalog, and, if the catalog exemplified these rules consistently, it would follow that the user could find his way around in the catalog with maximum ease. The measure of our success in this effort is set forth in the *Science and Technology Project List of Subject Headings.*

In our search for consistency and simplicity for the user's sake, we considered whether or not any of the generally accepted principles of subject headings were applicable to the field of descriptive cataloging. The Library of Congress Subject Cataloging Division and the Science and Technology Project agree in following the principle of direct and specific headings. This means that a work on analytical geometry is entered under the subject heading "Analytical geometry" and not under the heading "Mathematics—Geometry—Analytical." However, sometimes even the most specific heading seems to require subdivision, as, for example "Accelerometers—Mathematical analysis" and "Fibers—Fatigue." But it is a general rule in the Project that terms chosen as subdivisions rather than as specific entries must be capable of being subdivisions of many specific entries. Thus we have: "Aerial targets—Performance," "Rocket launchers—Performance," and "Turbojet engines—Performance."

Since these subdivisions are intended to be used under many different specific entries, both the Library of Congress proper and the Science and Technology Project maintain internally and have published lists of subject subdivisions to be used whenever suitable. From time to time new subdivisions are developed as they are required, and they are added to the existing lists. A subject cataloger does not have to guess whether or not a phrase or term can be used as a subdivision: he searches the list for it. If it is not on the list and he still wishes to use it, it must pass inspection not only for a particular and present use but for addition to the list for general and regular use.

When it came to the problem of descriptive entry, it was only natural to ask in the first instance whether or not the rule of specific entry, which seemed to work so well with reference to subject headings, could also be applied to this field. Any general rule applicable to both subject headings and author entries would, as we have said, *ipso facto* introduce the desired consistency in the overall task of cataloging.[38] Hence we set forth as our first rule of entry that the entry must be the specific agency or corporate body responsible for the report.[39] This rule provided that a publication of the National Cancer Institute should be cataloged under "National Cancer Institute" and not under "U.S. Federal Security Agency. Public Health Service. National Institutes of Health. National Cancer Institute." Our second rule holds that the specific agency responsible for the publication, and under which entry is to be made, is determined by information contained in the work being cataloged. The form of the entry given on the title-page or elsewhere in the work being cataloged may be modified in the entry only if a different form has already been established and used in the catalog. It can be seen that, taken together, these rules render unnecessary much of the research which is currently eating up the cataloging budget of the Library of Congress. Nor must it be supposed that by eliminating the research which is now presumably required to determine the proper entry and its form we are in any way advocating lower standards of cataloging; for here is what may be described as the great hoax of American cataloging practice: Research into the financial structure of an agency, in order to determine that its publications are properly entered under "U.S. Naval Asylum. Philadelphia" instead of under "Philadelphia Naval Asylum" (or, in the case of another agency, that its publications are properly entered under "Philadelphia. Naval Home" instead of "U.S. Naval Home. Philadelphia") may result in making cataloging consistent with budget statements, but it certainly introduces bibliographical inconsistencies into the catalog and results in a differentiation among forms of entry which is meaningless, if not actually confusing, to even the most erudite users of the catalog.

Although we arrived at our second rule independently, our investigations into cataloging theory and history disclosed that a similar rule was first promulgated by the British Museum in 1900.

> The choice of a heading for a main entry must be based on the information supplied in print in a perfect copy of the book itself, and on that only. An exception may be made in the case of reprints of recognized classics, where the author's name may be taken as the heading of the main entry, though it be not given in the book; e.g., a reprint of the Divina Commedia without the author's name should be cataloged under Dante, and a reprint of Robinson Crusoe under Defoe. But such cases are rare and very exceptional.[40]

It should be borne in mind that the motivation responsible for this rule is not a desire to save money or even to simplify cataloging but to insure against the intrusion into cataloging of bibliographically irrelevant information.

Our rule goes beyond the British Museum rule, although it is not inconsistent with it, in permitting a change in the form given on the copy being cataloged, if such a change is necessary to achieve consistency with a form previously used in our catalog. While granting that our rule provides for the internal consistency of our own catalog, one may argue that such consistency is not enough and that we should attempt to attain consistency between our catalog and the catalogs of other libraries. It may be said, further, that this wider consistency can be achieved if we are willing to consider previous entries not only in our own catalog but in other catalogs or in what are essentially the same things, reference books, printed bibliographies, indexes, etc. And it will be argued, finally, that this search for a consistent product by different catalogers in different places at different times justifies research beyond the book that is being cataloged and beyond previously established entries in any one library. In spite of a superficial plausibility, this whole argument is basically specious. Suppose that we agree to go beyond the book itself and beyond previously cataloged entries: How far do we go? It will be said that we should go to those reference books "readily at hand." But the reference books readily at hand in one institution may not be those readily at hand in another. And if different reference books are available in different institutions, we have no guaranty that a search through reference books will always produce identical entries. Indeed, our experience with co-operative cataloging ventures has demonstrated down to the hilt that catalogers in other institutions, following A.L.A. rules and using reference books available to them, do not always produce entries equivalent to the forms established by the Library of Congress. The Processing

Department of the Library has recently published the results of a study by the chief of the Descriptive Cataloging Division which purports to show conclusively that we cannot without checking and revision accept the entries supplied by other libraries.

Furthermore, the recent decision of the Army Medical Library and the Library of Congress to break off co-operative cataloging relations was occasioned in part by the realization that, unless the Army Medical Library was willing to use the Library of Congress official catalog in establishing authors (a practice which the Army Medical Library could not afford), the entries supplied by the Army Medical Library would not be consistent with those established by the Library of Congress itself. And it did not matter, in this connection, that the Army Medical Library was willing to follow our rules of entry and to use all reference books they thought necessary. Hence, unless we are willing to specify a common list of reference books to be used by all co-operating libraries each time an author entry is to be established, we have no reason to expect a gain in consistency by going beyond the sources allowed by Rule 2 of the Science and Technology Project.[41]

Our third rule concerns the subdivisions of corporate bodies whose names are not suitable for entries. It is obvious that certain kinds of administrative units are common to a great many agencies or corporate bodies and that, therefore, their names do not constitute acceptable entries. We refer to such names as "library," "personnel office," "information office," "department of physics," etc. This awareness undoubtedly led Cutter to allow exceptions to his rule of specific entry. Cutter's error and the error of the A.L.A. *Rules* consisted not in this recognition but in the attempt to supply a general description for the kind of names which should be treated as subdivisions. We can state categorically that such a description cannot be given. Hence the Science and Technology Project abandoned the attempt and sought a solution which differed in principle from all previous attempts. We solved this problem by establishing a list of unit names which are to be used as subdivisions and not as entries.

Thus, if we are confronted with a publication by the Yale University Department of Physics, our list will tell us that "Department of ——— under universities and colleges" is always a subdivision and never an entry. Similarly, if the National Cancer Institute has a library or a personnel office which issues publications, the list will tell us that the names of such offices are never entries and that entry should be made, therefore, under "National Cancer Institute." If we should be called upon to catalog a publication which is issued by a unit whose name we feel will not make a suitable[42] entry and if we then find that this name is not on our list of names to be used as subdivisions, one of two courses is open to us: We can either use the name as an entry or add it to our list and use it as a subdivision. It will be seen that in this practice, as in the rule of specific entry, we have sought and achieved a unification of theory of subject cataloging and descriptive cataloging.

Summary and Conclusions

In the final section of this paper we shall present our three rules for corporate entries in a consecutive and systematic order. But before we do so, it will be helpful to summarize the manner in which cataloging according to our rules, as contrasted with present practice, will fulfil the claims made earlier in this paper:

1. Cataloging will be faster because a considerable portion of the research, beyond the book in hand and the record of material already cataloged, is eliminated.

2. Research beyond the book in hand and the record of material previously cataloged does not contribute materially to the achievement of consistent entries and does introduce into the cataloging process extraneous considerations relating to administrative history, law, financial structure, etc., which have no bibliographical significance for the users of the catalog.

3. The number of necessary rules has been reduced from over a hundred, plus that many more exceptions, to three rules with no exceptions.

4. By virtue of (1) and (3), the cost of cataloging can be substantially reduced. Further comparative studies are necessary in order to arrive at a definite cost figure.

5. The elimination of exceptions and of the multiplicity of conflicting rules results in a more consistent and logical catalog. This point cannot be too strongly emphasized. Our primary concern has been to produce a better catalog. Our quarrel with present practice, therefore, is not that it is expensive but that it is uselessly so. In most of the literature on the cost of cataloging, catalogers have been arrayed against administrators. The latter have protested against high costs; the former have argued that simplification would destroy the scholarly character of cataloging. We should have realized, however, that the constant increase in complexity of catalog codes is a mark not of progress but of degeneration. Toynbee has reminded us lately that progress is always in the direction of simplification, of the larger generality and the more universal law; and in principle it does not matter whether the law concerns morals, physics, or so prosaic an affair as library cataloging.

6. Any user of a catalog who wishes to spare a few minutes' time can learn our rules of entry for corporate bodies and thus find his way around in any catalog constructed in accordance with these rules.

7. Similarly, catalogers can be trained in half a day to use our rules; thus the cost of cataloging in terms of high professional salaries will be considerably reduced.

In order to forestall precious and capricious criticism, we can admit at this point that there may be publications so unusual, with title-pages so misleading, and issued by corporate bodies so complex that they cannot be handled in accordance with our rules. Suppose we were to say that in such instances, if any, the cataloger could enter the publication in any way he pleases, provided that all necessary cross-references and authority cards are made. Such instances are not damaging to our general thesis unless they occur in a significant percentage of cases. We feel confident that they will not occur nearly so frequently as do exceptions to existing rules.

Appendix I
Rules for Corporate Entries in the Science and Technology Project

Specification.—Academies, institutes, associations, universities, colleges, societies, government bodies, corporations or other collective bodies of men under whatever name are to be considered and treated as authors of their official reports, proceedings, and other publications for which they are collectively responsible.

Rule 1.—Enter the publications of a corporate entity under its name.

Rule 2.—The form of the name is to be determined by information available in the work being cataloged and in authority lists from cataloging previous works and from these two sources only.

Rule 3.—If the title-page or other parts of the work being cataloged disclose that a division or part of a corporate body was responsible for the report, entry should be made under the division or part unless the *name* of the part is contained in a standard list of names not suitable for entries. In such cases entry is to be made under the next largest administrative unit or part. Names not suitable for entries may be used as subdivisions for filing purposes at the discretion of individual institutions.

Appendix II
A Note on the Choice between Corporate, Personal, and Title Entries

Many of the American Library Association rules for corporate entry are concerned with the choice between a corporate entry and an author entry (in the case of a monographic work) or a title entry (in the case of a periodical issued by a corporate body). The application of these rules requires the cataloger to determine whether the piece being cataloged is a "routine" or "nonroutine" publication. Now, even if the cataloger could make this determination accurately at all times, the distinction has no value from the point of view of the user of the catalog. The rules themselves recognize this fact by directing in many instances that, if the corporate name is chosen as the main entry, entry should also be made under the title or personal name, as the case may be, and vice versa.

The Science and Technology Project has solved this problem of making the general choice of corporate entry a matter of policy and not of rules. Entry under corporate name is more in accord with the purposes of the Project and the kind of use made of its catalog. For general libraries, however, we would recommend the use of corporate entries only in those cases in which a personal author is not given or is obviously unsuitable as an entry.

Appendix III
Author Headings for State Publications[43]

Since 1939 the Division of Classification and Cataloging of the American Library Association has had a Special Committee on State Author Headings: "The work of the Committee has consisted chiefly in attempting to interest individuals and national or state groups of catalogers in the compilation of lists of headings."[44] Many lists of state headings were begun, and several have been completed;

during 1948 there appeared Miss A. Ethelyn Markley's *Author Headings for the Official Publications of the State of Alabama.* In the *Annual Report* of the Special Committee on State Author Headings for 1947-48 it is stated that "the major accomplishment of the current year is the publication of the Alabama List. This is the first of the lists to be issued under A.L.A. sponsorship and, as such, will provide a model for all future lists."[4][5]

The general A.L.A. rule for official publications covers state publications as well as the publications of other jurisdictions. Miss Markley quotes this rule in full in her Introduction, in the form taken from the final prepublication draft of 1947. Since this version differs in arrangement from that which we have quoted previously from the 1941 *Rules,* we will follow Miss Markley and reproduce the new version here, together with her comments:

> In the matter of entering government publications A.L.A. *Cataloging Rules* (2d ed.) are clear and succinct. Careful study of them can leave little if any doubt in a cataloger's mind about the method of applying them. The guiding principles are set forth in General Rule No. 72 which states:
> "Enter under countries, nations, states, cities, towns, and other government districts, official publications issued by them or by their authority.
> "*a*) Enter publications from the various agencies of government under the names of the agencies (legislative bodies, courts, executive departments, bureaus, etc.) as subheadings (under country, or other jurisdiction) in the latest form in the vernacular. Refer from variant forms.
> "1) Use for a subheading the name of the office rather than the title of the officer except where the title of the officer is the only name of the office. Make whenever necessary a reference from the name of the head of a department to the name of the office.
> "*Exception:* Certain classes of institutions and other bodies created, maintained, controlled or owned by governments, but not direct agencies of government, are, however, to be treated according to the rules governing these bodies as authors, e.g., colleges, universities, schools, libraries, museums, galleries, observatories, agricultural experiment stations, hospitals, asylums, prisons, theaters, chambers of commerce, botanical and zoological gardens, banks, business corporations, churches, societies, etc."[4][6]

Miss Markley tells us further that "the rule is plain enough, but application to the particular body of material is not so simple because it is quite evident that in cataloging a collection of government publications or in compiling a list for an uncataloged collection, the successful use of this rule presupposes a knowledge of the names of the issuing offices."[4][7]

Unfortunately, we must assert that this rule plus the knowledge of the names is not enough. The 1941 *Rules* contain another rule which, in part, contradicts Rule 72. Rule 154 tells us to "enter state and provincial institutions of the U.S. and Canada under the name of the state or province."

According to Rule 72, the following entries are correct: "Talladega, Ala. Institute for Deaf and Blind"; "Auburn, Ala. Polytechnic Institute"; and "Birmingham, Ala. Business Industrial School." According to Rule 154, the above entries are wrong, and the following entries are correct: "Alabama. Institute for Deaf and

Blind, Talladega"; "Alabama. Polytechnic Institute, Auburn"; and "Alabama. Business Industrial School, Birmingham."

Contradictions of this sort seem to us to be sufficient to discredit the 1941 *Rules;* but in this work on author headings, officially sponsored by the Division of Cataloging and Classification of the American Library Association, confusion is twice confounded. Nowhere in the volume is there even the vaguest hint of the existence of Rule 154. We are told, however, that the 1941 *Rules* are "clear and succinct"; that Rule 72 is "plain enough"; and that a careful study of the rules "can leave little, if any, doubt in a cataloger's mind about the method of applying them." A cataloger's mind must be wonderful indeed, because the author headings in this volume exhibit a complete disregard for Rule 72 and follow absolutely the contradictory Rule 154 which, as we have said, is nowhere mentioned in the whole volume. *Quod erat demonstrandum.*

Notes

1. M. Taube, "New Tools for the Control and Use of Research Materials," *Proceedings of the American Philosophical Society,* XCIII, No. 10 (June, 1949), 248-52.

2. Washington, 1948.

3. M. Taube, "The Planning and Preparation of the Technical Information Pilot and Its Cumulative Index," *College and Research Libraries,* IX (July, 1948), 202-6.

4. M. Taube, "Memorandum for a Conference on Bibliographical Control of Government Scientific and Technical Reports," *Special Libraries,* XXXIX (May-June, 1948), 154-60.

5. *Ibid.,* pp. 157-58.

6. *Annual Report of the Librarian of Congress for 1946* (Washington: Government Printing Office, 1947), pp. 386-87. Since the limitation of this table to material in foreign languages applies to both descriptive and subject cataloging, the limitation does not affect the ratio of one to the other.

7. In addition to cataloging incoming material, the descriptive catalogers in the Science and Technology Project search all incoming material to eliminate duplicates, file temporary cards, and maintain the regular and permanent catalogs of the Project.

8. Julia Pettee, "The Development of Authorship Entry and the Formulation of Authorship Rules as Found in the Anglo-American Code," *Library Quarterly,* VI (July, 1936): 270-90.

9. *British Museum Catalogue of Printed Books* (London, 1841), I, v.

10. *Ibid.,* p. ix.

11. C. C. Jewett, *On the Construction of Catalogues of Libraries, and of a General Catalogue* (Washington: Smithsonian Institution, 1852), p. 42.

12. *Ibid.*

13. C. A. Cutter, *Rules for a Dictionary Catalog* (4th ed.; Washington: Government Printing Office, 1904), p. 41.

14. *Ibid.,* p. 42.

15.   These two publications will be hereafter referred to as the "1908 *Rules*" and the "1941 *Rules*."

16.   Logically superior because it is not constructed arbitrarily out of parts of the name.

17.   American Library Association and the (British) Library Association, *Catalog Rules: Author and Title Entries* (American ed.; Chicago, 1908), p. 17.

18.   American Library Association, *A.L.A. Catalog Rules: Author and Title Entries* (prelim. American 2d ed.; Chicago, 1941), p. 79.

19.   J. B. Childs, "The Author Entry for Government Publications," *Public Documents: Their Selection, Distribution, Cataloging, Reproduction and Preservation: Papers Presented at the 1934 Conference of the American Library Association* (Chicago, 1935), pp. 103-28.

20.   J. C. M. Hanson, "Corporate Authorship versus Title Entry," *Library Quarterly*, V (October, 1935), 457-66.

21.   *Op. cit.*, p. 131.

22.   *Ibid.*, pp. 132-33.

23.   *Ibid.*, p. 100.

24.   Buenos Aires, 1948.

25.   *Ibid.*, p. 48.

26.   *Op. cit.*, p. 135.

27.   *Op. cit.*, p. 288.

28.   *Op. cit.*, p. 42.

29.   *Op. cit.*, p. 42.

30.   *Ibid.*, p. 116.

31.   *Ibid.*, p. 118.

32.   *Op. cit.*, p. 18.

33.   *Ibid.*, p. 25.

34.   *Op. cit.*, p. 34.

35.   *Ibid.*

36.   *Ibid.*, p. 138.

37.   *Ibid.*

38.   Cutter also accepted the rule of specific entry for both subject and author entries. He believed that the use of specific entries in both categories was the essential mark of a dictionary catalog. This means that he departed from his own principles when, in certain instances, he advocated entries under place, in effect a device more suitable to a classed catalog.

39.   The rules presented below in the text are restated in Appendix I.

40.   British Museum, *Rules for Compiling the Catalogue in the Department of Printed Books at the British Museum* (London, 1900), Rule 4.

41.   In actual practice inconsistencies of entries as between libraries are usually occasioned not by the use of different reference books but by the inconsistencies actually present in the rules being followed. Furthermore, maximum consistency would be insured by strict instructions to adopt the term of entry on the title-page. Such a rule would lead to the separation of works by a given author in any one catalog, but it would certainly insure that library A and library B would have the same entries for copies of the same book.

42.   Names are regarded as not suitable for entries if they are completely general and nondescriptive. Thus "Library" is not suitable as an entry, whereas "Library of Congress" is. Now there obviously will be doubtful cases. Thus we may be certain that "Department of English" is not a suitable entry, but what about "Department of Agriculture" or "Radiation Laboratory (M.I.T.)"? The answer here is that *in principle* it does not matter what decision is made, so long as the decision is registered. Some decisions will be better than others in that they will result in more entries more easily found by more users of the catalog. But this aim cannot be expressed in a rule that would not beg the question.

43.   The following discussion has been placed in appendix because, while important as indicating certain characteristics of present-day cataloging, it does not contribute directly to the development of the main theme of the paper.

44.   A. E. Markley, *Author Headings for the Official Publications of the State of Alabama* (Chicago: American Library Association, 1948), p. vii.

45.   *A.L.A. Bulletin,* XLII (October, 1948), 443.

46.   *Op. cit.,* p. vii.

47.   *Ibid.,* p. viii.

The Cataloging of Publications of Corporate Authors: A Rejoinder

Since the spring of 1943, the Library of Congress has been actively review-ing and re-evaluating its cataloging rules and policies. One result of this effort was the revision of its rules for descriptive cataloging. For this purpose the objectives of descriptive cataloging were defined, the old rules re-evaluated in the light of these objectives, and the new rules accordingly redesigned. Like all change, the new rules originally evoked considerable opposition both within and without the Library of Congress and engendered discussion all over the country. Ultimately, however, they were adopted by the Library and approved by the profession.

What happened to the rules of description was to happen also to the rules of entry, and Dr. Taube's study published in the January, 1950, issue of the *Library Quarterly* must be recognized as an important step toward their revision. For, despite the zeal of his criticism and some questionable statements which will be challenged by catalogers, Dr. Taube demonstrates that the rules are not well rooted in logic, are productive of inconsistencies confusing to the cataloger as well as to the reader, and are needlessly complicated by irrelevant considerations which increase the cost of cataloging and reduce the effectiveness of the catalog. Dr. Taube's analysis should have dispelled whatever doubt still remained that our rules of entry are in need of revision, and it should be studied by all concerned with the subject of cataloging.

There are probably few who would take issue with Dr. Taube's criticism of our corporate rules of entry. However, Dr. Taube does not stop there but goes on to propose "three rules with no exceptions," which, he asserts, could replace the present "over a hundred [rules] plus that many more exceptions" and produce a more logical, consistent, and "bibliographically adequate" catalog at a fraction of the present cataloging cost. Actually, he could have gone further and dispensed with his first rule, *Enter the publications of a corporate entity under its name,* since the very first general rule in both the 1908 and 1941 codes reads: *Enter a work under the name of its author whether individual or corporate,* and thus main-tain that he had reduced all other rules for the cataloging of works of corporate authors to two rules. Moreover, these two rules were adopted by Dr. Taube from

Reprinted by permission of Seymour Lubetzky and The University of Chicago Press from *Library Quarterly* 21 (January 1951): 1-12.

subject cataloging practice and parallel the principles of subject entry and subdivision; thus he claims that he has not only solved the problems of entry but has also achieved "a unification of theory of subject cataloging and descriptive cataloging." Ordinarily, such claims would probably be passed up in disbelief. Coming as a conclusion of Dr. Taube's trenchant criticism, his claims deserve careful consideration. Let us, therefore, examine the principles advocated by Dr. Taube and their application in practice, test his rules in the realities of cataloging, and then consider the claims made and the issues involved.

Principles and Practice

In his search for "consistency and simplicity," Dr. Taube relates, he discovered in "the generally accepted principles of subject headings" a solution to the problems of corporate entry. "The Library of Congress Subject Cataloging Division and the Science and Technology Project," he explains, "agree in following the principle of direct and specific headings. This means that a work on analytical geometry is entered under the subject heading 'Analytical geometry' and not under the heading 'Mathematics–Geometry–Analytical'"; hence his first and basic tenet "that the entry must be the specific agency or corporate body responsible for the report" and, accordingly, "a publication of the National Cancer Institute should be cataloged under 'National Cancer Institute' and not under 'U.S. ... National Cancer Institute.'" Dr. Taube does not indicate in what respects the author entry is similar to the subject entry, which would make apparent the applicability of analogous rules; still, the author entry and the subject entry are similar in objective–which is to bring together under the same heading in the catalog the works of a given author or on a given subject–and the method used in the preparation of subject entries to achieve this objective might, therefore, also be appropriate for author entries. However, in focusing attention on the principles of subject cataloging, Dr. Taube appears to overlook their application in practice; and, in prescribing a rigid application of these principles to corporate entries, he deviates from, rather than follows, subject cataloging practice, where they are applied with considerable flexibility, tempered by the realities of the catalog and the conflicting needs of its users.

In the first place, it should be noted that our subject headings are not always direct but are often indirect. To take Dr. Taube's own example, the Library of Congress Subject Cataloging Division, with which he agrees "in following the principle of direct and specific headings," actually does *not* use the direct heading "Analytical geometry" but the inverted heading, Geometry, Analytic," thus bringing together under the heading "Geometry" the related subjects "Geometry, Algebraic," "Geometry, Analytic," "Geometry, Descriptive," "Geometry, Differential," "Geometry, Enumerative," "Geometry, Infinitesimal," etc. Moreover, the Subject Cataloging Division goes even further and subdivides this heading into "Geometry, Analytic–Plane," and "Geometry, Analytic–Solid," rather than use the direct headings "Plane analytical geometry" and "Solid analytical geometry." One may reasonably disagree with some or all of these headings; but one who invokes the principles of subject cataloging should also regard their application in practice. When one contemplates the numerous subdivisions under the heading "U.S.," ranging the whole gamut of the alphabet from "U.S.–Altitudes" to "U.S.–Territories," and then examines Dr. Taube's rules of corporate entry, one cannot escape the realization that, in forging a "unification of theory," Dr. Taube accomplishes a divergence of practice of descriptive and subject cataloging.

Nor can it be granted that the subject headings are always as specific as the subjects of the books to which they are assigned. If this were the case, our scheme of subject headings would be bewilderingly complicated, and most of the books would be scattered rather than brought together. For example, under the heading "Religion and science" one will find in the catalog works on

a)   religion and science

b)   Christianity and science
      morals and science
      God and science
      immortality and science

c)   evolution and religion
      nature and religion
      biology and religion
      sociology and religion

d)   Christianity and evolution
      Scriptures and geology
      Protestantism and capitalism
      faith and reason
      etc.

Here the subject heading is quite specific for example *a* but not for the other examples; "Religion" is obviously too broad for those under *b,* "Science" for those under *c,* and both for those under *d.* The reason is, of course, that the specificity of the subject heading is circumscribed by the underlying pattern of subject organization. To assign specific subject headings to all these and similar examples would obviously complicate greatly the subject structure of the catalog and would serve to scatter, rather than bring together, these related works. But that is exactly what Dr. Taube advocates for corporate entries.

The second principle adopted by Dr. Taube from subject cataloging practice concerns the problem of subdivision. This problem arises out of his recognition of the fact "that certain kinds of administrative units are common to a great many agencies or corporate bodies and that, therefore, their names do not constitute acceptable entries." In this case, too, Dr. Taube finds a solution in the principle followed in the preparation of subject subdivisions which he explains as follows:

> Since these subdivisions are intended to be used under many different specific entries, both the Library of Congress proper and the Science and Technology Project maintain internally and have published lists of subject subdivisions to be used whenever suitable. From time to time new subdivisions are developed as they are required, and they are added to the existing lists. A subject cataloger does not have to guess whether or not a phrase or term can be used as a subdivision; he searches the list for it. If it is not on the list and he still wishes to use it, it must pass inspection not only for a particular and present use but for addition to the list for general and regular use.

Thus Dr. Taube resolves the problem of subdivision under corporate bodies "by establishing a list of unit names which are to be used as subdivisions and not as entries."

The principle of subject division thus enunciated is without support in theory or in practice. There is no reason why any necessary or desirable subdivisions under any subject "must be capable of being subdivisions of many specific entries" or why they "must pass inspection not only for a particular present use but for addition to the list for general and regular use." There are many subject subdivisions—particularly geographical and form subdivisions—which can be used under many or all headings, but one need only refer to the Library of Congress list in *Subject Headings* to see the numerous subdivisions specifically designed for individual headings. The subdivisions "Plane" and "Solid" under "Geometry, Analytic," mentioned before, are examples of such subdivisions. The cataloger who provided for the subject heading "Blood" the subdivisions "Agglutination," "Circulation," "Coagulation," "Transfusion," etc., scarcely concerned himself with their qualifications to serve as subdivisions under many other subject headings. Nor is there any similarity in the character of Dr. Taube's corporate and subject subdivisions. The corporate subdivisions, by his definition, are those whose names are "not suitable for entries." There is no such criterion for subject subdivisions. The most common subdivisions—"Bibliography," "History," "Periodicals," etc.—and all geographical subdivisions are used as both main headings and subdivisions.

Dr. Taube's claim of having achieved a unification of descriptive and subject cataloging appears particularly vulnerable when one considers the basic practice of subject cataloging. In establishing a subject heading, the cataloger does not rely on the name by which the subject is called in the book in hand; that name may be obsolete, obscure, or even inaccurate. He investigates the various names by which the subject is known, selects the best known and most accurate name for the heading, and provides references from the other headings to the heading selected. This prevents dispersion of the material under various headings and guides all readers to the subject under whatever name they may look for it. This is precisely the method now followed in establishing author entries. But this is also diametrically different from Dr. Taube's rules, which prescribe that a corporate heading is to be established on the wholly fortuitous basis of the book cataloged.

Rules and Reality

One might forego the theoretical aspect of Dr. Taube's rules if their practical value could be granted; but an attempt to test them in the actual conditions of cataloging will be disillusioning. To reach for the nearest example, the Science and Technology Project, which, he indicates, was the laboratory of his rules, publishes a bulletin entitled *Technical Information Pilot*. Should this bulletin be entered under its title or under the name of the project responsible for it? Dr. Taube's Rule 1 says: *Enter the publications of a corporate entity under its name*, and his rules contain no qualifications or exemptions. Does it mean that no publications of corporate bodies are to be entered under their titles? If the bulletin is to be entered under the name of the project, as would appear from the rules and the note which follows them at the end of Dr. Taube's article, under which name should it be entered? The Science and Technology Project has since undergone a change of name and is now called Navy Research Section. Should the bulletin be entered under the former name, under the later name, or should the earlier issues be entered under the Science and Technology Project and the later under the Navy Research Section? One will search Dr. Taube's rules in vain for an answer to these pertinent questions. Suppose a cataloger decides to enter the bulletin under the Navy Research Section but feels that the name is "not suitable" for entry. Rule 3 instructs him: *In such cases entry is to be made under the next largest administrative unit;* but the bulletin does not disclose what is the next largest unit, and Rule 2 prohibits the cataloger from getting this information from another source, such as the *Annual Report of the Librarian of Congress.*

And there is another example. Should this *Annual Report of the Librarian of Congress* be entered under the "Librarian of Congress" as stated in the title, the "Library of Congress" which he represents, or the personal name of the librarian who officially signs it and is responsible for it? Here, too, Dr. Taube's rules will fail the cataloger. This paper was prepared for the Library of Congress by one of its employees and is released by the Library. Is it to be cataloged under the name of the Library, under that of the employee, or under both? And again Dr. Taube's rules will fail the cataloger. Or are all these titles illustrations of what Dr. Taube refers to at the conclusion of his article when he says, "There may be publications so unusual, with title pages so misleading, and issued by corporate bodies so complex that they cannot be handled in accordance with our rules."

At the beginning of his discussion of the subject, Dr. Taube admonishes earnestly: "Although it may seem at first glance that descriptive cataloging, as contrasted with subject cataloging or indexing, is or should be a relatively simple and straightforward affair, there are certain problems not always apparent to those who lack firsthand experience with the difficulty of devising uniform entries from the haphazard information which appears on the title pages of the various publications and reports requiring organization"; and he warns against "a blind rejection of the complexities of descriptive cataloging." Had Dr. Taube himself heeded this warning, his conclusions would probably be different; as it is, his rules will only serve to underline the importance of his warning. For, having demonstrated that the entry "U.S. National Cancer Institute" is unsound in logic and unwarranted in practice—and, by implication, all similar headings for government institutions—Dr. Taube proceeds without reservation to sweep away "the whole collection of special rules for government publications"; and in the next step, finding no reason for the distinction between societies and institutions, he goes on to discard all other corporate rules, replacing all of them by three distilled rules of his own. Had he examined more carefully the rules that he was ready to reject and the materials cataloged under them, he would probably have hesitated at the first corporate rule, whose practical value he could not overlook. This rule says: "Enter under names of countries, states, cities ... official publications issued by them or under their auspices." Under this rule various publications of the British government are appropriately entered under the heading "Great Britain," regardless of the form of name given in the publication or the absence of any name. If this rule were discarded and the cataloger were to follow Dr. Taube's rule prescribing that *the form of the name is to be determined by information available in the work being cataloged* ..., he would be confronted with such forms of name as "British Government," "Government of Great Britain," "Government of His Britannic Majesty,"

"Government of Her Britannic Majesty," "Government of the United Kingdom of Great Britain and Northern Ireland," "His Britannic Majesty," "His Britannic Majesty's Government," "Her Britannic Majesty," "Her Majesty's Government," and many other variations of name. Any one or several of these names, or none, might be given in the first book cataloged; how would it be entered under Dr. Taube's rules?

A survey of the publications issued by various countries, states, cities, etc., and their various legislative and administrative branches and offices will show how confusing these publications often are to the cataloger and will demonstrate the need of rules providing specific forms under which these generally amorphous publications could usefully be organized. Many of the rules discarded by Dr. Taube were designed precisely for this purpose, and their absence will not help the cataloger and will certainly not improve the quality of the catalog. In addition to the variant forms of name, the publications of foreign countries, cities, etc., will confront Dr. Taube's cataloger with the problem of the language of the heading. Should it be given in the language of the book cataloged or in the vernacular? If the heading is to be given in the language of the book cataloged, the publications of that body will obviously be scattered under the various languages. If it is to be given in the vernacular, how could the cataloger establish the heading under the restrictions of Dr. Taube's Rule 2 when the book in hand gives the name in translation only? And how is a cataloger to determine, under Dr. Taube's rules, what is the "corporate entity" under which the "Documents of the United Nations Conference on International Organization, San Francisco, 1945" should be entered. Is it the United Nations or the conference? If a conference is self-evidently a corporate body, how are the reports of the First, Eighth, or Thirteenth International Conference on – – – to be entered under these new rules—under "First International Conference ...," etc., or under "International Conference ..., First," etc.? And in what language should the heading of an international body be given? One could easily go on and extend this list of examples and questions which the rules leave unanswered. If in all these instances, following Dr. Taube's final suggestion at the end of his article, "the cataloger could enter the publications in any way he pleases ...," would the cataloging product really be "bibliographically more consistent, more logical, and easier to use"?

Dr. Taube's belief that all corporate rules of entry could be reduced to two or three rules is obviously based on the illusion that all corporate bodies and their various subdivisions could conveniently be divided into two categories: those whose names are "suitable" for entry and those whose names are "not suitable" for entry; the former could readily be entered directly under their names, the latter under the names of the "next largest" units. This is essentially all the guidance Dr. Taube's rules provide, leaving to the catalogers themselves to determine what is a corporate body (or "corporate entity"), what is to be regarded as the publication of a corporate body, when and what kind of additional entries are required, what is properly "the name" of the corporate body and what elements or words are to be omitted from the name, what kind of cross-references should be made to the name, etc., and ignoring the vexing problems arising from changes of name, the existence of variant forms of name, the various languages in which the name may appear, the organization of the elements of the name, the necessary qualifications of the name, and "the haphazard information which appears on the title pages" of which Dr.

Taube spoke earlier. However, for the first and basic question of the cataloger—what names are "suitable" for entry and what names are not?—Dr. Taube offers what he justly claims as an original solution: the establishment of "a list of unit names which are to be used as subdivisions and not as entries." Thus, Dr. Taube explains, "if we are confronted with a publication by the Yale University Department of Physics, our list will tell us that 'Department of ... under universities and colleges' is always a subdivision and never an entry."

To get an idea of what is involved in the preparation of such a "list of unit names," it may be well to pursue Dr. Taube's example a little further in the catalog. There one will find under "Yale University" also such unit names as Aeromedical Research Unit, Alumni Board, Associates in Fine Arts, Association of the Alumni, Bureau of Appointments, Catholic Club, Class of 1896, Clinic of Child Development, Committee on Transportation, Council on the Library and Museums, Directive Committee on Regional Planning, Divinity School, Elizabethan Club, Gallery of Fine Arts, Graduate School, Institute of International Studies, Labor and Management Center, Laboratory of Applied Physiology, Library, Medical Library, Mineralogical Society, Observatory, President's Committee on University Development, Psychological Laboratory, School of Engineering, University Press, etc. Proceeding to "Harvard University," one will find additional unit names, such as Archives, Board of Overseers, Botanical Museum, Bureau for Economic Research in Latin America, Bureau of Vocational Guidance, Chinese-Japanese Library, Committee on Economic Research, Dramatic Club, Faculty of Arts and Science, Germanic Museum, Graduate School of Arts and Sciences, Library of the Departments of Landscape Architecture and Regional Planning, Museum of Comparative Zoölogy, Russian Research Center, Semitic Museum, etc. These two samples will indicate how numerous and varied are the names of university units alone, most or all of which would have to be examined, selected, and listed. If one stops to think of the names of the subdivisions and units found under the infinite number and constantly growing and changing variety of corporate organizations all over the world and in the various languages, one cannot seriously concede that such a list as that recommended by Dr. Taube could really be prepared and maintained without research and without an extravagant cost, that the preparation and maintenance of such a list is of "bibliographical significance," or that it would facilitate the use of the catalog by the reader, who would scarcely be able to absorb this list with Dr. Taube's rules in "a few minutes' time."

Fact and Fancy

At the conclusion of his article Dr. Taube undertakes to summarize and explain how cataloging under his rules would achieve the claims made by him earlier. Let us now examine the facts enumerated by him in the light of the foregoing discussion.

    1.   Cataloging will be faster because a considerable portion of the research, beyond the book in hand and the record of material already cataloged, is eliminated.

Obviously, if the research done in cataloging is to be limited to the book in hand and the record of previous cataloging, the rate of cataloging will rise.

However, this is not a matter of cataloging rules but of regulative cataloging policy. If this limitation is defensible, it could be applied also to the cataloging rules now in effect, with the prospect of a corresponding gain. Such a limitation need not be construed as contrary to the present rules but should be regarded, rather, as a policy to be followed in the application of the rules. The essential justification of present cataloging research, as indicated above, is to enable the cataloger to select the most appropriate form of name for the author heading and to provide the necessary references from the other names under which the corporate body may be known and from related bodies, in order to avoid dispersion of the publications of this body and related bodies and to guide all readers to these publications regardless of the names under which the readers may look for them. If this objective can be dispensed with or can be achieved to a reasonable degree without verification in other sources, then Dr. Taube's proposed limitation on research should be applied also under the present cataloging rules. If not, Dr. Taube's rules will fall short of this objective and will be inadequate. A study of the effect of a similar limitation on cataloging research is discussed later.

2. Research beyond the book in hand and the record of material previously cataloged does not contribute materially to the achievement of consistent entries and does introduce into the cataloging process extraneous considerations relating to administrative history, law, financial structure, etc., which have no bibliographical significance for the users of the catalog.

The two parts of this statement must be considered separately. Dr. Taube's assertion that research "does not contribute materially to the achievement of consistent entries" must be regarded as dubious. He demonstrates from the experience in co-operative cataloging that research in sources other than the book in hand does not insure uniformity of entry by various libraries; it does not follow by logical deduction that cataloging without research would not produce "materially" less consistent entries within any library and between libraries. As already mentioned, the effect of such limitation on research is considered later.

The second part is surprising as a patently illogical allegation in a case based largely on logic. To assert that research beyond the book "does introduce into the cataloging process extraneous considerations" is to ascribe to an instrument the faults of some of its users. Obviously, research itself does not introduce any considerations, it merely reveals them. If irrelevant facts are introduced, the fault is clearly that of the cataloger or of the rules followed by him. To restrict cataloging research on such grounds is to imply that it is bad for a cataloger to know more about an item he catalogs than is revealed by the books handled by him.

3. The number of necessary rules has been reduced from over a hundred, plus that many more exceptions, to three rules with no exceptions.

The foregoing examination does not bear out Dr. Taube's claim that he has reduced the number of *necessary* rules. As has been shown before, his rules leave many questions unanswered and are quite insufficient for the requirements of the materials ordinarily cataloged in a general library. Earlier in his article Dr. Taube quotes a memorandum of his own, setting forth that "a code for cataloging scientific reports ... should be detailed, as is required by the material to be cataloged...." It would be difficult to maintain that Dr. Taube's three rules meet this requirement.

4.   By virtue of (1) and (3), the cost of cataloging can be substantially reduced.

Nobody could dispute this conclusion—if the virtues of (1) and (3) were indisputable. Unfortunately, this is not the case, as has already been indicated in the discussion of these points.

5.   The elimination of exceptions and of the multiplicity of conflicting rules results in a more consistent and logical catalog....

This is also incontestable in principle. In practice, however, the mere elimination of exceptions and conflicting rules does not, in itself, create a logical and consistent code; it may produce something worse than an inconsistent code, namely, a vacuum. This appears to be precisely what Taube accomplished when he swept out wholesale the present rules with their inconsistencies and irrelevancies but failed to provide other rules adequate for the materials cataloged under the present rules.

6.   Any user of a catalog who wishes to spare a few minutes' time can learn our rules of entry for corporate bodies....
7.   Similarly, catalogers can be trained in half a day to use our rules....

At this point these claims are irrelevant, for, if Dr. Taube's rules are of no avail, there is no virtue in the fact that they can easily be learned by the cataloger as well as by the reader. In pursuit of simpler and more consistent rules, Dr. Taube appears to have given insufficient consideration to the fact that the present multiplicity of rules sprang not from pure caprice but from the variety of the materials encountered, although he has very persuasively demonstrated the fissures in their logical structure and the flaws in their practical design.

Issues in Balance

Beyond the questions of the validity of Dr. Taube's principles, the practicability of his rules, and the merits of his claims, three of the issues raised by him deserve special attention.

Question of Entry

The first issue relates to the distinction, made in the present corporate rules, between governments, institutions, and societies. Exploiting the names of the National Cancer Institute, which is entered under "U.S.," and the British Museum, Bibliothèque Nationale, and the Library of Congress, of which the first is entered directly under its name, the second under the name of the city, Paris, and the third under the name of the country, "U.S.," he argues very cogently that these distinctions are irrelevant to the purposes of the catalog and the needs of its users, that they complicate and increase the cost of cataloging, and that they make the catalog more difficult to understand and use. Here Dr. Taube has pointed out a fundamental weakness in the structure of our cataloging rules and a way of making them more logical, more simple, and more purposeful. One cardinal principle which underlies the establishment of author and subject headings is to enter material under the names and the headings under which it is most likely to be looked for in the catalog by the reader. Is there any reason why we should expect a reader to look for material on the National Foundation for Infantile Paralysis under this name but the National Cancer Institute under "U.S."; the National Committee on Atomic Information under its name but the National Committee on Radiation Protection under "U.S."; the National Film Music Council under its name but the National Film Library under "London"? Is there any bibliographical significance in the fact that an institution is supported by private or public funds which would require that it be entered differently in each of these cases? Of course, we plant a sign under "National Cancer Institute" to direct the reader to look for it under "U.S." But should we not do it the other way around? Here Dr. Taube makes a constructive contribution to the revision of our rules.

Question of Subdivision

Having achieved considerable simplification by extending the principle of direct entry to all corporate bodies regardless of origin, character, and source of income, Dr. Taube proceeds to extend it further, vertically, to the subdivisions and parts of a corporate body *unless the name of the part is contained in a standard list of names not suitable for entries.* The practical considerations involved in the preparation of such a list were considered before, but what are the intrinsic merits of this rule? Here, too, doubts will arise.

In the first place, the publication of a minor unit is not always associated with the name of that unit. There may be a statement inside the book indicating the unit which prepared the publication, but the title-page may give prominence only to the larger division or the corporate body responsible for it. Also, there is often an overlapping responsibility, and it is difficult to decide whether the publication should be regarded as the work of the larger division or of the smaller unit. Such publications will be referred to and looked for by some under the name of the larger division and by others under the name of the smaller unit. In this case the present rules are more helpful to the reader by bringing together the publications of the major division and its minor subdivisions. Under Dr. Taube's proposal these publications might be scattered under the names of the individual units and lost to the reader.

Second, minor subdivisions of corporate bodies, even if their names are "suitable for entry," are often unknown to those interested in them. For example, the readers of the *Library Quarterly* may occasionally be interested in the reports and surveys of various university libraries. They can now find them without difficulty under the names of the universities; but how many are sufficiently familiar with the special names of the various university libraries and their branches, named after their donors, faculty members, special functions, etc., to find their reports under these names? In this case, too, the present rules entering all such subdivisions under the names of the universities, whether or not their names are suitable for entry, are obviously more helpful than Dr. Taube's proposal would be most for users of the catalog.

Third, it must be recalled that corporate headings, like all other author headings, serve not only an author function but also a subject function. They are consulted by those who want publications *by* these organizations as well as by those who want publications *about* them. It is apparent that the interests of the latter would not be well served by Dr. Taube's proposal, which would separate the publications of and about the various subdivisions of an organization from those of and about the organization as a whole whenever the subdivisions had names suitable for entry. Of course, what Dr. Taube sought in this rule was to spare the cataloger the question of what is a major division, which should be entered under its own name, and what is a minor subdivision, which should be entered under the name of the organization; but in this case he would relieve the cataloger at the expense of the users of the catalog. The subject cataloger is frequently faced with a similar question in deciding whether to enter a subject heading directly or indirectly. He may decide that American, French, and German literature are major subjects and enter them as "American literature," "French literature," and "German literature," but he may regard American, French, and German folklore as subdivisions of the subject "Folklore" and enter them as "Folklore, American," "Folklore, French," and "Folklore, German." His decision will not always be right and will never conform to everyone else's, but it is calculated to meet most frequently the approach of most users of the catalog. The criterion of "suitable" and "unsuitable" names, as defined by Dr. Taube, is inadequate for determining direct entry or subdivision.

Question of Research

As noted before, Dr. Taube combines cataloging rules and policy, and his three rules provide not only how corporate names should be entered but also that these names "be determined by information available in the work being cataloged and in authority lists from cataloging previous works and from these sources only." The relevance of this provision to his other rules was considered before. Here the merits of this issue will be considered.

A rigid application of this policy, as required by Dr. Taube, is scarcely desirable or practicable. To impose a blanket restriction which would prohibit the cataloger from consulting a readily available reference work when the information in the book cataloged and in the authority list is clearly inadequate of confusing is to substitute rigid rule for balanced reason. Applied with reasonable flexibility, it may not be without merit. It has actually been in effect in the Library of Congress since April, 1949, but its application is restricted to personal names. The Processing Department Memorandum No. 60, which was reproduced in *Cataloging Service* (Bull. 20) and is authority for this policy, prescribes:

> New personal name entries to be used in all cataloging shall hereafter be established on the basis of "no conflict," that is, a personal name shall be established in the form given in the work being cataloged without further search, provided that, as given in the work being cataloged, the name conforms to the A.L.A.

rules for entry, and is not so similar to another name previously established as to give a good basis for the suspicion that both names refer to the same person. When the nationality of an author must be established and his period identified for subject cataloging purposes, the search will be made by the descriptive cataloger.

The reluctance to extend this "no conflict" policy to corporate authors is due to the fact that the longevity of corporate bodies is ordinarily greater than that of individuals, that their names are more frequently changed, that they are not infrequently known and referred to under varying forms of names at the same time, and, consequently, that the application of this policy to corporate names would do more damage to the catalog than it does in the case of personal names. To determine what would be the effect on the catalog if the "no conflict" policy were extended to corporate authors, a sample study was recently made by Mr. Joseph S. Allen, editor of the card catalogs, Catalog Maintenance Division. His study and conclusions are summarized in the following extracts:

The publications of 90 corporate bodies entered in the public card catalog of the Library of Congress were selected as the basis of the comparison. The aim in the selection was to obtain a representative group of various types of corporate entities: societies, private institutions, and governmental agencies and institutions.

The headings are divided as follows: societies, 45; institutions, 45 (subdivided thus: private institutions, 17; governmental agencies and institutions, 28).

The corporate bodies are established by the Library of Congress in the following languages:

	Societies	Private Institutions	Govt. Agencies	Total
English	27	. . .	9	36
French.	9	13	2	24
German	3	2	9	14
Spanish	1	1	8	10
Swedish.	5	. . .	. . .	5
Portuguese	. . .	1	. . .	1
Total.	. . .	. . .	. . .	90

Under these 90 corporate headings there are a total of 783 entries, composed of main entries, added entries, and subject entries.

In the publications of and about these 90 corporate bodies 237 different forms of name appear. In other words, for every body there is an average of slightly less than 3 forms of name. For 37 bodies there is but one form of name; this is 41% of the total. The remaining 53 bodies account for 200 forms of name; 22 have 2 forms of name, 10 have 3 forms, 8 have 4 forms, 5 have 5 forms, 4 have 6 forms, 2 have 8 forms, 1 has 12 forms, and 1 has 17 forms.

The following table lists the languages in which name changes and variant names occurred:

	Total No. of Corporate Bodies in Survey	No. with Name Changes and Variant Names	Per Cent
English	36	20	56
French	24	10	42
German	14	9	64
Spanish	10	8	80
Swedish.	5	5	100
Portuguese	1	1	100
Total.	90	53	59

The publications of the 90 corporate bodies in the experiment were examined in order to apply the "no conflict" method to these corporate names.

Instead of 90 headings the "no conflict" method produced 118 headings.

Publications of 72 of the 90 bodies remain under one heading when the "no conflict" method is employed. 13 of the 90 are divided under 2 headings, 3 are divided under 3 headings, 1 under 4 headings, and 1 under 7 headings.

The 28 incorrect headings consist of earlier or later names and variant names of 17 different corporate bodies and one anonymous entry. Of these 17 bodies, 9 underwent changes in name. These are divided as follows: 6 societies, 1 private institution, and 2 governmental agencies. In the other 8 bodies variant names occurred; these are composed of 3 societies, 4 private institutions, and 1 governmental agency. One of the bodies which underwent name changes also had variant names.

The following point cannot be too strongly emphasized. In many instances, the two forms of name (variants or name changes) have been identified as one corporate body by means of information in *only one* publication. If the Library did not happen to possess this one publication, or in the case of a serial one particular volume of a set, the cataloger would not discover that the two forms represent a single organization, and thus the publication would be separated under two headings.

If the Library of Congress had not received the publication or certain volumes of serial titles containing the information concerning changes in name and variations in name, 46 incorrect headings would have been established. This total is in addition to the 28 incorrect headings established by the use of all the publications in the library under the 90 headings.

These results must be further examined and evaluated, the indications being that certain categories of corporate names have greater stability than others, but they must give one pause before extending the limitations on research in cataloging to corporate authors.

To take issue with Dr. Taube's principles and rules is not to minimize in the slightest the value of his criticism of our present rules. Those who are aware of the inadequacies of our rules and are looking forward to their revision and reformation will be grateful to Dr. Taube for having illuminated the situation and for having stimulated the search for ways to make cataloging more rational, purposeful, and economical.

Literary Unit versus Bibliographical Unit

Eva Verona

Editor's Introduction

The Yugoslavian librarian, Eva Verona, achieved world-wide recognition at the International Conference on Cataloguing Principles (ICCP) held in Paris in 1961. Respected for her extensive knowledge of catalog codes as well as for her ability to conceptualize issues, she continued for many years to be an active participant in international cataloging meetings. In her writing, she is perhaps best known for her commentary on the *Paris Principles* and for her examination of corporate headings. The following selection was published in 1959, when Verona was head of the Department of Printed Books at the University Library, Zagreb. The paper presents her in one of the roles she played at the ICCP, that of an earnest protagonist in the unfolding drama of the function of main entry in modern catalogs. Her antagonist in the drama was Seymour Lubetzky.

Verona and Lubetzky agree on what the objectives of a catalog should be. In Verona's formulation, these objectives are to (1) locate a particular book, (2) identify all editions, translations, etc. of a given work, and (3) provide information on all works by a given author. They differ on the function of the main entry vis-à-vis the objectives of the catalog. Verona's position is that the main entry should be used to identify bibliographic units, Lubetzky's that it should be used to assemble literary units. A catalog based on the primacy of the bibliographic unit is seen as favoring the first objective of the catalog, whereas one based on the literary unit is seen as favoring the second.

Leonard Jolley characterizes the bibliographic versus literary unit debate as a face-off between expediency and principle: while using the main entry to assemble literary units might produce a more consistent catalog, using it to identify bibliographic units would produce a catalog at lesser cost.* But this characterization is not fair to Verona because it implies that she believes literary units are unnecessary. Verona never questions the second objective of the catalog; she only relegates the achieving of it to added entries rather than to main entries.

Verona's strongest argument for bibliographic units, one she reiterates, is based on user convenience. In bibliographic unit cataloging, the title used for purposes of entry is the one that appears on the title page of the publication in hand. Literary unit cataloging, on the other hand, enters the publication under a uniform title, normally the original title of the work. Verona feels the literary unit approach fails to respond to the needs of the great majority of users, who come to the catalog with requests for particular items. Unfortunately, her argument is based upon hyopthesis. While there have been studies showing the kinds of data users bring to the catalog, none of these has adequately explored the helpfulness of main entry assembled literary units. Today, with the advent of online catalogs, the controversey is not primarily concerned with which of the objectives of the catalog the main entry should favor; rather, it centers on the relative effectiveness of the various devices that can be used in a machine environment to achieve the collocating function of the catalog. As the environment changes, so do the questions, and the drama is recast.

ES

---

*Leonard J. Jolley, "The Function of the Main Entry in the Alphabetical Catalogue; a Study of the Views Put Forward by Lubetzky and Verona," in International Conference on Cataloguing Principles, *Report: International Conference on Cataloguing Principles, Paris, 9th-18th October, 1961* (London: Organizing Committee of the International Conference on Cataloguing Principles, 1963), 159-63.

Further Reading

Lubetzky, Seymour. "The Function of the Main Entry in the Alphabetical Catalogue—One Approach." In International Conference on Cataloguing Principles, *Report: International Conference on Cataloguing Principles, Paris, 9th-18th October, 1961*, 139-43. London: Organizing Committee of the International Conference on Cataloguing Principles, 1963.

States the position that the main entry for a publication should show it as a representation of a certain work.

Verona, Eva. "The Function of the Main Entry in the Alphabetical Catalogue—a Second Approach." In International Conference on Cataloguing Principles, *Report: International Conference on Cataloguing Principles, Paris, 9th-18th October, 1961,* 145-57. London: Organizing Committee of the International Conference on Cataloguing Principles, 1963.

A restatement of the position presented in the selection reprinted in the following pages, but differently organized and in some places more closely argued.

Literary Unit versus Bibliographical Unit

I. Introduction

Recent papers on the revision of cataloging codes have also brought forth new discussions on the objectives of the alphabetical catalogue for author and title entries. As a rule the following three objectives are mentioned:

1) the rapid location of a particular book;
2) the provision of information concerning all editions, translations etc. of a given work as far as they exist in the library;
3) the provision of information concerning all works by a given author as far as they exist in the library.

In practice these three objectives will often conflict with one another, especially as far as the first two are concerned. In order to make this statement quite clear we shall examine the three objectives separately. We shall furthermore describe the general outlines of catalogues built up—in so far as that is possible—on the basis of only one of these objectives.

A catalogue designed for the first objective and neglecting the other two will have as its basic element the individual book, i.e. the bibliographical unit. In such a catalogue the choice of the main headings as well as the compilation and arrangement of the main entries will have to be concentrated exclusively on that element. That is to say that, in such a catalogue, the main headings will be chosen from the particular book itself (i.e. various editions and translations of a certain anonymous work entered according to their particular titles regardless of whether the author can be ascertained or not; names of authors given in the form which appears in the particular book); the descriptions of the particular books will be such as to differentiate them from other works and other editions of the same work without necessarily giving any information concerning their relation to other editions or other works; finally in the sub-arrangements under author headings the various editions and translations of the authors' works will be filed according to their particular titles.

Reprinted by permission of Eva Verona and Munksgaard from *Libri* 9 (1959): 79-104. © 1959 Munksgaard International Publishers, Ltd., Copenhagen, Denmark.

A catalogue compiled in such a way, taking into consideration the first objective only, will be, primarily, a finding list for particular books. It will be an efficient help to those users who know exactly which particular book or bibliographical unit or which edition or translation of a certain work they are looking for and what the title of that book is. The catalogue will enable an easy and quick location of such a unit.

Let us now examine a catalogue which is designed for the second objective only and which neglects both the first and the third. The second objective is concentrated on the location of literary works, also called literary units, which are thus accepted as basic elements of the catalogue. Hence particular books will not be considered as single items but as representatives of a whole group of similar items, all belonging to the same literary unit. In this case the choice of the main headings, as well as the compilation and arrangement of the main entries, will not be centred on the elements determining particular books, but mainly on those designating whole literary units. Hence the procedure of cataloguing a particular book for such a catalogue will have to be preceded by the identification of the literary unit to which the book belongs, i.e. by the identification of the title and author of the literary unit. Considered from this point of view a particular book will often have two different titles: its own, and the original or best known title of the literary unit to which it belongs (filing title, standard title, Einordnungstitel). It is the filing title which will serve as basis for the procedure of cataloguing; it will provide the heading for the main entry, it will be mentioned in the description of the particular book and it will determine the place of the main entry in the sub-arrangement under an author heading.

A catalogue compiled in this way and taking into consideration the second objective only will be, primarily, a finding list for literary units. It will be of great help to users who approach the catalogue in order to look for a literary work in whatever edition, translation or excerpt it may exist in the library. On the other hand it may disappoint those who seek information about a certain book and who know only its particular title.

Now let us consider the last objective. A catalogue aiming at this objective has to bring together under a uniform heading all works by a given author in so far as they exist in the library, also including, naturally, works published anonymously or under a pseudonym. The third objective is not concerned with the attitude of the catalogue towards literary and bibliographical units and therefore does not enter more deeply into the structure of the catalogue. Hence this objective by itself will not be enough to determine the nature of the catalogue but will always have to be accompanied by one of the first two objectives. In practice we shall often find the method of assembling works by a given author adopted by catalogues which recognize literary units. Some authors even consider these two objectives to be inseparable, or mention the third objective as an essential condition for the identification of literary units. But such an assumption does not seem to be correct and is not in accordance with the fundamental nature of the two objectives. Indisputably, it remains true that, if all works by a given author are entered under a single heading, all items of a certain literary unit belonging to this author will be brought closer together. However, although this fact might in certain cases enable or facilitate their identification, it will not necessarily do so. Without the help of added entries or notes on the main entries, the user of the catalogue will sometimes find it quite impossible to ascertain whether a particular translation or edition belongs to the literary unit he is looking for. Thus we see that it is possible to bring together all works by a given author without identifying literary units. Theoretically the reverse can also be envisaged: we might enter all editions and translations belonging to a certain literary unit under that form of the author's name under which it had been originally published, thus recognizing literary units without bringing together all works by a given author under a single heading.

In this paper examining the attitude of the alphabetical catalogue for author and title entries towards literary and bibliographical units we shall be mainly concerned with the first two objectives. The third will be taken into consideration only as far as proves necessary.

From what has been said before, it clearly follows that all three objectives are very important for the alphabetical catalogue for author and title entries, and that no good catalogue can risk neglecting any of them entirely. But since the first two objectives are in many cases mutually conflicting it is not possible for any catalogue to take them both into account to the same degree. Only one objective, considered as primary, can be met by main entries while the other has to be relegated to added entries.

Before attacking this problem from the theoretical point of view, it will be useful to provide a brief historical background; this will help us to understand the attitude of some current cataloguing codes towards literary and bibliographical units.

II. Historical Part

The role of the above mentioned objectives in *Anglo-American cataloguing practice* has been discussed by J. Pettee[1] and S. Lubetzky[2].

J. Pettee sees in T. Hyde's rules[3] the first formulation of the idea of assembling literary units under a single heading. Yet it has to be pointed out that Hyde did not provide for a real identification of literary units but only for the assembling of the works by a given author (with the exception of works published under a pseudonym) under a uniform heading. Under such a heading titles were as a rule arranged in a chronological sequence.

Hyde's method was further developed by British 18th century catalogues. But in the 19th century we meet a new conception. In the series of rules laid down by H. H. *Baber* in 1834, and intended for the compilation of a new catalogue of the British Museum, preference is almost entirely given to the particular book, and to the form of the author's name as it appears in the book. There is but one exception, which concerns the surnames of noblemen (rule IV).[4]

A similar attitude is expressed in *Panizzi's* 91 famous rules though with less consistency. These rules have been analysed both by J. Pettee and S. Lubetzky. If we examine them from the point of view of the three different objectives mentioned in the Introduction, we shall see that Panizzi takes into account the third objective only in connexion with authors who appear in the book under different forms of their real name (rules X, XIV, XV) or who have changed their names (rule XI). On the other hand if the book is published under the author's initials (rule XXXII), under a pseudonym (rules XLI, XLII) or anonymously (rule XXXIX) the heading will be based on the information given in the book, irrespective of whether the author has been ascertained or not.

The second objective, the identification of literary units, is fully recognized only for various editions of the Bible which are all brought together under this heading (rule LXXIX). In the sub-arrangement under authors, or under other headings, Panizzi tends towards the recognition and assembling of literary units (rules LXXV, LXXVI, LXXVIII); but, since the same author appears in certain cases under different headings, such assembling is obviously possible only in a restricted measure. An exception is made for partial editions of a particular work if the complete edition does not exist in the library; in this case the partial edition is not filed under the title of the complete edition but after the whole series of single works (rule LXXVI). No provision is made for the various editions and translations of anonymous works in general; they are apparently treated as single items according to the first objective.[5]

The cataloguing instructions published in 1881 and in 1883 by the *Library Association of the United Kingdom* go a step further in the recognition of the second and third objectives: the names of identified authors of anonymously published works are accepted as headings (rule 10); in addition the identification of literary units is extended to all kinds of sacred books (rules 19, 20).[6]

The later editions of the *British Museum* rules do not introduce fundamental innovations though, in some details, the recognition of the second and third objectives is also somewhat extended. Thus the editions of recognized classics are, as an exception, entered under their names even if these names do not appear in the book (rule 18); if an author has written almost exclusively under one pseudonym all editions of works, originally published under the pseudonym, are entered under this even though the author's real name occur in the book (rule 20); all editions of the work De imitatione Christi are entered under a fixed heading (rule 17 h).

Thus we see that the main principle expressed in rule 4 of the new code: "The choice of a heading for a main entry is, as a rule, based on the information supplied in print in a perfect copy of the book itself, and on that only" is not applied consistently but shows a great number of exceptions.[7]

The new British Museum rules do not introduce any provision for sub-arrangement under author headings. But the printed British Museum catalogue shows a fundamental agreement with Panizzi. It is interesting to note that these sub-arrangements are concentrated on the recognition of literary units to such a measure that the location of bibliographical units is often quite neglected. Thus no added entries are made for the titles of translations which are filed immediately after the original text.

The *Bodleian Library* rules reveal a certain influence of the tradition laid down by Hyde and thus differ in several points from the British Museum rules. The second objective is fully accepted and all works by a given author, even those published anonymously, under a pseudonym or under initials, are brought together under a single heading (rules 15-17, 19). In addition the recognition of anonymous literary units is extended to old romances (rule 17) and to all kinds of sacred books (rule 27).[8]

Panizzi's rules were taken over and modified by Ch. C. *Jewett*. Compared with the original rules, Jewett's modification published in 1852 goes considerably further in the recognition of the second and third objectives. Thus anonymous and pseudonymous works are entered under the identified author if any edition, continuation or supplement has been published under his name (rules XXVIII, XXIX); all translations (including translations of anonymous works) are entered under the heading of the original text irrespective of the fact whether the original text exists in the library or not (rule XXIII).[9]

The most important contribution to American cataloguing theory were Ch. A. *Cutter*'s rules published first in 1876. These rules introduce a fundamental innovation: along with the assembling of all works by a given author under one heading, the recognition of literary units is for the first time accepted almost completely, and extended to personal and title entries as well. Thus all works by a given author whether issued under his name, under a pseudonym or anonymously, are brought together under a single heading (rules 1, 2, 7); revisions, translations, excerpts of any given work are entered under the author or under the title of the original text, respectively, and filed immediately after it (rules 17-19, 123, 124, 131, 132, 144, 246, 331). But Cutter allows a variation in the case of translations, which may be entered under their title if the original text does not exist in the library (rule 331). In his insistence on the recognition of literary units Cutter goes so far as to neglect in some cases added entries which might facilitate the ready location of a particular book (rules 132, 331).[10]

If we wish to understand completely the attitude of the cataloguing practice generally current in the United States of America towards the three objectives, we have to examine the three main cataloguing codes regulating this practice. These provide for the choice of headings, the description of books and the filing of catalogue cards.[11]

In the Introduction to the *Rules for author and title entry* we find the following statement (p. XX): "The principle on which the cataloguing is planned is the use as main entry of the author, personal or corporate, considered to be chiefly responsible for the creation of the intellectual content of the work. Thus the finding list function of the catalog is extended beyond what is required for location of a single book to the location of literary units about which the seeker has less precise information.... Added entries serve also to complete the assembling of related material as part of a literary unit."

This statement by itself shows a certain inconsistency in relation to the three objectives. While the extension of the finding list function towards the location of literary units is in the first part attributed to main entries, the second part allots a portion of this function to added entries. Moreover this statement does not reveal a clear conception of the second and third objectives. This fact has already been discussed in general in the Introduction to this paper and we need not dwell further upon it.

The rules themselves show a full recognition of the third objective. Thus all works by a given author including various editions, translations, abridgements, etc., whenever they remain substantially his, are brought together under a single form of his name, whether or not this form appears in the book itself (rules 2, 20-22, 32, 36).

For anonymous works two different methods are adopted: while anonymous classics are treated as literary units and entered under a uniform heading (rules 33-35), other anonymous works are treated as bibliographical units and their translations are entered under their particular titles with references from the original titles (rule 32 G).

Now let us see what the American rules say about the arrangement of the works under author headings.

The *Rules for descriptive cataloging* prescribe bibliographical notes concerning the relationship of the particular book to other works or other editions of the same work (rule 3:15 C 9). These notes include the original or earliest known title of a work reissued, the original title of translated works (but only if the translated title is not a literal translation of the original title) etc. This rule has been restricted to a certain degree by Supplement 1949–51 (p. 13, III).

The *Rules for filing* give alternatives for the arrangement under author headings: translations are either arranged alphabetically according to their language, immediately after the corresponding original title or filed according to their own titles in one alphabetical sequence with the original titles. In the first case provisions are made for cross references from the titles of the translations (rule 25 a). For classic authors or writers whose output is exceptionally large a grouping of entries is adopted. Here again two alternatives are given for the filing of translations of single works: either immediately after the original text or in a separate group following the entire body of original texts (rule 26).

The entire attitude of the current cataloguing practice in USA toward literary and bibliographical units can be summed up as follows: The practice is clearly in favour of literary units, the main inconsistency being the treatment of anonymous translations. A further inconsistency which might be mentioned, is the custom of some libraries to file translations according to their own titles.

The first instructions for the compilation of an alphabetical catalogue for author and title entries to be found in *German* library literature are, as far as we know, given in the preface to the *Zürich catalogue*.[12] The compiler mentions Hyde's catalogue as a model and imitates him as far as the assembling of works by a given author is concerned.

It was M. *Schrettinger* who introduced the first systematic and more detailed survey of the main problems concerning the compilation of an alphabetical catalogue for author and title entries written in German. With him it is definitely the bibliographical unit which seems to be considered as the most important element of the catalogue. In accordance with this general attitude the heading has to be chosen, as a rule, from the title of the particular book. As far as author headings are concerned Schrettinger's attitude is almost identical with the one expressed some years later by Panizzi and shows the same inconsistencies. With regard to the sub-arrangement under author headings Schrettinger's first manual gives full preference to literary units; all editions of a certain work are brought together and the works are filed chronologically according to the years of their first editions. But in his Handbuch Schrettinger is more consistent, giving preference to bibliographical units also in the sub-arrangements: translations follow in a separate sequence after all original texts; in both sequences titles are filed alphabetically.[13]

Most German library manuals published during the first half or about the middle of the 19th century agree with Schrettinger in so far as their attitude towards the three mentioned objectives is concerned. Yet there are some exceptions tending towards a more or less strict recognition of the third objective (assembling of all works by a given author). Such an attitude is to be found e.g. in P. A. Budik,[14] J. A. F. Schmidt,[15] A. A. E. Schleiermacher[16] and J. G. Seizinger.[17] In addition, some of the above mentioned authors also propose a certain, though very restricted, recognition of literary units. Thus Budik gives preference to literary units in the sub-arrangement under author headings, while Seizinger adopts this method for various editions of the Bible, which are thus brought together under a uniform heading.

The change in the general attitude towards the objectives of the catalogue, which had thus been gradually prepared for by the above mentioned manuals, was still more stressed in C. *Dziatzko's* rules. Dziatzko's view is best expressed by rule 181 concerning anonymous works. "Die verschiedenen Title betreffen verschiedene Ausgaben derselben, im Grunde unveränderten Schrift. Dann hat im wesentlichen die allgemeine Regel Geltung, dass man, wie die Schriften desselben Verfassers unter einem Namen, so die auf dieselbe (anonyme) Schrift bezüglichen Titel nach Möglichkeit unter einem OW zu vereinigen sucht." Similar rules are given for translations (rules 184, 185) for excerpts (rule 191) and, in exceptional cases, for adaptations (rule 178). In the sub-arrangement under author headings Dziatzko as a rule recognizes literary units (rules 334, 335) but with certain exceptions.[18]

The last step towards the full and consistent recognition of the second and third objectives (identification of literary units, assembling of all works by a given author) was realized by the *Prussian instructions*. These fundamental principles are clearly and simply stated by the following rules:

§ 30. Massgebend für die Einordnung der Schriften ist der Name des Verfassers; wenn dieser weder genannt noch ermittelt ist, der Sachtitel.

§ 78. Derselbe Verfasser wird stets unter demselben Namen eingeordnet.

§ 181. Dieselbe Schrift wird stets unter demselben Titel eingeordnet.... (Cf. also § 217, 221, 230).[19]

It has to be noted that the last rule applies to anonymous works as well as to works entered under an author heading.

The above mentioned principles are adopted throughout the rules with great consistency. The recognition of literary units is further amplified by the fact, that the filing title is supplied in the body of the main entry. According to H. Fuchs[20] it had been the original intention to give this title in a special line between the heading and the body of the main entry in order to make it more conspicuous. Later on this intention was changed; since then the filing title is as a rule mentioned in brackets in the body itself, immediately after the particular title of the bibliographical unit.

Bibliographical units are taken into consideration by the Prussian instructions only through added entries. According to Fuchs[21] added entries are omitted if there seems to be no practical necessity for them (e.g. for works entered under an author heading represented in the catalogue only by a few titles).

Several German codes agree with the Prussian instructions in essential points concerning the attitude towards the above mentioned objectives, but disagree in detail; for instance, *München*,[22] (but no provisions are made for the sub-arrangement under author headings) and *Basel*,[23] but with the exception that under a certain author heading translations are filed according to their own title if the original text does not exist in the library (rule 274).

The new code for the *Swiss National Library* brings two parallel solutions to our problem. The so-called primary heading intended for the current Swiss bibliography is chosen on the basis of the information given by the particular book itself. In addition there is a secondary heading intended for the catalogue of the Swiss National Library as well as for the Swiss retrospective bibliography and which eliminates the primary heading. Through this secondary heading various bibliographical units belonging to the same literary unit, as well as works by a given author, are brought together under a uniform heading.

While the rules for the primary heading show an almost consistent recognition of bibliographical units as basic elements, the rules for the secondary heading are less consistent in their recognition of the second and third objectives. Thus authors writing under their real name but using a pseudonym for a certain class of works (e.g. for fiction) are listed under two different headings (rule 16); as a rule only translations of an anonymous work into one language are assembled under a uniform heading, and it is only in more important cases that all such translations, irrespective of the language, are assembled (rule 110).[24] The code gives no prescription for the sub-arrangement under author headings but according to the introduction of the Schweizer Bücherverzeichnis 1948-1950 original texts and translations are filed in separate groups according to their languages.[25]

In addition there exist some older German codes which differ from the Prussian instructions in their fundamental attitude towards the given problem. Thus the former codes of the *Landesbibliothek Kassel*[26] and of the *Württembergische Landesbibliothek Stuttgart*[27] gave full preference to the particular book in every detail. This method was theoretically defended by Mecklenburg.[28]

More interesting is the code of the *Austrian National Library* now adopted only for books published before 1930. While observing a strict recognition of the third objective (all works by a given author are brought together under a uniform heading) it gives preference to bibliographical units.[29]

It is interesting to point out that the practice of cataloguing various editions and translations according to their own titles seems to have been a characteristic trait of the older Austrian cataloguing practice in general. It is also followed to-day in most Austrian libraries in the case of books published before 1930-1933.[30]

One of the first *Italian* librarians to mention something about the compilation of alphabetical catalogues for author and title entries was G. B. Audiffredi. In the preface to his catalogue he describes his own method; as well as entering all works by a given author under a single heading, he endeavours to bring together various editions and translations of the same work.[31]

We do not know anything about the further development of this method in Italian catalogues of the 18th and 19th centuries. But a hundred years later G. Fumagalli was to draw up cataloguing rules which show a strict recognition of the second and third objectives and which might almost be based on Audiffredi's tradition.[32]

The *official Italian code* first published in 1922 is less consistent. Though in general preference is given to literary units, there are some exceptions: translations of Slavonic or Oriental anonymous works may be entered under their particular titles (rule 88); in the sub-arrangement under author headings translations are filed in special groups after all original texts (rule 150). The new edition reveals even a certain deviation from the third objective: if the names of corporate authors have changed, each work is entered under the name which was in use at the time when the particular work was published (rule 65).[33]

The *Vatican rules* adopt in general the American cataloguing practice and show the same inconsistency with regard to translations of anonymous works.[34]

Finally we shall examine some *French* cataloguing regulations. In doing so we shall take into consideration also the directions drawn up by the Danish bibliophile F. *Rostgaard,* but written in French and published in Paris. These directions were intended for a classified catalogue accompanied by an alphabetical index. They are, nevertheless, mentioned here, on account of two characteristic features appearing in them: anonymous works are entered under the identified author and translations filed after the original text, regardless of the fact whether, by this procedure, the chronological order recommended by Rostgaard is interrupted. These recommendations reveal a fairly clear recognition of the second and third objectives.[35]

The *French code of 1791,* an outcome of the French Revolution, brought regulations for the cataloguing of books from which became the property of the State. This code differs fundamentally from Rostgaard's proposal: nothing is said about the identification of authors; it is always the particular book which provides the information for the entry.[36]

Such an attitude seems to be more or less characteristic of the French 19th century cataloguing theory. Thus P. *Namur* is definitely in favour of bibliographical units and his attitude coincides almost completely with Schrettinger's as expounded in the latter's first manual.[37] Several other French library manuals e.g. Cousin's[38] and Rouveyre's[39] simply reproduced Namur's recommendations without any great changes. A somewhat different attitude is to be found in A. *Maire's* manual but only in so far as the third objective is concerned; works by a given author are brought together, but no effort is made to identify literary units. In the sub-arrangement under author headings, original texts and translations are filed in two separate groups.[40]

L. *Delisle* fully accepts the third objective and shows moreover a certain tendency towards the recognition of literary units, though only with regard to better known anonymous works. But he emphasizes the fact that such a treatment has to be considered as an exception and does not accord with the general character of the alphabetical catalogue for author and title entries.[41]

There is a striking difference between these opinions expounded more or less theoretically in the 19th century, and the *French cataloguing* rules drawn up in the 20th century and representing the practice of the most important Parisian libraries. These rules are clearly in favour of literary units.[42] There is but one exception in the newest cataloguing code which, along with the French practice, mentions also the Vatican rule to enter translations of anonymous works under their titles, while anonymous classics are to be treated as literary units.[43]

Summing up in brief what has been expounded in this chapter we may say that in the 17th and 18th centuries a strong inclination to bring together the works by a given author was shown, and that there existed modest signs of a tendency towards the identification of literary units. Approximately at the beginning of the 19th century a more or less general change took place and during the first half of this century preference was generally given to the particular book, frequently also with regard to the form of its author's name.

Obviously the above mentioned practice and the first cataloguing directions were not yet based on deeper theoretical considerations about the function of the catalogue. We must not forget that, at the time when these directions were drawn up, there did not yet exist any theory of cataloguing. So how can the above mentioned attitude be explained? In connexion with this question it might perhaps be worth while to record the significant coincidence of the change in the catalogues' attitude towards literary and bibliographical units with the change in the role of those units in library acquisition policy.

It is a well known fact that during the 17th and 19th centuries the acquisition policy of libraries was focused exclusively on the collecting of certain works i.e. literary units. Different editions of the same work were ususally considered as duplicates and discarded from the library.[44] Still at the end of the 18th century A. Ch. Kayser expresses the opinion that, among various editions of a certain work, only the best should be kept in the library; moreover he recommends that particular works by a given author should be discarded if his collected works exist in the library.[45]

It was the 19th century which broke definitely with the old tradition. This century was significant for the history of libraries in general. It introduced the great development of national libraries, the definite determination of their main function as being the collecting of the complete national printed production, new and improved copyright regulations, as well as the beginning of national bibliographies. It seems natural that these facts could not occur without exerting a deep influence on library acquisition policy in general. In addition they settled the role of bibliographical units in this policy. This characteristic change was reflected by several 19th century manuals which now began to stress the fact that different editions of the same work should not be considered as duplicates.[46]

We cannot state a definite connexion between the above mentioned change which occurred in acquisition policy and the similar change in the attitude of the catalogue towards bibliographical units. However, it seems to be significant that both took place more or less at the same time.

Along with the development of the theory of cataloguing and the drawing up of cataloguing codes in the second half of the 19th century and the beginning of the 20th century, a new change in the attitude of catalogues towards literary and bibliographical units occurred: the general opinion began to veer gradually towards the recognition of literary units.

However, even at that time, the attitude of the catalogue towards literary and bibliographical units was not expressly formulated as a fundamental problem of the catalogue. Even those codes which reveal a complete understanding of the importance of this problem (e.g. the Prussian instructions) do not define their attitude towards it as a governing principle. Regulations concerning this attitude are concealed under specific rules and can be detected only by a more intensive study of the code.

But even this statement applies only to a very small number of codes. Most of them do not seem to envisage the problem as a whole and, consequently, do not adopt a fixed attitude towards it.

III. Theoretical Part

In the Introduction two main objectives of the alphabetical catalogue for author and title entries have been pointed out. We have emphasized the importance of both objectives as well as the fact that no good catalogue can risk neglecting either of them.

From what has been said in the Historical part we see that most current codes, though recognizing both objectives, show a definite preference for the second. Thus literary units are as a rule brought together by main entries, while the location of bibliographical units is mostly relegated to added entries. However it has to be pointed out that only very few codes adopt this method consistently. Most of them make exceptions and, in some cases, entirely neglect the location of bibliographical units.

We do not wish to dwell on the problem as to whether or not cataloguing rules have to be consistent. S. Lubetzky has recently discussed this question and has proved the necessity of consistency. Logical and consistent rules are not only easier to apply but also easier to understand. Lubetzky has furthermore pointed out that most shortcomings and complexities of our modern cataloguing codes are due simply to their internal inconsistency.

Lubetzky's conclusions might also be applied without reservation as far as our problem is concerned. Surely a catalogue showing a consistent attitude in dealing with literary and bibliographical units would render better service to its users than most present catalogues succeed in doing.

Nevertheless, it has to be stressed that, in the opinion of the author, consistency by itself is not enough to make a good catalogue, if the basic principles are not such as will best respond to the needs of the great majority of users.

This assumption seems to need further analysing. Of late it has been frequently stated, that the various needs and habits of readers should not be allowed to interfere with the consistent observance of the basic principles of the catalogue.[47] Though this statement and the opinion expressed by the author seem to be in mutual contradiction, they may easily be reconciled if interpreted in the right way. We should thus come to the following conclusion: basic principles must be such as to correspond to the normal approach to the catalogue i.e. to satisfy the needs of the majority of readers. Once such principles are determined they should be applied consistently throughout the code, even if they do not meet with the entire approval of some readers, and regardless of special cases which might perhaps benefit from the application of other principles. We are quite convinced that basic principles determined and handled in such a way will soon be acknowledged by the readers and will make the catalogue a useful and efficient instrument.

Now let us return to our problem. It has been mentioned that, as far as main entries are concerned, most current codes show preference for literary units, but are not consistent in the application of this principle. Since we consider consistency indispensable, it must be considered whether a strict recognition of literary units (in the way adopted e.g. by the Prussian instructions) responds best to the needs of modern libraries?

Some authors take the identification of literary units in alphabetical catalogues almost for granted, at least where their own country is concerned, or consider it indispensable for large libraries and research libraries. Most of them assume that this identification has to be obtained through main entries.[48] As far as we know the possibility of relegating the identification and assembling of literary units throughout the catalogue to added entries and of concentrating main entries on bibliographical units has not yet been examined systematically.

Some of the exceptions introduced by various codes as mentioned in the Historical part of this paper, tend towards such a method. Furthermore, in the attempt to economize and accelerate cataloguing procedures, some current practices show a growing tendency to neglect in certain cases the identification of literary units, irrespective of the provisions made by their codes. Thus the search for original titles of translations has been restricted in some libraries to more important works or to cases easily solved.[49] Some German libraries have adopted for the sub-arrangement under author headings the Berghoeffer system or a method very similar to it, assembling all works by authors with the same name and surname, and filing them according to their particular titles.[50] Recently the usefulness of treating certain translations as literary units has also been questioned theoretically.[51]

It stands to reason that all these attempts which tend to neglect literary units or identify them through added entries, were only meant as simplifications of certain cases, and might render the catalogue still more inconsistent. On the other hand, it is significant that all these attempts are really directed against the recognition of literary units through main entries as a fundamental principle of the catalogue. Hence it is clear that this principle does not fully correspond to the demands of modern catalogues.

It is the purpose of this chapter 1) to examine how far this conclusion is correct, and 2) to evaluate the alternative method (concentration of main entries on the location of bibliographical units and identification and assembling of literary units through added entries) and to weigh its advantages and disadvantages from the point of view of the needs of modern libraries.

The question as to which basic attitude towards literary and bibliographical units should be chosen for the alphabetical catalogue for author and title entries, is closely connected with the priority of the first two objectives of the catalogue mentioned in the Introduction. If the primary function consists in the location of literary units, a consistent application of the method adopted by the Prussian instructions would obviously remain the best solution. But if we consider the location of particular books to be the primary function of the catalogue, then the alternative method mentioned above would seem to be preferable.

It is interesting to note that most authors, irrespective of their attitude towards the identification of literary units, mention the location of particular books as the primary function of the alphabetical catalogue or, at least, in enumerating the various functions, put this function in the first place. Even the most ardent defenders of the recognition of literary units by main entries accept this order. These facts are rather puzzling in their contradiction. It almost seems as if, in these cases, the function of the catalogue and its attitude towards literary and bibliographical units were considered as facts without any logical relation.

It stands to reason that what has been said about the necessity of considering the needs of the users, as far as the basic principles of the catalogue are concerned, also applies to the determination of its functions. Therefore it seems that an accurate evaluation of the two objectives of the catalogue could be carried out only on the basis of statistical data showing the numerical proportion between the requests concerning literary units and those concerning particular books. Such statistics do not exist. Therefore we can but attempt to give a general idea of what the proportion may be.

In 1919 W. Frels pointed out that anonymous works published round about that time were almost exclusively looked for under their titles, even if the author had been ascertained. On the other hand, older anonymous works the author of which had been already mentioned in bibliographies or other reference works were often looked for under their authors.[52] This statement seems to remain true for any period.

There is a certain analogy with regard to translations, excerpts, new editions with changed titles etc.: editions of recently published works will be looked for, as a rule, under their particular titles while older works, which may be already known as literary units, will be looked for as such.

A generalization based on these facts would result in the conclusion that newer publications are usually requested by the users as particular determined items, while requests about literary units concern, as a rule, older works. This will especially apply to classical authors and the so-called anonymous classics.

It is natural that the great majority of requests will be for more recent publications. In 1912 Milkau pointed out that 90% or more of all requests were for the newest books.[53] Experiments carried out in the Budapest Town Library in 1913, over a period of two weeks, mostly concerning social sciences, gave a result that was only slightly lower (66,8% for publications of the 13 preceding years).[54] In the present age with the enormous development of sciences and technology this proportion is probably very much higher.

The last two statements, considered together, lead to the conclusion that the number of users approaching the catalogue with requests concerning particular books, will be much higher than the number of those looking for literary units. This supports the alternative method (concentration of main entries on the location of bibliographical units and identification of literary units through added entries).

The advantage of this method can be still more convincingly demonstrated by examining the nature of recent publications entering libraries. If we compare pre-war and post-war accessions we shall find a considerable change not only in the number of books (the influx tends to increase in all libraries) but also in their scope and general characteristics.

Improved cultural relations the world over have resulted in a greater interest, on the part of libraries, for foreign publications, even those in less well known languages. Moreover, the number of translations increases steadily, a fact easily proved by a perusal of the Index translationum. The number given for 1957 is almost five times greater than that given for 1933. But it is not only the total number of translations all over the world which is increasing, a fact which might be partly due to the inclusion of data from new countries into the Index translationum. With a few fluctuations the Index shows a steady increase in the translating activity in all countries. In addition, there is a change in the subject of translated works. While the proportion between translations of scientific, juridical and social works to the total number of translations increases, the same proportion diminishes slightly as far as fiction is concerned. Furthermore, parallel with the increase of anonymous publications in general, an increase of translations of anonymous works can be detected. Finally the number of translations from less well known languages (Chinese, Japanese, Yiddish, Hebrew, etc.) is also increasing.

It seems only natural that among the accessions entering libraries, there will also be a great number of translations. It will be mostly translations from foreign languages into the national language or from a less well known foreign language into one more generally known. According to what has been said before, the greater part of these translations will be known and looked for under their particular titles. But in a catalogue giving preference to literary units they will be entered under their original titles. Thus the reader looking in a German library for the publication "Der gegenwärtige Stand der Strukturtheorie in der organischen Chemie" will be referred to the original title "Sostojanie teorii himičeskogo stroenija v organičeskoj himii". The reader looking in a Yugoslav library for the work "Veterinarski leksikon za praktičnu terapiju i profilaksu" will be referred to the main entry "Lexikon der praktischen Therapie und Prophylaxe für Tierärzte" etc. Is this really the most efficient way of helping the user of the catalogue?

The reason for asking this question will be still more justified if we remember the change in the users' attitude towards library catalogues which has taken place during the last decades but has become especially conspicuous since the last war. A larger number of readers interested in sciences and technology, a larger number of those who have no definite bent of interest and finally the increased tempo of life in general—all these factors affect the demands of the public towards the catalogue and ask for a simple and quick service. In the cases mentioned above it is certainly the alternative method (concentration of main entries on bibliographical units and assembling of literary units through added entries) which will guarantee such a service.

It seems to be a further advantage of the alternative method that it proves equally convenient for all kinds of libraries: large academic libraries, special libraries and public libraries. It will only be the number of added entries which will have to vary from case to case.

Similar reasons apply to works whose relation to other works, for one reason or another, it is not necessary to discover. These are as a rule catalogued according to a simplified method. In a catalogue giving preference to literary units this simplified method will necessarily differ fundamentally from the normal method. While according to the normal method main entries will be based on original (filing) titles of literary units, those compiled in a simplified way will take the titles of the particular books as a basis. On the other hand in a catalogue established on the basis of the alternative method there will be no fundamental difference between the cataloguing of books with or without ascertained original titles. All main entries will be based on the particular titles of books. The chief difference will be in the fact that, in certain cases, no added entries will be made.

It is quite obvious that all that has been said applies equally to translations of anonymous works as to translations of works published under the name of their authors.

Finally the method of identifying literary units solely through added entries seems also to have certain advantages when considered from the point of view of the cataloguer or from the point of view of rationalisation in cataloguing. At the moment when a newly published translation, or an edition with a modified title, comes into the library it will not be possible, often, for the cataloguer to ascertain their original titles. Hence the translation or edition will have to be catalogued according to its own title. Later on, when the original title comes to be known, libraries giving preference to literary units will have to make a new main entry and an additional secondary one. On the other hand, in libraries which assemble literary units by means of added entries, the original title will simply be added in a note on the main entry and only an additional secondary entry will have to be established.

However, there is no denying the fact, that the method of identifying and assembling literary units solely by means of added entries has also a certain disadvantage: the various editions and translations of the so-called anonymous classics, mostly known and looked for as literary units, will be in the catalogue assembled only through added entries, while their main entries will be scattered all over the catalogue. But if we remember what has been said about the numerical proportion of requests, it seems better to accept this disadvantage than to have modern works catalogued as literary units. We certainly cannot approve of the method adopted by some codes of treating anonymous classics differently from other anonymous works. Surely such inconsistency will prove a greater disadvantage than would be the case were anonymous classics to be treated in a way analogous to the one adopted for anonymous works in general.

Summing up what has been said in this chapter, we clearly arrive at the conclusion that the so-called alternative method (identifying and assembling of literary units through added entries and concentration of main entries on the particular book) is much more convenient if considered from the point of view of modern library catalogues. According to our opinion this fact should also be taken into consideration in discussions concerning the international co-ordination of cataloguing principles.

Finally we wish to stress once more the fact that the critique expounded in this chapter concerns exclusively the identification of literary units through main entries. We have no intention of advocating the neglect of original titles in general, nor do we agree with those who question the usefulness of the second objective in general.[55] In the Introduction to this paper the recognition of literary units has been mentioned as one of the fundamental tasks of the alphabetical catalogue for author and title entries. In accordance with this task we consider it indispensable to make added entries under the original titles for almost all translations of anonymous books as well as for re-edited anonymous works with modified titles. Moreover, added entries are also, in certain cases, useful, or even necessary, for translations or re-editions of works published under the name of an author.

Even in the case of translations, the original text of which it is most unlikely will ever come into the library, added entries as a rule should not be omitted. But the author agrees with L. Sickmann who has pointed out the illogicality of entering such translations under the original title as main entry.[56] Here again the method of identifying literary units by means of added entries seems to be more convenient.

Furthermore it has to be emphasized that the recognition of literary units is not only a fundamental but also a typical function of the alphabetical catalogue for author and title entries, and therefore cannot be relegated to the classified catalogue.

In some libraries the classified catalogue is built up in such a way as to bring together various editions and translations of the same work.[57] However, in the classified catalogue this fact is not intended to facilitate the location of a given literary unit and, in practice, will not do so. In this catalogue the given literary unit is included in a chronological sequence of similar units all belonging to the same class of knowledge. Hence, from the point of view of a reader looking for a certain literary unit and knowing its title, this unit will be lost among other similar units; its location will be possible only through the exact knowledge of the class into which the work has been put, as well as of the date when the given work was published for the first time. Thus the fact that various editions and translations of a given work are brought together in the classified catalogue should not be allowed to influence the structure of the alphabetical catalogue for author and title entries or to relieve it from the duty of fulfilling one of its fundamental functions.

IV. The Croatian Cataloguing Practice and Its Attitude towards Literary and Bibliographical Units

In this chapter we wish to point out that the alternative method (concentration of main entries on bibliographical units and identifying and assembling of literary units by means of added entries) has stood the test of many years in the Croation cataloguing practice.

More than 20 years ago the Zagreb University Library, not altogether content with its cataloguing practice, began to take into consideration certain modifications. Together with other improvements the Library was eager to introduce a change in the attitude of the catalogue towards literary and bibliographical units. The main motive for this tendency was the wish to bring greater consistency into the treatment of the various editions and translations of anonymous works. Until then the much used method had been employed of treating most anonymous classics as literary units, while the various editions of other anonymous works were catalogued as separate bibliographical units. Obviously there were only two possibilities of avoiding this inconsistency: either the extension of the treatment of anonymous classics to all anonymous works or the reverse process of extending the treatment of anonymous works in general to anonymous classics. We decided to accept the second alternative. The reasons leading to this decision need not be considered here; they have been discussed at full length in the previous chapter. However, we have to point out that, 20 years ago, some of the above mentioned considerations had not yet the full weight they have now.

It stands to reason that, as long as the tendency was towards logical and consistent cataloguing rules, the above mentioned decision could not remain an isolated fact but had necessarily to introduce along with it further changes. All such considerations and reconsiderations led finally towards the decision to adopt the following two fundamental principles:

1) assembling of all works by a given author under a uniform heading;
2) concentration of main entries on bibliographical units, together with the assembling of literary units through added entries.

These two governing principles are still valid in the Zagreb University Library to-day and since 1945 they have been accepted, together with the general cataloguing practice of this library, by most Croatian academic libraries.

Whenever those two principles come in practice into mutual contradiction, preference is given to uniform author headings. In this way all works by a given author are brought together without any exceptions, regardless of whether a particular edition has been published under the name of the author, or anonymously or under some pseudonym.

From the point of view of what has been said in the previous chapter about older and more recent anonymous works this preference for uniform author headings might perhaps be criticised. From this point of view it might be considered more convenient for the users to find in the catalogue all anonymous works, even those whose author has been ascertained, under the particular title of each edition as main entry. But the above mentioned decision was stimulated by the conviction that the assembling of all works by a given author has still greater advantages even from the users' point of view and that it will facilitate a greater number of requests than the convenience mentioned before.

Naturally in the sub-arrangement under author headings main entries are filed according to their particular titles and literary units are brought together only through added entries. Such added entries have been somewhat neglected during latter years and will have to be supplemented as necessary.

In order to facilitate the recognition of literary units and to explain the relation of certain added entries to their corresponding main entries, the original title of literary units are mentioned in the body of the main entries. Thus the difference between the Croatian practice which recognizes the location of bibliographical units as a primary function of the catalogue and the practice of other catalogues which give priority to the recognition of literary units is mainly reduced to the choice of headings for main and added entries.

Considered from the point of view of card catalogues which use unit cards, and thus provide the same information under main and added headings, this difference will be a purely theoretical question and will not be of great importance as far as the needs of the users are concerned. But it will be quite another matter with catalogues which make, for one reason or another, separate entries under secondary headings. This applies e.g. to card catalogues using typed cards or to those printed in book form. Such catalogues will have to economize over labour or space and will thus be compelled to make their added entries as short as possible. Hence users coming across an added entry will not always find there all the information for which they are looking and will be obliged to look up the corresponding main entry as well. In such a catalogue the choice of the main headings is therefore especially important and they should be adapted as much as possible to the needs and the habits of the majority of readers.

With regard to the treatment of bibliographical units and with regard to the assembling of the works by a given author, the Croatian cataloguing practice seems to approach most nearly the older Austrian cataloguing practice. However, there is a significant difference: while the Croatian practice also takes into consideration the identification and assembling of literary units though only by means of added entries, the older Austrian practice seems to neglect them totally.

As far as the two mentioned principles are concerned the Croatian practice has proved very satisfactory. Though it is intended, in the near future, to revise and improve upon this practice, there seems to be no reason to alter the two underlying principles.

Notes

1. Pettee, J.: The development of authorship entry and the formulation of authorship rules as found in the Anglo-American code. The Library Quarterly, 1936:6:270-290.

2. Lubetzky, S.: Cataloging rules and principles. Washington 1953, p. 37-41.

3. Hyde, Th.: Catalogus impressorum librorum Bibliothecae Bodleianae in Academia Oxoniensi. Oxonii 1674.

4. Francis, F. C.: A reconsideration of the British Museum rules for compiling the catalogues of printed books. I. In: Cataloguing principles and practice. Ed. by M. Piggott. London 1954, p. 32-33.

5. Règles à suivre pour la confection du Catalogue du Musée britannique. Bulletin du bibliophile, 1845-46:7:299-308, 338-347.

6. Katalogisirungs-Regeln der Library Association of the United Kingdom. Neuer Anzeiger für Bibliographie und Bibliothekwissenschaft, 1882: 53-57; 1885: 166-172.

7. Rules for compiling the catalogues of printed books, maps and music in the British Museum. Revised ed. London 1936.

8. Bodleian Library, Oxford. Cataloguing rules. (Revised ed.) Oxford 1939.

9. Jewett, Ch. C.: Della compilazione dei cataloghi per biblioteche. Firenze 1888.

10. Cutter, Ch. A.: Rules for a dictionary catalog. 4th ed. 1904. Republished. London 1948.

11. A. L. A. Cataloging rules for author and title entries. 2nd ed. Chicago 1949. – Rules for descriptive cataloging in the Library of Congress (adopted by the American Library Association). With Supplement 1949-51. Washington 1949-1952. – A. L. A. Rules for filing catalog cards. Chicago 1942.

12. Catalogus librorum Bibliothecae Tigurinae. Tiguri 1744. T. 1-2.

13. Schrettinger, M.: Versuch eines vollständigen Lehrbuchs der Bibliothek-Wissenschaft. München 1829. Bd. I, Heft 2, p. 33-43, 70-71. – Schrettinger, M.: Handbuch der Bibliothek-Wissenschaft. Wien 1834, p. 53, 57-62, 77. – It was not possible for the author to consult the statements concerning the alphabetical catalogue in the work A. Ch. Kayser, Ueber die Manipulation bey der Einrichtung einer Bibliothek, Bayreuth 1790, which, therefore, have not been taken into consideration.

14.   Budik, P. A.: Vorbereitungsstudien für den angehenden Bibliothekar. Wien 1834, p. 41-42, 49-50.

15.   Schmidt, J. A. F.: Handbuch der Bibliothekswissenschaft, der Literatur- und Bücherkunde. Weimar 1840, p. 297-298.

16.   Schleiermacher, A. A. E.: Bibliographisches System der gesammten Wissenschaftskunde mit einer Anleitung zum Ordnen von Bibliotheken. Braunschweig 1847, T. 1, p. 48.

17.   Seizinger, J. G.: Bibliothekstechnik. Leipzig 1855, p. 31, 39. – Seizinger, J. G.: Theorie und Praxis der Bibliothekswissenschaft. Dresden 1863, p. 202-203, 209.

18.   Dziatzko, C.: Instruction für die Ordnung der Titel im alphabetischen Zettelkatalog der Königlichen und Universitäts-Bibliothek zu Vreslau. Berlin 1886.

19.   Instruktionen für die alphabetischen Kataloge der preussichen Bibliotheken vom 10. Mai 1899. 2. Ausg. in der Fassung vom 10. August 1908. Berlin 1909.

20.   Fuchs, H.: Kommentar zu den Instruktionen für die alphabetischen Kataloge der preussichen Bibliotheken. Wiesbaden 1955, p. 51.

21.   Fuchs, Op. cit., p. 165.

22.   Katalogisierungs-Ordnung der Bayerischen Staatsbibliothek München. 2. Ausg. München 1922, rules 19, 27, 44-46, 87. However, it has to be pointed out that this edition differs in several points from the older drafts, the first of which dates from 1849; the older tradition was more in favour of the particular book. Cf. W. Frels, Die bibliothekarische Titelaufnahme in Deutschland. Leipzig 1919, comparative tables at the end of the book.

23.   Katalog-Instruktion der Universitätsbibliothek Basel. Basel 1914, rules 5, 65, 68, 188, 190, 191, 192, 272.

24.   Schweizerische Landesbibliothek Bern. Entwurf einer neuen Katalogisierungsintruktion für die Schweizerische Landesbibliothek, Oktober 1956.

25.   Schweizer Bücherverzeichnis. Katalog der Schweizerischen Landesbibliothek 1948-1950. Zürich, 1951, 1.

26.   Regeln für die Aufnahme, Druck und Ordnung der Buchtitel bei der Ständ. Landesbibliothek in Kassel. 1893. In use until the publication of the Prussian instructions. Cf. Frels, Op. cit., p. 21-22 (see reference no. 22).

27.   Existing only in manuscript. Cf. Frels, Op. cit., p. 25 and comparative tables.

28.   Mecklenburg: Ueber alphabetische Anordnung. Centralblatt für Bibliothekswessen, 1885: 2: 354-355.

29.   Vorschrift für die Verfassung des alphabetischen Nominal-Zettelkatalots der Druckwerke der k. k. Hofbibliothek. Wien 1901, § 19, 21, 38, 40.

30.   Kammel, K.: Österreichische Katalogisierungsvorschriften. Biblos, 1957:6:156-159. – Cf. also Instruction für die k. k. Universitäts- und Studienbibliotheken, 23. VII. 1825, in F. Grassauer, Handbuch für österreichische Universitäts- und Studien-Bibliotheken. Wien 1883, p. 202, which seems implicitly to show the same attitude, as well as Grassauer's own recommendations, p. 89-95.

31.   Audiffredi, G. B.: Bibliothecae Casanatensis catalogus librorum typis impressorum. Romae 1761, T. I.

32.   Fumagalli, G.: Cataloghi di biblioteche e indici bibliografici. Firenze 1887, p. 20, 30, 51, 123.

33.   Ministero dell'educazione nazionale, Direzione generale delle academie e biblioteche. Regole per la compilazione del catalogo alfabetico. (Ristampa.) Roma 1932, rules 15, 36, 40, 51, 84, 85, 88-92, 150. – New edition: Regole per la compilazione del catalogo alfabetico per autori nelle biblioteche italiane. Roma 1956.

34.   Biblioteca apostolica Vaticana. Norme per il catalogo degli stampati. Città del Vaticano 1931. – 3ª ed. 1949, rules 1, 38, 189, 190-221, 472.

35.   Rostgaard, F.: Projet d'une nouvelle méthode pour dresser le catalogue d'une bibliothèque. 2ᵉ éd. Paris. 1698.

36.   Cf. Norris, Op. cit., p. 195-196.

37.   Namur, P.: Manuel du bibliothécaire. Bruxells 1834, p. 73-75, 92.

38.   Cousin, J.: De l'organisation et de l'administration des bibliothèques. Paris 1882, p. 40, 46.

39.   Rouveyre, E.: Connaissances nécessaires à un bibliophile. 5ᵉ éd. Paris 1899. T. 9, p. 87, 102.

40.   Maire, A.: Manuel pratique du bibliothécaire. Paris 1896, p. 120, 153.

41.   Delisle, L.: Instructions élémentaires et techniques pour la mise et le maintien en ordre des livres d'une bibliothèque. Lille 1890. Reprinted in: Revue des bibliothèques, 1908: 18: 320-322, 325-326.

42.   Association des bibliothécaires français. Règles et usages observés dans les principales bibliothèques de Paris pour la rédaction et le classement des catalogues d'auteurs et d'anonymes, 1912. Revue des bibliothèques, 1913: 23: 145 f, rules 72, 74, 115. – Ledos, E. G.: Usages suivis dans la rédaction du Catalogue général des livres imprimés de la Bibliothèque nationale. Revue des bibliothèques, 1923: 33: 133 f, rules 188, 190. – Nouv. éd. refondue par A. Rastoul. Paris 1940, rules 153, 200.

43.   Association francaise de normalisation. Direction des bibliothèques. Code de catalogage des imprimés communs. Dictionnaire des cas. Paris 1945.

44.   Cf. e. g. E. G. Ledos, Histoire des catalogues des livres imprimés de la Bibliothèque nationale. Paris 1936, p. 21-22.

45.   Kayser, A. Ch.: Ueber di Manipulation bey der Einrichtung einer Bibliothek und der Verfertigung der Bücherverzeichnisse. Bayreuth 1790, p. 50.

46.   Cf. e. g. M. Schrettinger, Versuch eines vollständigen Lehrbuchs der Bibliothek-Wissenschaft. München 1829, Bd. I, Heft 2, p. 73. – Delisle, Op. cit., p. 313 (see reference no. 41).

47.   Dunkin, P. S.: Criticisms of current cataloging practice. The Library Quarterly, 1956: 26: 301. – Wagman, F. H.: The administrator and the research library catalog. Journal of Cataloging and Classification, 1955: 11: 192.

48.   Pettee, Op. cit., p. 271 (see reference no. 1). – Wright, W. E.: Some fundamental principles in cataloging. Catalogers' and Classifiers' Yearbook, 1938: 7: 29, 34-35. – Fuchs, H.: Für und wider die Preussichen Instruktionen. Zeitschrift für Bibliothekswesen und Bibliographie, 1954: 1: 184-185. – Lubetzky, S.: Comments on discussion of cataloging rules and principles. Journal of Cataloging and Classification, 1953: 9: 139.

49.   Bauhuis, W.: Katalogfragen. Zeitschrift für Bibliothekwesen und Bibliographie, 1954: 1: 187. — Rules for descriptive cataloging in the Library of Congress, Suppl. 1949-1951, p. 13.

50.   Sickmann, L.: Aktuelle Probleme des alphabetischen Katalogs. Zeitschrift für Bibliothekswesen un Bibliographie, 1957: 4: 256-257. — Berghoeffer, Ch. W.: Der Frankfurter Sammelkatalog. Zentralblatt für Bibliothekswesen, 1925: 42: 450-451.

51.   Sickmann, Op. cit., p. 257. — Working group on the co-ordination of cataloguing principles. Report on anonyma and corporate authorship. Libri, 1956: 6: 289, 293.

52.   Frels, Op. cit., p. 34-35 (see reference no. 22).

53.   Milkau, F.: Die Bibliotheken. In Die Kultur der Gegenwart. Hrsg. von P. Hinneberg. Berlin & Leipzig 1912, T. I., Abt. 1, p. 623.

54.   Benutzungshäufigkeit. Zentralbaltt für Bibliothekswesen, 1913: 30: 351.

55.   Ellsworth, R. E.: Notes on the Lubetzky report. Journal of Cataloging and Classification, 1953: 9: 130-131.

56.   Sickmann, Op. cit., p. 257 (see reference no. 50).

57.   Kammel, Op. cit., p. 159 (see reference no. 30).

Statement of Principles

International Conference on Cataloguing
Principles, Paris, October 1961

Editor's Introduction

As early as the 1870s, there were attempts to promote international uniformity in cataloging. If such uniformity were ever achieved, the librarian's dream of a universal bibliography might be achieved. Unfortunately for librarians, cataloging traditions had developed independently in the various countries suppporting national libraries and bibliographies. For instance, corporate entry was usually not allowed in the cataloging codes of German-speaking countries and Sweden, but was in the codes of English-speaking countries. This disparity existed in spite of the fact that both cataloging traditions originated in Panizzi's ninety-one rules. Regarding the descriptive part of a cataloging entry, the situation was even more chaotic.

Three factors intervened to change the effect of national cataloging traditions on international bibliography. The first was that the catalogs of many German libraries were destroyed during the Second World War; the existence of large catalogs no longer hindered German-speaking librarians from changing their cataloging rules. The second was that time had revealed deficiencies in the elaborate provisions for generating title entries in the German catalogs; German librarians felt that acceptance of corporate entry would be a useful reform.

The third was an increase in the number of nations capable of supporting library systems; they needed the assistance of cataloging agencies in other nations, provided the outputs of those agencies were mutually compatible.

Partly as the result of Lubetzky's work in the United States, it became evident that the formulation of a set of cataloging principles, around which future cataloging codes might be written, would be possible. After much preparatory work, the International Conference on Cataloguing Principles (ICCP), comprising delegations from fifty-three countries and twelve international organizations, met in Paris 9 through 18 October 1961. The goal of the ICCP, or, as it is often called, the Paris conference, was to agree on an internationally acceptable set of principles.

Because of divisions among the delegations, some of the draft sections of the conference's *Statement of Principles* were revised to effect a compromise. This is especially noticeable in the provisions for works entered under the names of corporate bodies (section 9) and collections (section 10.3), although other portions contain wording sufficiently vague to suggest an effort to cover more than one position. Because of these ambiguities, many codes produced after the conference and claiming compatibility with the *Statement of Principles* diverge widely from each other. For example, the provisions for corporate main entry change radically in the two editions of the Anglo-American Cataloguing Rules (AACR), and are themselves very different from the provisions found in the German *Regeln für alphabetische Katalogisierung*. As another example, the AACR rules for entry of compilations changed substantially in 1974; the older rule originated from the exception taken by the American delegation to the text of section 10.3.

At the time the *Paris Principles* were composed, there was some awareness that computers might change cataloging; the direction of this change could not then be imagined. It remains to be seen whether this change will require the composition of a new set of principles, this time without ambiguity or compromise.

MC

Further Reading

International Conference on Cataloguing Principles. *Report: International Conference on Cataloguing Principles, Paris, 9th-18th October, 1961,* 22-90. London: Organizing Committee of the International Conference on Cataloguing Principles, 1963.

Discussion of the draft statement and the positions taken by the various delegations.

—————. *Statement of Principles Adopted at the International Conference on Cataloguing Principles, Paris, October 1961.* Annotated ed. London: IFLA Committee on Cataloguing, 1971.

An annotated commentary on the *Paris Principles* by Eva Verona, assisted by Franz Georg Kaltwasser, P. R. Lewis, and Roger Pierrot. Includes descriptions of many post-Paris codes.

Statement of Principles

1. *Scope of Statement*

    The principles here stated apply only to the choice and form of headings and entry words—i.e. to the principal elements determining the order of entries—in catalogues of printed books[1] in which entries under authors' names and, where these are inappropriate or insufficient, under the titles of works are combined in one alphabetical sequence. They are framed with special reference to catalogues enumerating the contents of large general libraries: but their application to the catalogues of other libraries and to other alphabetical lists of books is also recommended, with such modifications as may be required by the purposes of these catalogues and lists.

2. *Functions of the Catalogue*

    The catalogue should be an efficient instrument for ascertaining

    2.1   whether the library contains a particular book specified by
         (a) its author and title, *or*
         (b) if the author is not named in the book, its title alone, *or*
         (c) if author and title are inappropriate or insufficient for identification, a suitable substitute for the title; and

    2.2   (a) which works by a particular author and
         (b) which editions of a particular work are in the library.

3. *Structure of the Catalogue*

    To discharge these functions the catalogue should contain

    3.1   at least one entry for each book catalogued, and

    3.2   more than one entry relating to any book, whenever this is necessary in the interests of the user or because of the characteristics of the book—for example:

Reprinted by permission of the International Federation of Library Associations from International Conference on Cataloguing Principles. *Report: International Conference on Cataloguing Principles, Paris, 9th-18th October, 1961*. London: Organizing Committee of the International Conference on Cataloguing Principles, 1963, p. 91-96. © 1963 International Federation of Library Associations.

3.21 when the author is known by more than one name or form of name, *or*

3.22 when the author's name has been ascertained but is not on the title-page of the book, *or*

3.23 when several authors or collaborators have shared in the creation of the book, *or*

3.24 when the book is attributed to various authors, *or*

3.25 when the book contains a work known by various titles.

4. *Kinds of Entry*

Entries may be of the following kinds: *main entries, added entries* and *references.*

4.1 One entry for each book—the *main entry*—must be a full entry, giving all the particulars necessary for identifying the book. Other entries may be either *added entries* (i.e. additional entries, based on the main entry and repeating under other headings information given in it) or *references* (which direct the reader to another place in the catalogue).

5. *Use of Multiple Entries*

The two functions of the catalogue (see 2.1 and 2.2) are most effectively discharged by

5.1 an entry for each book under a heading derived from the author's name or from the title as printed in the book, *and*

5.2 when variant forms of the author's name or of the title occur, an entry for each book under a *uniform heading*, consisting of one particular form of the author's name or one particular title, or, for books not identified by author or title, a uniform heading consisting of a suitable substitute for the title, *and*

5.3 appropriate added entries and/or references.

6. *Function of Different Kinds of Entry*

6.1 The *main entry* for works entered under authors' names should normally be made under a *uniform heading.* The main entry for works entered under the title may be *either* under the title as printed in the book, with an added entry under a uniform title, *or* under a uniform title, with added entries or references under the other titles. The latter practice is recommended for the cataloguing of well-known works, especially those known by conventional titles (see 11.3).[2]

6.2 Entries under other names or forms of name for the same author should normally take the form of *references*; but *added entries* may be used in special cases.[3]

6.3 Entries under other titles for the same work should normally take the form of *added entries;* but *references* may be used when a reference can replace a number of added entries under one heading.[4]

6.4   *Added entries* (or in appropriate cases *references*) should also be made under the names of joint-authors, collaborators, etc., and under the titles of works having their main entry under an author's name, when the title is an important alternative means of identification.

7.   *Choice of Uniform Heading*

The *uniform heading* should normally be the most frequently used name (or form of name) or title appearing in editions of the works catalogued or in references to them by accepted authorities.

7.1   When editions have appeared in several languages, preference should in general be given to a heading based on editions in the original language; but if this language is not normally used in the catalogue, the heading may be derived from editions and references in one of the languages normally used there.

8.   *Single Personal Author*

8.1   The *main entry* for every edition of a work ascertained to be by a single personal author should be made under the author's name. An added entry or reference should be made under the title of each edition in which the author's name is not stated on the title-page.

8.2   The *uniform heading* should be the name by which the author is most frequently identified in editions of his works,[5] in the fullest form commonly appearing there, *except that*

8.21   another name or form of name should be taken as the uniform heading if it has become established in general usage either in references to the author in biographical, historical and literary works, or in relation to his public activities other than authorship;

8.22   a further identifying characteristic should be added, if necessary, to distinguish the author from others of the same name.

9.   *Entry under Corporate Bodies*

9.1   The main entry for a work should be made under the name of a *corporate body* (i.e. any institution, organized body or assembly of persons known by a corporate or collective name)

9.11   when the work is by its nature necessarily the expression of the collective thought or activity of the corporate body,[6] even if signed by a person in the capacity of an officer or servant of the corporate body, *or*

9.12   when the wording of the title or title-page, taken in conjunction with the nature of the work, clearly implies that the corporate body is collectively responsible for the content of the work.[7]

9.2   In other cases, when a corporate body has performed a function (such as that of an editor) subsidiary to the function of the author, an *added entry* should be made under the name of the corporate body.

9.3   In doubtful cases, the main entry may be made *either* under the name of the corporate body *or* under the title or the name of the personal author, with an added entry in either case under the alternative not chosen for the main entry.

9.4   The *uniform heading* for works entered under the name of a corporate body should be the name by which the body is most frequently identified in its publications, *except that*

9.41   if variant forms of the name are frequently found in the publications, the uniform heading should be the official form of the name;

9.42   if there are official names in several languages, the heading should be the name in whichever of these languages is best adapted to the needs of the users of the catalogue;

9.43   if the corporate body is generally known by a conventional name, this conventional name (in one of the languages normally used in the catalogue) should be the uniform heading;

9.44   for states and other territorial authorities the uniform heading should be the currently used form of the name of the territory concerned in the language best adapted to the needs of the users of the catalogue;

9.45   if the corporate body has used in successive periods different names which cannot be regarded as minor variations of one name, the heading for each work should be the name at the time of its publication, the different names being connected by references;[8]

9.46   a further identifying characteristic should be added, if necessary, to distinguish the corporate body from others of the same name.

9.5   Constitutions, laws, and treaties, and certain other works having similar characteristics, should be entered under the name of the appropriate state or other territorial authority, with formal or conventional titles indicating the nature of the material. Added entries for the actual titles should be made as needed.

9.6   A work of a corporate body which is subordinate to a superior body should be entered under the name of the subordinate body, *except that*

9.61   if this name itself implies subordination or subordinate function, or is insufficient to identify the subordinate body, the heading should be the name of the superior body with the name of the subordinate body as a subheading;

9.62   if the subordinate body is an administrative, judicial or legislative organ of a government, the heading should be the name of the appropriate state or other territorial authority with the name of the organ as a subheading.

10. *Multiple Authorship*

When two or more authors[9] have shared in the creation of a work,

10.1 if one author is represented in the book as the *principal author,* the others playing a subordinate or auxiliary role, the *main entry* for the work should be made under the name of the *principal author;*

10.2 if no author is represented as the principal author, the *main entry* should be made under

10.21 *the author named first on the title-page,* if the number of authors is two or three, *added entries* being made under the name(s) of the other author(s);

10.22 *the title of the work,* if the number of authors is more than three, *added entries* being made under the author named first in the book and under as many other authors as may appear necessary.

10.3 *Collections*[10]

The *main entry* for a collection consisting of independent works or parts of works by different authors should be made

10.31 under *the title of the collection,* if it has a collective title;

10.32 under *the name of the author,* or under *the title, of the first work in the collection,* if there is no collective title;

10.33 in both cases, an *added entry* should be made under the name of the *compiler* (i.e. the person responsible for assembling from various sources the material in the collection) if known.

10.34 *Exception:* if the name of the *compiler* appears prominently on the title-page, the main entry may be made under the name of the compiler, with an added entry under the title.

10.4 If successive parts of a work are attributed to different authors, the *main entry* should be made under the author of the first part.

11. *Works Entered under Title*

11.1 Works having their *main entry* under the title are

11.11 works whose authors have not been ascertained;

11.12 works by more than three authors, none of whom is principal author (see 10.22);

11.13 collections of independent works of parts of works, by different authors, published with a collective title;

11.14 works (including serials and periodicals) known primarily or conventionally by title rather than by the name of the author.

11.2 An *added entry* or *reference* should be made under the title for

11.21 anonymous editions of works whose authors have been ascertained;

11.22 works having their main entry under the name of the author, when the title is an important alternative means of identification;

        11.23 works whose main entry is made under the name of a corporate body, but which have distinctive titles not including the name of the corporate body;

        11.24 collections whose main entry is made exceptionally under the compiler.

11.3   The *uniform heading* (for main or added entries, see 6.1) for works entered under titles should be the original title or the title most frequently used in editions of the work,[11] *except that*

        11.31 if the work is generally known by a conventional title, the uniform heading should be the conventional title.

11.4   The *uniform heading* for works of which successive parts or volumes bear different titles should be the title of the first part, unless the majority of the parts or volumes bear another title.

11.5   When a *serial publication* is issued successively under different titles, a *main entry* should be made under each title for the series of issues bearing that title, with indication of at least the immediately preceding and succeeding titles. For each such series of issues, an added entry may be made under one selected title.[12] If, however, the variations in title are only slight, the most frequently used form may be adopted as a uniform heading for all issues.

11.6   Multi-lateral international treaties and conventions and certain other categories of publications issued with non-distinctive titles may be entered under a uniform conventional heading chosen to reflect the form of the work.[13]

12.   *Entry Word for Personal Names*

When the name of a personal author consists of several words, the choice of entry word is determined so far as possible by agreed usage in the country of which the author is a citizen, or, if this is not possible, by agreed usage in the language which he generally uses.

Notes

1.   In this statement, the word "book" should be taken to include other library materials having similar characteristics.

2.   The principles established for treatment of works entered under title may be followed also in arranging entries under any particular author heading.

3.   e.g. when a particular group of works is associated with a particular name.

4.   e.g. when a particular variant title has been used in a number of editions.

5.   Subject to section 7.1.

6.   e.g. official reports, rules and regulations, manifestoes, programmes and records of the results of collective work.

7.   e.g. serials whose titles consist of a generic term (Bulletin, Transactions, etc.) preceded or followed by the name of a corporate body, and which include some account of the activity of the body.

8.   It is a permissible alternative, when it is certain that the successive names denote the same body, to assemble all the entries under the latest name with references from the other names.

9.   In this section the word "author" is used to include a corporate body under whose name entries are made (see section 9).

10.   A large minority of the Conference did not accept the text of 10.3 but favoured the following alternative text:
    10.3   The *main entry* for a collection consisting of independent works or parts of works by different authors should be made
        10.31   when the collection has a collective title
            10.311   under the name of the *compiler* (i.e. the person responsible for assembling from various sources the material in the collection) if he is named on the title-page;
            10.312   under the title of the collection, if the compiler is not named on the title-page;
        10.32   when the collection has no collective title, under *the name of the author,* or under the *title, of the first work in the collection.*
        10.33   An added entry should always be made under the *name of the compiler* (if known), when not chosen as heading for the main entry; and under the *title,* if the main entry is under the compiler.

11.   Subject to section 7.1.

12.   If it is desired to collect information about the serial publication as a whole in one place in the catalogue.

13.   If it is desired to group these publications in one place in the catalogue.

The Objectives of the Catalog

Seymour Lubetzky

Editor's Introduction

Seymour Lubetzky was born around the year 1898 in Zelwa, a town alternately in Poland and the Soviet Union. After coming to the United States in 1925, he graduated with a certificate in librarianship from the University of California at Berkeley in 1934. Later, he worked as a cataloger at UCLA where he wrote articles questioning cataloging practices of the time. The articles attracted the attention of the new administration at the Library of Congress, which hired him in 1943 to examine the current practices of bibliographic description. Later, Lubetzky was assigned to study the rules for entry. From his studies of the 1949 *A.L.A. Cataloging Rules, Author and Title Entry, Second Edition,** which is commonly known as the "red book," he wrote the 1953 classic *Cataloging Rules and Principles.*† In this book, Lubetzky proposes a design for a new code. Lubetzky himself was later appointed editor of the new code, the monumental, but unfinished, achievement in three draft editions called *Code*

---

*American Library Association, Division of Cataloging and Classification, *A. L. A. Cataloging Rules for Author and Title Entries,* 2d ed., edited by Clara Beetle (Chicago: American Library Association, 1949).

†Seymour Lubetzky, *Cataloging Rules and Principles: A Critique of the A. L. A. Rules for Entry and a Proposed Design for Their Revision* (Washington, D.C.: Library of Congress, 1953).

*of Cataloging Rules.*** The new code had a strong influence on the 1961 Paris International Conference on Cataloguing Principles, whose well-known *Statement of Principles* is reprinted in this volume. Although Lubetzky was unable to complete the revision of the cataloging codes, he summarized his views in a 1969 report, *Principles of Cataloging,* from which "The Objectives of the Catalog" is taken.

In reading "The Objectives of the Catalog," one may want to question whether it makes sense to speak of principles for a catalog, to discuss further the exact status of *works* as opposed to *texts* or *books,* and to try to see why authorship has become the usually accepted way of identifying library materials. Lubetzky's discussion brings these questions, as well as many others fundamental to cataloging, to the forefront.

Some catalogers think that Lubetzky's discussion of the nature of works parallels that of Pettee. Others assert that the genesis of the distinction between *book* and *work* might be found in the discussion of arrangement or filing in Cutter's rules. Although the historical claims are intrinsically interesting, what is more important is the validity and useful- ness of the distinction, however it is made. Other ways of defining *book* and *work* are to be found in the paper by Verona, reprinted elsewhere in this volume. Evidence of the practical importance of the distinction between the two is found in the ICCP *Statement of Principles,* especially section 3.25. A challenge to its validity is found in the Wilson paper, also in this volume.

MC

Further Reading

Carpenter, Michael. *Corporate Authorship: Its Role in Library Cataloging,* 28-71, 118-20. Westport, Conn.: Greenwood Press, 1981.

The first passage cited here describes Lubetzky's role in code revision only with respect to the development of

---

**Seymour Lubetzky, *Code for Cataloging: Authors and Titles* rev. ed., partial draft (Washington, D. C., 1956-1957).

_____. *Code of Cataloging Rules: Bibliographic Entry and Descrip- tion* (n. p., 1958).

_____. *Code of Cataloging Rules: Author and Title Entry* (Chicago: American Library Association, 1960-1961).

the concept of corporate authorship. The second passage deals with problems surrounding the use of terms like *book* and *work*.

Wilson, Patrick. *Two Kinds of Power: An Essay on Bibliographical Control.* 6-19. Berkeley: University of California Press, 1968.

Describes another distinction between *book* and *work*.

The Objectives of the Catalog

The concept of the catalog as a guide designed to tell an inquirer not only whether the library has the particular book he wants, but also what related materials it has that might well serve his purpose, implies that the materials of a library have significant aspects by which they can be related to enhance their effective use. What, then, are these aspects?

Contemplating the most typical of library materials—the book—and its use, one is led to recognize two distinct and important aspects. One is *the origin and identity of the book* as a phenomenon, entity, or product; and the other is *the character of its contents* as on a particular subject or of a particular type. The former is referred to as the "bibliographical" aspect of the book, and the latter as its "subject" aspect—though the terminology leaves much to be desired. It will also be observed that those who come to consult the catalog are normally either after particular books, of particular authors or titles, or after books on a particular subject or of a particular type—that is, the users of the catalog exhibit either a "bibliographical" or a "subject" interest in the materials sought by them.

The problem involved in providing for the subject needs of the catalog users is the province of "subject cataloging" and "classification," which are beyond the scope of this study. The provision for the users' bibliographical needs requires a prior consideration of the genetics of library materials—as exemplified by the book.

The book, it should be noted, comes into being as a dichotomic product— as a *material* object or medium used to convey the *intellectual* work of an author. Because the material *book* embodies and represents the intellectual *work,* the two have come to be confused, and the terms are synonymously used not only by the layman but also by the cataloger himself. Thus catalogers refer to *the author and title of a book* instead of, more accurately, to *the author of the work and the title of the book embodying it,* and the inquirer searching the catalog for a *particular book* is more often than not after *the work* embodied in it, although he is very likely unaware of the distinction between the two. But the distinction between the *book* and the *work* is not purely an academic one. It is, rather, of

Reprinted by permission of Seymour Lubetzky from his *Principles of Cataloging. Final Report, Phase I: Descriptive Cataloging* (Los Angeles: Institute of Library Research, 1969), pp. 11-15.

basic importance to an understanding of the nature of the problem of cataloging and of the objectives which the catalog should be designed to serve. This is due to the fact that the existence and the vicissitudes of the *work* are not confined to any particular *book*; that the book is actually only *one particular edition,* or representation of the work embodied in it—which may be found in the library in various editions of special interest (as first, latest, well edited, illustrated), in various translations, in various media (as books, tapes, discs), and sometimes, in addition, under different titles or different names of the author. The question that must then be faced at the outset—and that has been faced since Panizzi, though beclouded by the failure to distinguish clearly and consistently between the *book* and the *work*—is whether the objective of the catalog should be merely to tell an inquirer whether or not the library has the *particular book* he is looking for, or whether it should go beyond that and tell him also what other editions and translations—or other representations—of the *work* the library has so as to help him more effectively to determine whether the library has what he needs and to select what might best suit his purposes. The answer to this question is necessarily to be found in the library's general function. If, as Butler maintained and as has been increasingly recognized, the function of the library is to provide for its users not only the materials needed by them but also the "bibliographical" guidance they require to help them make optimum use of the materials, then the catalog will have to be made to tell an inquirer in search of a book not only whether the library has that book but also what other editions and translation of the work the library has.

The interrelation between the various representations of a work—as editions or translations—is an immediate and intimate one; but there is yet another "bibliographical" relation of both direct and indirect interest to many catalog users: it is the interrelation between the works of an author. To show what works the library has of a particular author is of direct interest to many users concerned, not with any particular book or work, but rather with a particular author who may be represented by his works in the library. Indirectly, this is of interest to many more users who are uncertain, or may have an inaccurate citation, of the title of the book or the work they want, but could recognize it in a list of the author's works. In fact, only such a list makes it possible for one to determine with certainty whether or not the library has a particular work of a certain author. It is probably in recognition of these facts that the major codes of cataloging rules since Panizzi have generally provided for the catalog to show what works, or "books," the library had of a particular author, although the means they employed to accomplish it have not been the same.

In summary, then, it must be recognized that, genetically, a *book* is not an independent entity but represents a particular *edition* of a particular *work* by a particular *author*; and that, consequently, it may be of interest to different users either as a particular *edition*, or as a representation of a particular *work,* or as a representation of the work of a particular *author.* If all these users are to be served—and it is further realized that even those who look for a particular book would generally better be served if informed at the same time of the other editions of the work and of the other works of the author which the library has—then the book will have to be represented in the catalog as an edition of a particular work by a particular author and related to the other editions (and translations) of that work and to the other works of that author. This is the essence of the objectives evolved in the preparation of the new *Anglo-American Cataloging Rules* and sub-sequently adopted by the International Conference on Cataloging Principles. In the "unfinished draft" of the former they read:

"The objectives which the catalog is to serve are two:

First, to facilitate the location of a particular publication, i.e., of a particular edition, of a work, which is in the library.

Second, to relate and display together the editions which a library has of a given work and the works which it has of a given author."[2]

In the *Report* of the latter they are reworded to read:

"The catalogue should be an efficient instrument for ascertaining

1. whether the library contains a particular book ... and

2. which works by a particular author and which editions of a particular work are in the library."[3]

Comparing these objectives with the corresponding "Objects" of Cutter cited above, it will be noted that the first objective "to facilitate the location of a particular book" is substantially identical with Cutter's "To enable a person to find a book." The use of the phrase "to facilitate" for Cutter's "To enable" was intended to emphasize the choice of cataloging methods which not only *enable* but *facilitate* the location of the material sought. The emphasis was directed at such former rules as those which prescribed the entry of an author under *his full and real name* instead of the name by which he is *commonly identified in his works* as provided in the new rules. The former *enabled* a person to find the author desired in the cata-log, but often by means of references to the full and real name; the latter is intended to facilitate the location of the author by using the name under which he is most likely to be looked for. The second objective, however, is significantly different in specifying *the editions of a work* and *the works of an author* for Cutter's vague *what the library has by a given author.* Cutter's unqualified *what* is expressive of the failure to distinguish clearly and consistently between the *book* and the *work* in his rules, and characterizes also the old Anglo-American rules which were based on them; and the differences noted between Cutter's "Objects" and the objectives evolved in the preparation of the new *Anglo-American Catalog-ing Rules* reflect some of the fundamental differences between the old and the new Anglo-American Cataloging Rules.

Notes

1.   Butler, Pierce. "Bibliographical Function of the Library," *Journal of Cataloging and Classification* 9:7 (March 1953).

2.   Lubetzky, Seymour. *Code of Cataloging Rules, Author and Title Entry;* and unfinished draft ... Chicago, American Library Association, 1960, p. ix.

3.   International Conference on Cataloguing Principles, Paris, 1961. *Report.* London, 1963, p. 26.

Editor Entries and the Principles of Cataloguing

Ákos Domanovszky

Editor's Introduction

"It is the duty of theory and terminology to distinguish clearly between things and concepts that *are* different, and carefully to avoid any confusion between them."* These are the words of Ákos Domanovszky, who, as Deputy Librarian of the University Library, Budapest, was the Hungarian representative to the International Conference of Cataloguing Principles (ICCP). What he means by these words is elucidated in the article reprinted here, which deals with the concept of editor entries. Domanovszky asks whether there is any bibliographical condition under which the making of main entries under editors is optimal. His response takes two directions: first, an evaluation of editor entries, using as measures principles that have guided catalog code construction in the past; second, a philosophico-linguistic analysis of Rule 4 (AACR67). Only the first of these responses is reprinted in this volume.

Domanovszky's evaluative measures, adapted from A. H. Chaplin, may be summarized as user expectations, logic and clarity, and tradition. With regard to user expectations, Domanovszky argues that there are cases where there are no generally prevailing ones. Cutter's canon, which states that books should be entered under author, or, failing this, under

---

*Ákos Domanovszky, "Editor Entries and the Principles of Cataloging," *Libri* 23 (1973): 314.

title, is valid for only two classes of publications: periodicals and works written by a single, personal author. All other works (about one-third of what is published) represent bibliographic conditions for which there are no generally prevailing user expectations. Works produced under editorial direction certainly fall into this class. Such works are complex: being characterized by more formal distinguishing marks than single-author works, they engender a wide diversity of user expectations.

According to Domanovszky's scheme, where there are no user expectations, decisions should be made on the basis of logic and clarity. Logic would demand that all works of multiple authorship, where an editor is present, be entered according to a uniform rule. To attempt to distinguish cases where an editor's role is significant from those where it is not would proliferate rules and exceptions to rules; the user would be perplexed. Therefore, Domanovszky argues that such works should be uniformly entered under editor or title. But the former alternative (entry under editor) is not acceptable because the editor's role in a large number of cases is often intellectually insignificant. Thus, entry under title is the better option. The third measure, appeal to tradition, confirms the wisdom of this decision. In the matter of editor entries, traditions vary with locality. Since there is no norm, it is only reasonable that variant practices be sacrificed for an overriding principle, that of international uniformity. Domanovszky concludes: "Tested by Chaplin's principles, the editor entry proves to be an unequivocally inexpedient catalog device, of which a further preservation is theoretically unwarrantable."†

Domanovszky's arguments are an excellent and somewhat rare example of the deductive or rationalistic approach to decision making in cataloging matters. Perhaps from an empiricist's point of view, Domanovszky's premise in his first evaluative measure can be challenged: is it really true that there are no prevailing user expectations in the case of works of multiple authorship produced under editorial direction? Ironically, Domanovszky was one of those at the ICCP who urged that collections be entered under editorial compiler; his reason was that there was a century-old tradition of entry under compiler.**

---

†Ibid., 319.

**International Conference on Cataloguing Principles, *Report: International Conference on Cataloguing Principles, Paris, 9th-18th October, 1961* (London: Organizing Committee of the International Conference on Cataloguing Principles, 1963), 64.

Domanovszky ends his article on a prophetic note, viz. that the type of analysis he brings to bear on editor main entries might also be applied to corporate author main entries, and that they, too, would be found wanting. Thus, he heralded the failure of the Anglo-American tradition to stretch the definition of *author* beyond its meaning in common usage. As a result, editors in 1974 and corporate bodies in 1978 ceased to be considered authors.

ES

Further Reading

Pettee, Julia. "The Development of Authorship Entry and the Formulation of Authorship Rules as Found in the Anglo-American Code." *Library Quarterly* 6 (July 1936) 270-90.

Reprinted in this volume. In discussing the evolution of the authorship principle in Anglo-American cataloging, Pettee shows how the concept of author was stretched to include editors and corporate bodies.

International Conference on Cataloguing Principles. *Report: International Conference on Cataloguing Principles, Paris, 9th-18th October, 1961,* 62-65. London: Organizing Committee of the International Conference on Cataloguing Principles, 1963. London: International Federation of Library Associations, 1963.

Reports the proceedings of the Conference dealing with the question of entry under editorial compiler, a question on which there was considerable difference of opinion.

Domanovszky, Ákos. "Code Making: a Criticism and a Proposal." *Vjesnik Bibliotekara Hrvatske* 14 (1968): 58-65.

A critique of the first edition of *AACR* including a discussion of entry under editor.

Editor Entries and the Principles of Cataloging

This paper is devoted to an examination of the question, whether or not it is expedient in library cataloguing to use "editor entries", i.e. *main entries* made under the name of an editor. The word "editor" will be used to denote only personal, never corporate, editors. In consequence of the relationship between the respective activities of editors and compilers, most of what will be said about editor entries will also apply to compiler (main) entries, which some codes regard and treat as an entry category separate and distinct from the editor entry.

Before embarking on a discussion of the subject proper, a point of general import must first be clarified. Currently an increasing number of authors think it feasible to dispense with the concepts "main entry" and "main entry heading", and maintain that these have been doing more harm than good long enough. The theme of this paper shows that I hold the opposite opinion, which is, doubtless, still far more widespread. I am convinced that the traditional main entry heading still fulfills a series of very important functions, and will surely continue to do so for a long time to come. Even if it will have become widely replaced in some kinds of catalogues by the ISBN, other materials—printed catalogues, bibliographies, book-sellers' lists, etc.—are bound to stick to their traditional arrangement by names and titles. The advantages of this arrangement have been brilliantly pointed out by Seymour Lubetzky, and recently again emphasized by the introduction of the AACR; so there is no need to repeat them. Nor is it necessary here to enlarge upon the theme that it is desirable that the arrangement by names and titles should obey uniform rules throughout the world.

There is, thus, no occasion to muse upon a vanishing validity of the maxim that for main entries the most appropriate headings should always be chosen. Code-makers must still continue to take the utmost care when making rules providing for main entry headings; they must never fail to select the most suitable of all the available formal distinctions of books for this rôle. The cogency of this basic principle of code-making, however old-fashioned a minority of authors might consider it, remains not only unimpaired, but increases persistently. Necessarily so: the

Reprinted by permission of Munksgaard International Publishers from *Libri* 23 (1973): 307-320, 328-330. © 1973 Munksgaard International Publishers, Ltd., Copenhagen, Denmark.

progress of international uniformity in cataloguing also involves a spreading of the use of an identical main entry heading for the same book, and in proportion to this the importance also increases of choosing this heading as happily as possible.

Having settled this preliminary question, we may now reformulate the question raised at the outset, by putting it in the following, more concrete manner: are there any bibliographical conditions under which one may regard an editor entry as optimal, and the editor heading as superior to all the other alternately available main entry headings? A negative answer would, of course, imply that it is preferable to drop the editor entry altogether, and to relegate the editor's name—in spite of its being an extremely characteristic formal distinguishing mark of certain kinds of books and works, endowed with an outstanding retrieval value—consistently to the heading of added entries.

I propose to answer this question by testing the editor entry according to the principles of revising and constructing cataloguing rules as formulated by A. H. Chaplin.[1] To facilitate reference to them, I shall venture to add an ordinal numbering to Chaplin's own statement of his principles.

According to his first principle, cataloguing rules should be adapted to the catalogue-users' expectations, and should even follow the development, the changes, of these expectations.

According to the second, rules should conform to the general logical principles of the construction of catalogues. This principle often clashes with the first, mainly in consequence of the inconsistency and variability of the expectations of the users of catalogues; only some of these expectations being able to be fulfilled by the system to which the rules must necessarily conform. Chaplin discerns the solution of this dilemma in the creation of *general* rules which conform to the users' *generally* prevailing expectations. Exceptions might be made, but only for important and clearly definable categories of material. The users' generally prevailing expectations of specific rules for "the odd isolated case", as well as the expectations of minorities of users, should not be allowed to disturb the general pattern; they should be taken care of by means of added entries and references.

Thirdly, the code-maker should take into consideration the cataloguers' traditions, but only if these do not clash with the users' expectations.

In my opinion, every really experienced and unbiassed cataloguer must agree that with the formulation of these three principles Chaplin has hit the mark admirably: he has succeeded in summing up the fundamental precepts of which a reviser or maker of cataloguing rules must never lose sight, not only correctly, but also as aptly and concisely as nobody before. Hence, I think, that most cataloguers will also approve of the method I propose to avail myself of in the succeeding investigation of the expediency of editor entries: testing this expediency by the standard of Chaplin's principles. Since, however, Chaplin has confined himself to stating his principles very concisely, I must first interpret a few points of his principles, and now and again even develop them in greater detail.

To begin with, there are two remarks of a general nature. Firstly, Chaplin's principles apply, of course, in the first instance to the choice of headings for main entries. And secondly, despite its obviousness, it is not superfluous to point out that in formulating his principles Chaplin did not have the revision or construction of local, individual codes in mind, but the construction of rules fit to be applied uniformly throughout the world. A rule that conforms, e.g. to his second principle, only with respect to a particular local code, while standing in the way of international uniformity, cannot, of course, be considered to conform to his second principle.

Now let us inspect his three principles one by one.

On closer examination the field of application of the first principle proves to be much narrower than at first glance. There are in fact not more than two kinds of expectations which can be regarded as "generally prevailing", that is to say, as held by a large majority of catalogue-users, or more appropriately, of readers. The first of these expectations is that the editions of a work written entirely or principally by one personal author will be retrievable in the catalogue under that author's name; the second, that a periodical will be recorded under its title. An overwhelming majority of readers are already familiar with the fact that cataloguing rules to that effect are generally applied. Regarding other bibliographical conditions there exist no such large majorities, and generally not even small ones for that matter. In other words, those two bibliographical situations are the only ones in relation to which Cutter's famous canon can be regarded as uncontestably valid.

The principal reason for this is that in most other bibliographical situations the book, and the work of which the book forms an edition, are together equipped with several, often quite a number of formal distinguishing marks fit to catch the reader's attention. The more such marks are attached to a particular item, the more multifarious will be the expectations and the behaviour of the readers searching the catalogue for that item. Which implies, obviously, a correspondingly diminishing chance of one type of expectation being generally prevalent. Obviously this is even more valid for a bibliographical condition embracing a great many of such single items.

Sporadically there do occur, of course, individual items in regard to which readers' expectations happen to be nearly, or even entirely, uniform, in spite of several formal marks being attached to them. These cases are, however, of no account, since sporadic, unusual cases, as already mentioned, must not be allowed to disturb the pattern of a code. Besides, rules are never made for individual, but for whole groups of items, and so we are concerned only with the expectations relating to groups, and with the question whether or not the rules providing for the treatment of these groups correspond to expectations. Among the old-fashioned rules drawn up for certain types of books (e.g. for chrestomathies) there may be one or two which do actually correspond to the expectations of a majority; but I doubt even that. As to the more up-to-date kind of rules, tailored—in accordance with the principle so very rightly stressed by S. Lubetzky—not for types of books, but for bibliographical conditions, there is certainly no chance of their being in harmony with the *generally* prevailing expectations of readers (excluding the two exceptions mentioned above). Naturally so, as the rules of this type are more comprehensive than those of the older type, and embrace even larger varieties of books, even greater numbers of different combinations of formal distinguishing marks attached to these books. Within the very wide range of the entire coverage of such a rule, the individual readers' expectations are correspondingly bound to vary widely, according to their turn of mind, their education, their bibliographical experience, the assortment of their pertinent information, etc. Thus it is almost unthinkable that there should arise any generally prevailing readers' expectations of the whereabouts of a majority of the constitutent items of such a coverage.

All of this by no means implies a rejection of Cutter's canon; only a restriction of its validity to a limited field in which generally prevailing expectations of readers *do* exist. To give an idea of the comparative magnitude of this restriction, we might perhaps venture to estimate that at present Cutter's canon cannot be applied to about one third of the books subjected to standard cataloguing, in consequence of the considerable discrepancies between readers' expectations. Twice this amount, constituted by the editions of one-author-works and by the periodicals, is, however, still left to be catalogued in strict pursuance of Cutter's canon: in harmony with the readers' generally prevailing expectations.

To where then shall the code-maker turn for guidance when he sets about composing rules for the treatment of the problematical one third of cases?

Let us see, first of all, whether or not he may obtain some help, if only partial, from Chaplin's first principle, also in this particular respect. Could there be any advantage, if not unequivocal, at least not quite negligible, in meeting the expectations of some minor group of readers? If there is no generally prevailing expectation to be met, nor one entertained by a small majority, is it not the code-maker's duty to fulfil at least the expectations of the largest among the readers' minority groups?

In my opinion, decidedly not. Firstly, because the primacy of the first principle is valid only if an expectation is *generally* prevailing, but vanishes as soon as there are only insignificant differences in size between the groups of readers maintaining divergent expectations—which is, of course, the case if there are no groups other than minority groups. Secondly, because as yet we possess no adequate method of measuring and comparing minor differences between the respective magnitudes of the groups of readers entertaining diverse anticipations.

Consequently, if the code-maker cannot reckon upon a generally prevailing expectation, he must usually act upon the second principle, according to which the rules of a code should form a strictly consistent and—we may also add—a lucidly articulate system.

This implies, first, that the rules of a code must not be contradictory; if with respect to some adjacent peripheral parts of their respective fields of application they cannot be prevented from being so, the code must include rules for resolving these contradictions. Secondly, it implies that the meaning of all its rules should be as clear-cut as possible; which includes in its turn the requirement that the field of application of each rule should be delimited with the greatest possible exactitude. Thirdly, there must be no rule in the code which does not enhance its efficiency and the efficiency of the catalogues it underlies.

The first two requirements are self-evident and need no justification. The third follows from the fact that the lucidity of a code, and therefore its efficiency too, vary in inverse ratio to its length and complexity: the fewer the rules, the easier will the reader find his way in the catalogues. From this one must obviously conclude that if for a specific type of books a minority of readers expect a specific heading, presupposing a rule which would form an exception to a higher-ranking more general rule, the code-maker must always take the side of the general rule and consistency, refraining from allotting a special type of publications a special treatment. That is to say, he must refrain from conceding to the anticipations of even the largest minority group of readers.

The maxim is almost generally valid that the bibliographical conditions which, owing to the absence of generally prevailing readers' expectations, cannot be dwelt with on the ground of the first principle of rule-making, must be handled according to the second. There are, so far as I can see, no exceptions to it other than the few cases offering an opportunity to proceed on the grounds of the third principle: an opportunity to pick one's way in accord with cataloguer's traditions.

This third principle of rule-making is based upon the consideration that the maintenance of continuity always offers some advantages. Irrespective of all the shortcomings it might have had, the discarding or the modification of a cataloguing rule in use for some time past baffles those of the public who were aware of its existence and had grown accustomed to it; besides, it is costly, as it involves the adaptation of operating catalogues. The propensity to cling to old-established rules and practices is, therefore, strong and easily comprehensible. Codifiers, however, should never do their job without keeping an eye on the future; and should not, therefore, cling to devices and rules, however time-honoured, which have already proved or become sub-optimal.

This means that an occasion for acting on the grounds of the third principle does not present itself to code-makers except in cases left unsettled by the higher-ranking first two principles, that is to say, when the possible alternatives are equally unobjectionable to the latter. Chaplin did not explicitly state that he regarded his third principle as subordinate not only to his first, but also to his second principle; in other words, that he considered its application, the preservation of traditional practices, permissible only if not in conflict with his second principle, either. Nevertheless, his train of thought leaves no doubt about his taking this position.

All this does not mean, of course, that only very rarely are the revisers or makers of a code able to retain an old rule. In fact, most of the rules they adopt are old rules they preserve, but preserve on the grounds of either the first or of the second principle. In such cases, we cannot consider the third principle to have come into operation, to have influenced the code-maker. This we can only do, as we saw, in cases left entirely unsettled by the first two principles. Such cases being, however, very rare, let us give an example of their occurrence.

A code prescribing that the editions of works by a single author should be entered under that author's name, and further that periodicals should be entered under title, must not fail to provide for the treatment of a periodical written entirely by a single author. Each of the two possible alternatives for the construction of that particular rule conforms to one of the code's two fundamental rules referred to above, and contradicts the other. So judged by our second principle (the claim for the code's logical consistency), both alternatives are just as permissible as objectionable. The same applies if we test them by the first principle: I do not think that there exists any generally prevailing expectation of any particular mode of entry for one-author periodicals. So here it is indeed only the third principle on which the code-maker can and should base his decision: he should decide in accord with the cataloguer's tradition—provided that one exists.

Let us now inspect the advantages and drawbacks of the editor entry, and see how they balance in the light of Chaplin's principles.

The editor main entry is a venerable, time-honoured device of author-title cataloguing, very probably brought into existence by two different motives. Firstly, the early cataloguers' grasp of the facts they dealt with was in all probability less firm, and their ideas, their concepts, the denotation of their terms, less clear-cut and exacting, than ours are today. Now, the boundary line between authorship and editorship, even in the codes of our own days, has many blurs—at the time of birth of the editor entry, in the heroic age of cataloguing, these blurred sections were surely far more numerous. The obscurity of ideas was liable to lead not only directly, but also indirectly, to an extension of the practice of treating editors as if they were authors. Directly, because librarians did not draw a clear line of division between authors and editors; and indirectly, since it is a rather common phenomenon in the development of cataloguing practices that if a device with fluid boundaries of application has once been employed, these boundaries are bound steadily to expand. On these grounds, the editor entry, too, was gradually employed also for editors whom nobody would mistake for an author.

The second motive for the introduction of editor entries was presumably the fact that of all formal distinguishing marks of books and works it is the personal name which—being the most concise, striking and easily recalled—furnishes the best headings, the most serviceable, most efficient handles of entries. In all probability, cataloguers kept striving to extend the utilization of this most advantageous class of headings also beyond the limits of the domain of author entries, by using them in bibliographical conditions too in which the persons involved have nothing in common with authors.

At first glance this tendency is apt to strike one as not only natural, but also rather sound. In earlier stages of cataloguing it may have been so indeed; but in modern times, in which the rapid growth of catalogues has rendered the need of a rigid consistency in their organization increasingly urgent, the balance of the advantages and drawbacks of editor entries—let us state that anticipatively already at this point—was being reversed gradually but thoroughly, until their application became directly detrimental. In our days it not only severely impairs the consistency of catalogues, but also generates trouble in the realm of theory. As an example we may mention that it has induced theorists to fabricate—by way of subsequently supplying an old practice with a theoretical foundation—the artificial construction, generally adopted nowadays, that the editor of a work of multiple authorship, though not the author of any of the contributions in the work, may nevertheless be regarded as the author of the new literary entity he produced by combining these contributions to form a new organic unity. In this way theory came to operate with two different concepts of authorship, the second of which includes some kinds of editorship too. This was a fatal mistake which, of course, could not help generating further confusion. It is the duty of theory and terminology to distinguish clearly between things and concepts that *are* different, and carefully to avoid any confusion between them. To consider and to call an editor "an author in a wider sense" makes no sense, since cataloguing theory, as well as practice, cannot do at all without either of these two concepts, which they must, therefore, set apart clearly and sharply. The construction in question, oblivious of all this, is a typical instance of those not at all rare, untidy manipulations of words which cataloguers seem so very disinclined to forgo—especially if they have grown accustomed to employ them in disguising the defects of their less felicitous ingrained ideas or practices—and for which they have always heavily to pay.

Now we approach the verification of our already anticipatively stated negative opinion of the editor entry, by means of putting that entry to the test of Chaplin's principles.

To begin with, the editor entry does not meet the criterion for the suitability of main entry categories derived from Chaplin's first principle. There are surely many readers who do expect to find a particular book under its editor's name, but, no less certainly, they constitute only a minority of all the readers looking for books or works produced with the participation of an editor. The same applies to the items produced with the participation of a compiler. The books and works under consideration comprise a great variety of different types; they range from encyclopedias to anthologies, from serials to the transactions of conferences, etc. With the single works, and even more so with the single books pertaining to these types, there may be connected, along with the editor's name an almost infinite variety of combinations of other formal distinguishing marks, composed of different kinds of titles (alternative title, cover title, striking subtitle, series title), of the names of various numbers of bodies which have participated in the production of either the work or the book, of the names of co-authors or of authors of the contributions, of the names of revisers, translators, etc.

The readers' expectations concerning the heading of the entry for a particular book, i.e. for a particular edition of a particular work, will thus waver, even within the same type of publication produced with the assistance of an editor, between the different formal distinguishing marks connected with either the work or the book. We may confidently assume that within the sum total of the readers looking for a book produced with the assistance of an editor, the proportion of those who anticipate an editor entry will vary roughly in inverse ratio to the number of the conspicuous formal distinguishing marks connected with that book *and* with the work it contains. And since the formal distinguishing marks other than editors' names, with which such a book is generally equipped, considerably outnumber the editors' names connected with it, one may also assume that the readers who expect to find that book under an editors' name are bound to be a minority.

The question whether the minority of readers anticipating an editor entry is or is not the largest among several minority groups entertaining different expectations of the main entries of the books produced with editorial assistance, is in this context of no relevance: as we have already seen, the expectation of the largest minority, or even of a bare majority, cannot in itself be considered sufficient justification for the employment of a separate main entry category to meet it.

Thus the editor entry lacks the characteristic that could render it, on the authority of the first principle, eligible for the rôle of main entry. Let us now test its eligibility by the standard of the second principle.

As we saw, the second principle demands a careful fitting of each rule into the system of the code. This implies that every rule must satisfy the three requirements specified above in the course of our interpretation of this principle [p. 198]. The first of these requirements we need not enlarge upon.

According to the second requirement, the meaning of each rule has to be made perfectly clear.This implies first of all that its field of application must be sharply delimited, by means of exact and explicit definitions of the conditions of this application.

As a matter of fact, not one of the numerous rules by which the diverse codes have tried to regulate the use of editor entries has managed to satisfy this requirement. It is an old-established cataloguers' tradition that editor entries are never prepared indiscriminately for *all* books of multiple authorship produced with the assistance of an editor, but only for certain kinds of them. So all the rules providing for the employment of this entry category are bound to divide this class of books into two distinct sections. The division is, however, never based on purely formal criteria, on formal characteristics of the *books*, but always on some sort of distinction made between two different classes of *editors* performing two diverse kinds of functions. Even today this method is still steadily applied, though experience has long proved it to be unsatisfactory. It is applied in numerous diverse variants, which are different in tenor, but without exception akin in clearly demonstrating its unsatisfactoriness. Unable to draw a definite line of division between the two classes of editors that are to be treated differently, all these variants are flat failures.

It is not difficult to realize that this persistent failure was a necessary outcome of the very nature of the bibliographical condition which those prolonged efforts have been made to deal with. The multifarious types and forms of publications produced with the assistance of an editor, and together with them also the numerous kinds of editorial activities, form a continuous chain, each link of which is closely related to its immediate neighbours. There is no break in the chain which could divide it into two contrasted, or at least satisfactorily delimitable, sections. Consequently, it is impossible to find a clear-cut criterion whereby to divide up the hosts of editors into two sharply delimited, distinctly different classes. There exists no natural, no obvious way of accomplishing that division, no way that could satisfy all cataloguers, and impel them to accept it generally. Generations of codemakers, unsatisfied with their predecessors' arbitrary handling of the task, have had their try at it in turn, and have invariably failed; they have only kept adding new items to the long series of already existing unsatisfactory, and even detrimental, earlier solutions.

The real losers in this long-drawn, futile struggle are, obviously, the readers. An overwhelming majority of them have not even a faint idea of the distinctions made between two contrasted classes of editors which underlie the diverse variants of a discriminative employment of editor entries. They realize only that many books *are* entered under their editor, and also that the selections of books that the diverse catalogues and bibliographies do enter in this way are very differently composed. Bewildered, they become inclined to seek also such kinds of books under the editor's name which no cataloguer would ever dream of entering in this way.

Merely for the sake of argument, let us assume that there *does* exist a possibility of constructing a rule for a restricted, discriminative employment of editor entries which, so far as it goes, i.e. so far as it positively provides for the application of editor entries, *does* conform to the expectations of a great majority of readers. But even if we succeeded in designing such a rule, the drawbacks it entailed would still very probably outweigh its benefits, as many of the readers in need of a book having an editor but *not* entered under him, would now, owing to the existence of that rule, hesitate in their expectation of the location of the entry they need. It is, thus, only a comparatively small group of readers which would benefit by this hypothetical rule, while the majority would find it detrimental.

Along with the readers needing a book covered by the rule, but entertaining expectations that do not conform to its provisions, this rule would also disappoint all those whom the now bifurcated practice would induce to look also for such books under their editor's name which the rule does *not* cover. So, in all probability, the bargain would be a bad one even in this hypothetical case.

We may now conclude our theoretical examination of the cataloguing instrument of a discriminative employment of editor entries by an unequivocally unfavourable verdict. Later an example will illustrate not only the validity of our explanation of the continuous failure to find an appropriate formulation for the rule necessitated by that instrument, but also the fact that even at present great efforts are made to attain this unattainable end.

After reaching the above conclusion, we must not omit to raise the question of the possible expediency of an indiscriminative and consistent employment of editor main entries for all books of multiple authorship having an editor. Would or would not such a policy conform to the second requirement included in Chaplin's second principle? For logical completeness we must not omit this question, in spite of the fact that, at least so far as I know, no modern code has adopted such a policy.

At first glance, a rule prescribing that all the books of multiple authorship produced with the assistance of an editor (or compiler) whose name is known should be entered without exception under that name, seems to be clear and definite enough, and so, judged by the standard of that particular requirement, not inferior to a rule prescribing that all such books should be entered consistently under title. The same applies also to a restrictive rule, the restriction being confined to an exclusion of only those books not naming their editor on the title page. Parenthetically, we might also add that with regard to the books in question both the title entry and the indiscriminatively applied editor entry seem to be equally superior to all other alternatives, to all entries made under another formal distinguishing mark. The argument upon which this is based is the following: 1) all these books are equally equipped with a title as well as an editor's name; 2) for the time being we are unable to ascertain whether the anticipation of an editor entry or of a title entry actually prevails, and are therefore impelled to resort to mere mathematical probability; and finally 3) no other kind of formal distinguishing mark shares with these two the property of being without exception attached to all the books under consideration.

On second thoughts, however, we are obliged to withdraw the above favourable verdict. Even if employed indiscriminatively, the editor entry has, in the light of the second requirement, an unequivocally unfavourable effect. It necessarily involves a dividing up of the area outside the domain of application of author entries into two separate and distinct fields, assigned to the editor and title entries, respectively; and this necessitates the fixing of a boundary line separating these two fields. Experience shows, however, that all such boundary lines unfailingly involve the emergence of doubtful borderline cases, even if they are delineated with the utmost care and efficiency. A device which eliminates a boundary line is, therefore, according to our second requirement, always preferable to one which necessitates the establishment of such a line. This would hold true even in respect to a hypothetical indiscriminative employment of editor entries entailing only a comparatively harmless boundary line—a line that could be drawn without any greater difficulty, with a relatively high degree of exactness, and of which the draw-backs could be thus outweighed, if only the policy of an indiscriminative use of editor entries would give in some other respect at least a slender compensatory advantage—as this policy would yield no advantage whatsoever. On the contrary, it would embody also a second, and even graver, deficiency of another nature: it would involve the entry of very many books, manifestly in conflict with the first principle, under the name of an editor who had no intellectually significant part in producing them. This is, of course, also the reason why code-makers have always consistently refrained from adopting this policy.

We come now to testing the editor entry by the third requirement included in the second principle—the requirement that codes should contain no rules which do not contribute to the efficiency of catalogues.

The editor entry cannot pass this test, either: it increases the intricacy of the structure of codes and catalogues, without offering any adequate compensation for the resulting decrease in their efficiency. The validity of the second part of this statement has already been demonstrated above: we have shown that, tested by the first principle, the editor entry proves at best to be indifferent; while if tested by the second requirement of the second principle, it turns out to be directly detrimental. The first part of the statement is, on the other hand, self-evident. If code-makers could decide to abandon the editor entry (together with the compiler entry), their rules for the choice of main entry headings could be cut down to a more delimitation of the area, and a determination of the modes, of the application of author entries, primarily in the various cases of multiple and principal author-ship. The domain of the title entry would then automatically include the whole area not assigned to author entries, that is to say, it would become residual in character, and thus require no direct delimitation, no additional rules. Whereas the use of editor entries inevitably entails the introduction of two further groups of rules, and the fixing of two new boundary lines: one separating the fields assigned to the editor and the author entry, the other those assigned to the editor and the title entry, respectively. A code-maker who also adopts similar compiler entries, as a separate entry category with rules differing from those providing for the use of editor entries, must also put up with the addition of three further rules or groups of rules. Such a proliferation of the cardinal rules governing the choice of main entry headings, i.e. the structure of catalogues, is of course proportionately bound to perplex the reader.

That basic rules should be applied consistently, with as few exceptions as possible, is a widely recognized axiom, not only explicitly emphasized by Chaplin, but also turned into one of the pillars of the "philosophy of filing" adopted recently by the Library of Congress.[2] The use of editor and compiler entries is at variance with this axiom—this is one of the reasons why these entry categories are theoretically indefensible. Code-makers should at last recognize that.

We must now conclude our analysis by casting a quick glance at the question whether or not Chaplin's third principle—according to which if a rule is rooted in cataloguing tradition this may justify the code-maker's retaining it—also applies to the editor entry.

We have already seen that this principle is valid only in regard to rules which are not irreconcilable with either of the first two principles, and also that editor entries *are* irreconcilable with the second principle. This would already be sufficient to exclude a positive answer to our question. But the editor entries must be rejected even on the strength of the third principle itself. As already stressed above, in our times characterized by strenuous efforts to attain international uniformity in cataloguing, Chaplin's third principle cannot apply to local traditions thwarting these efforts. The tradition of using editor entries is, however, of this nature: it has numerous local variants, widely differing in regard to the field of application they allot to these entries. Their speedy removal is thus desirable not only because of their own intrinsic vagueness, but also by reason of their multifariousness obstructing the progress of international uniformity. If, however, they are to be sacrificed, then they must be sacrificed in the most rational way possible. Undoubtedly, this should entail their general and complete removal, since—irrespective of the impossibility of finding them a really satisfactory positive application—it must be easier to attain uniformity by means of this negative step, than by replacing all the widely diverging national rules by a single uniform provision of positive character.

To sum up: tested by Chaplin's principles, the editor entry proves to be an unequivocally inexpedient cataloguing device, of which a further preservation is theoretically unwarrantable.

Chaplin himself reached this conclusion long before he explicitly proclaimed his principles in the form recorded above. In his Draft Statement of Principles prepared for the Paris Conference—and supported by M. Braun's working paper—he had already discarded this entry category, thus summarily rejecting all the solutions offered by former codes, and boldly taking a new—the right—course.[3] This courageous launching of a radical innovation had only a slight flaw: it was not sufficiently uncompromising. In section 10.34 of his Draft Principles, Chaplin allowed that the main entry of those collections (in which term he included also composite works), of which the name of the compiler (or the editor) is generally known, may exceptionally be made under that name. This concession is not in harmony with his precept, as formulated in 1966 and cited above, that exceptions from general rules should be made "only for important and clearly definable categories of material". Nor is it a happy one, since liable to give rise to inconsistent practices. Of course, in Paris Chaplin had to compromise for the sake of his chief aim—to reach international agreement. Besides, his section 10.34 is only a concession, not a command. Nevertheless, one has only to recall J. Tait's commentary on the Paris Principles to realize how harmful compromises of this sort can be. According to Tait, the difference between the two alternative formulations of section 10.3 of the Paris Principles was "more apparent than real because of the concessions which each makes to the other"[4]—in other words, there was no essential difference between these two in fact directly opposite standpoints! Is it possible to conceive of a more telling demonstration of the dangers embodied in a permission to make optional exceptions than the one furnished by this amazing misinterpretation of the rules and positions under consideration?

Of course, it is a fact htat Chaplin and the small majority of the Paris Conference participants did not express the opinion of the majority of the world's cataloguers. Obviously, the latter as yet are not prepared to drop the editor entry definitively—the post-Paris codes demonstrate this fact quite plainly. The reason for this attitude of the cataloguers is obvious: they wish to save the continuity of their already existing catalogues. This is, however, only a matter of transitory policy with which we are not at all concerned, our subject being confined to the *theoretical* examination of the question whether there are or not any bibliographical conditions under which the editor entry has to be considered as optimal amongst all alternatively disposable main entries.

We have reached the end of our theoretical inquiry into the utility and expediency of the editor entry. The result of this inquiry is unequivocally negative. Among the three fundamental principles of code-making we find not one which could warrant a preservation of this entry category. This is a theoretical finding that automatically includes the conclusion that the editor entry will have to be discarded in practice, if not sooner then later, in spite of the existing catalogues in use.

· · · · ·

We conclude this article by pointing out an inference to be derived from its findings. Although this inference concerns an issue outside the proper scope of our subject, we cannot omit it in view of its utmost importance.

Everything said about the obstacles thwarting all attempts at finding adequate formulae for the provisions of regulating the use of editor and compiler entries, as well as about the untoward effects of even the least objectionable variants of these formulae upon the simplicity and lucidity of the cataloguing codes and author-title catalogues, and finally about the great advantages to be gained by relegating the utilization of the editor's and the compiler's name entirely to the competency of the added entry—all this also applies, almost without qualification, to the corporate main entries, and applies to them to a considerably greater degree than to the editor entries. Very striking new evidence for the validity of these propositions was furnished by the 1969 Copenhagen International Meeting of Cataloguing Experts, which confessed to the utter insuitability of the Paris rules providing for the limits of application of corporate main entries, without having made even the slightest attempt to replace them by less inadequate ones.[12] In consequence of the undeniable inexpediency of all variants of the rules providing for these limits, the corporate main entries impair the consistency and lucidity of our catalogues far more gravely than even the editor and compiler main entries. Their complete abandonment, and a transfer to the added entry of the inestimable retrieval handle offered by the corporate names connected with the books, would be a real blessing to the users of author-title catalogues.

It is exclusively the cataloguers' tradition—their vested interests—the weakest among the three possible foundations upon which a cataloguing device and rules for its application may be based—which prevent the editor, compiler, and corporate main entries from being discarded altogether. But any device having so poor a basis is doomed sooner or later to succumb when confronted by one of more solid foundation. Concerning the three main entry categories in question, this confrontation is already in progress.

Notes

1. Chaplin, A. H.: Tradition and Principle in Library Cataloguing. Univ. of Toronto School of Library Science, 1966. *The Bertha Bassam Lecture in Librarianship.* No. 1. p. 10-11.

2. Cf. Rather, J. C.: Filing Arrangements in the Library of Congress Catalogs. *Library Resources and Technical Services.* Vol. 16. (1972). no. 2, p. 247.

3. It may be mentioned that in his 1966 paper (see note 1) Chaplin did not explicitly disapprove of the editor and the compiler entry being retained in the new Code, the completion of which was at that time already at hand. But that he nevertheless maintained his original standpoint implied in his statement that the search for a rule for multiple authorship that would produce a heading likely to be associated with the work by the user of the catalogue, and at the same time be unambiguous and certain in its application, had been so far unsuccessful, and that it was difficult to choose between the solutions offered (see op. cit., p. 20).

4. Tait, J. A.: *Authors and Titles.* London, Clive Bingley, 1969. SBN 85157 082 8. p. 118.

. . . . .

12. According to a statement of its mimeographed report (p. 2), "The Meeting recognized the unsatisfactory nature of sections 9.11, 9.12 and Footnote 8 [of the Paris Statement of Principles], and wished to point out that no codes evolved since the Paris Conference have found it possible to formulate rules consistent with both these sections".

The Role of a
Machine Based Authority File
in an Automated Bibliographic
System

S. Michael Malinconico

Editor's Introduction

Adapting library catalogs to a machine environment requires a mind not only informed about catalog requirements and automation, but also one with the vision to imagine what has never been. S. Michael Malinconico has such a mind. After obtaining a Master's Degree in physics and working as a systems analyst for the National Aeronautics and Space Administration, he joined the New York Public Library, and there distinguished himself on several counts. Most notable was his role in designing and implementing a machine-based authority file. His reports of this project, at once technical and philosophical, influenced the development of authority control systems both in this country and in Canada. In 1978, he was awarded the Esther J. Piercy award "in recognition of his work as an advocate of the application of computer technology as a tool for facilitating the cataloging process, preserving cataloging principles, and enriching bibliographic access and control."*

In the selection that follows, Malinconico describes authority control in an online environment. Like Cutter and Lubetzky before him, he reflects on the intellectual organization of the catalog. But his language differs from theirs.

---

*Esther J. Piercy Award, 1978: S. Michael Malinconico," *Library Resources and Technical Services* 22 (Fall 1978): 418.

It is a machine-oriented language. The catalog is a *database* made up of a *bibliographic file* and an *authority file*, the latter an automated version of Cutter's *syndetic structure.* The two are linked by an *authority control system*, whose purpose is to collocate related material, to integrate records for new items into an existing catalog structure, and to maintain the integrity of the catalog as a bibliographic tool.

When computer technology is introduced into a discipline, it often brings with it a new *Weltanschauung,* a new way of looking. The discipline of cataloging is no exception: the development of machine-based authority files has introduced a new way of looking at catalog structures, and this, in turn, has raised questions. One question concerns the data elements susceptible to authority control. Is it cost effective, as Malinconico suggests, to provide authority treatment for all data elements that are not item specific? Another question concerns bibliographic relationships. Cutter's concept of collocation called for subject, author, and edition relationships. Lubetzky refined this concept by elaborating the notion of a *work*. The present MARC linking technique characterizes bibliographic relationships as hierarchical, vertical, and chronological.† What relationships should be recognized in an online environment, how should they be represented, and which database management system should be used to implement them? A third question concerns the design of authority records. Is it possible to design such records with alternative uniform name headings, in order to meet the demands of local usage, and at the same time not adversely affect the exchange of bibliographic data in an international network environment? These are some of the questions raised by the development of machine-based authority files, questions whose answers can advance our understanding and point to the design of future catalogs.

ES

Further Reading

Heymans, Frans. "How Human-Usable Is Interchangeable? Or, Shall We Produce Catalogues or Babelographic Towers?" *Library Resources and Technical Services* 26 (April/June 1982): 156-69.

---

†Sally H. McCallum, "Marc Record-Linking Technique," *Information Technology and Libraries* 1 (September 1982): 281-91.

Discusses the INTERMARC authority file format and the use of an International Standard Control Form as a means of interchanging bibliographic data while at the same time accommodating local usage.

Goossens, Paula. "Hierarchical Relationships in Bibliographic Descriptions: Problem Analysis." In *Hierarchical Relationships in Bibliographic Descriptions*, edited by Ahmed H. Helal and Joachim W. Weiss (INTERMARC Software-Subgroup Seminar, March 25-27, 1981; Publications of Essen University Library, Vol. 2), 18-128. Federal Republic of Germany: Gesamthochschulbibliotek Essen, 1981.

Conceputalizes linking structures abstractly and presents practical examples of bibliographic relationships of various levels of complexity. Particularly notable in attempting to devise a consistent approach to handling part-whole relationships in machine authority files.

Gorman, Michael. "Cataloging and the New Technologies." In *The Nature and Future of the Catalog,* edited by Maurice J. Freedman and S. Michael Malinconico, 127-36. Phoenix: The Oryx Press, 1979.

Reprinted in this volume. Discusses how cataloging in a machine environment releases us from the tyranny of the main entry; in such an environment cataloging becomes the constructing of linked packages of information.

The Role of a Machine Based Authority File
in an Automated Bibliographic System

The Library Catalog

In order to understand the role of an authority file in a cataloging system, we should first examine the role of the library catalog. The catalog might be said to serve three basic functions: (1) provide access to an item in the collection, (2) organize the collection, and (3) assist the user with information regarding its own organization.

The first function is obvious; the user is provided with a location identifier, by which he may either request the item in a closed stack environment, or find it himself in an open stack library. Even in this mode a certain amount of organizational assistance is provided when the collection is shelved according to some classification scheme. This is due to the fact that the material itself is organized as a subject added entry. Thus, for the purposes of this discussion we can ignore this mode of collection access.

The second function is perhaps the most important, and least addressed by automated systems. The catalog, as we all know, represents a surrogate of the collection. More importantly, it represents several simultaneous surrogates. The alternate access points thus created, of course, also provide assistance in locating a specific item. However, the added entry structure represents much more than simply an alternate route to a particular item. It provides us with the possibility of presenting in one sequence all items which partake of a particular organizational attribute. Alternate sequences could, naturally, not possibly be provided by physical organization of the material. Thus, from the point of view of the catalog's utility, the ability to review a comprehensive sequence under a given heading is of importance at least equal to the ability to access a particular item.

The researcher is rarely satisfied with access to a predefined list of documents. Rather, he appproaches the catalog as a representation of the collection; he will then, according to his needs, survey under various categories the material which the library holds in order to determine what may be of use to him. He may be

Reprinted by permission of S. Michael Malinconico and the Canadian Library Association from *Automation in Libraries: Papers Presented at the CACUL Workshop on Library Automation, Winnipeg, June 22-23, 1974.* (Ottawa: Canadian Library Association, 1975). © 1975 Canadian Library Association.

interested in what has been written about a particular subject, in how a particular idea evolved, in how a particular author's thinking evolved, in how a particular author's writings affected others, etc. Each of these requirements dictate that when he makes a query of the catalog that the resultant response be complete in terms of the collection, and not result in extraneous citations. Thus, it should be obvious that the library catalog is considerably more than another manifestation of simple document retrieval. Representing the relationship of one item to others in the collection is perhaps more important than providing access to a single item. This, after all, is the primary role of the cataloger. He attempts to integrate each new item into the catalog in the context of what already exists in the collection. As the catalog grows in size, and consequently in complexity, and as time causes terminology to change, the cataloger must alter the contextual setting in order to integrate new material. The goal, however, remains the same. The cataloger attempts to add all new material in a manner consistent with an evolving structure.

Here we begin to note a dichotomy of interests. The catalog must possess a rigid, consistent structure at any given instant of time. It must also be capable of accepting material added to it over a considerable span of time. Thus, we are asking for a rigid structure which it is expected will need to be manipulated. It is almost as if we were asking that a building be created with structural integrity, yet be capable of accommodating a varied multiplicity of spatial requirements in the course of its existence. Naturally, in the case of an architectural structure, this would be accommodated by periodic reconstruction. Frequent physical reorganization of a building, just as frequent reorganization of a catalog can prove extremely expensive. Ohmes and Jones address the problems of maintenance of the catalog in an article entitled, *The Second Half of Cataloging.*[1] They point out that the clerical effort of altering bibliographic data in order that it may be integrated into an existing catalog is only half, the simple and relatively inexpensive half, of cataloging. They express the opinion that automation has only addressed the clerical aspects of preparing new data to fit into a catalog, and has completely ignored those aspects of cataloging which are of professional concern to the cataloger. They point out that with relative ease one can modify, for example, an LC record of an earlier era to conform to more recent practice. However, automation has not attacked the more profound problems of reorganizing a catalog to reflect the newer practice represented by a recent LC record.[2] Nor, has it offered any solution to the simpler problems of guaranteeing integrity of the catalog when no intentional change in form has occurred.[3]

The problems of maintaining a coherent catalog are grieviously exacerbated by an automated system. Machine logic is of the most literal nature. Even though week after week we pass the most profound record of human intellectual endeavor through its electronic circulation system, it will always return in its untutored ignorance to insist that *Yeats, William Butler* and *Yeats, William B.* are different people. If we attempt to break it of this habit it will, in its unbridled desire to please, insist that perhaps we should not overlook *Cellophane* when inquiring about the *Cello*. The problems of absolutely literal retrieval are seriously aggravated by the other components of an electronic system. A CRT display, for example, normally provides only about 25 lines of 80 characters each. The scan range thus presented is extremely limited; rendering an item only slightly misfiled inaccessible. In a manual system if a cataloger committed a transposition such as in *Yeats,*

William Bulter, there is the possibility that it would escape the notice of the cataloging revisor. For virtually the same reason, it would escape the notice of the filer, and he would, as a consequence, file it into the correct sequence in the catalog. Further, the user when he accessed the record would probably be equally impervious to the error. The important point being that since the source of the error, the placement of the record into the data base, and its retrieval are all subject to compatible error thresholds the system functions despite the error. The machine, of course, does not even possess the literary acumen of the least erudite filing clerk, hence, in the man-machine interface there is an imbalance of error tolerance. In an on-line environment, of course, the equivalent error might prove disastrous, as *Bulter* would sequence ahead of *Butler* and would perhaps never be seen again. If we consider a display medium with a much wider scan range; e.g. a book form catalog, the problem is only slightly less severe. If the error is only of the magnitude just described, the record will be found. Nonetheless the user is still subjected to a search of two sequences. A slightly more serious error can produce a disproportionately greater problem. For instance, between *Horse* and *Horses* there are 33 primary headings and 7 cross references listed in the seventh edition of the LC Subject Heading Guide. Since the entire display must be completely created at one time, and due to the expense of production must last for a considerable period of time, there is no room for ad-hoc fine tuning. Every inconsistency will inexorably produce a double file.

I would like to offer one final point on data accuracy. If one were to assume that a keyboarder can achieve an accuracy rate of 99.9%, which seems to be about the norm, then in the course of keying 400 character records, we can expect that one-third of all records will have at least one error in them (see figure 1). If we restrict ourselves to a consideration of only the access point data; i.e. main entry, uniform and series titles, added entries and subject headings, we have about 116 characters of data susceptible to error, which implies that about 11% of all records will have at least one faulty access point.[4] Thus, in addition to the problems of establishing headings consistently, we must also take into account this inevitable human frailty when considering the management of a machine readable bibliographic data base.

I should now like to return to the problems of intentional changes in the form of headings. Changes occur for many reasons: corporate bodies change name, political entities come and go, national policy changes with respect to recognition of existing political entities, women authors' names may undergo several transmutations as a result of the institutions of marriage and divorce, an author may be known by several different pseudonyms, each with varying degrees of popularity at different times, use of the language changes, making subject terms anachronistic (for example, the standard laugh-getters: *Computers* see *Electronic Calculating-Machines,* or *Airplanes* see *Aeroplanes*), etc.

Each of these cases are equally problematical in manual, and automated systems. There is, however, a large category of changes which generally cause only minor disruption in a manual system, but which wreak havoc in an automated system. This situation is most often characterized by the discovery of more complete information regarding an entry after it has already been used several times in its incomplete form. Examples might be: discovery of the complete form of middle name, e.g. *Walsh, Edmund A.* is determined to be *Walsh, Edmund Aloysius,*

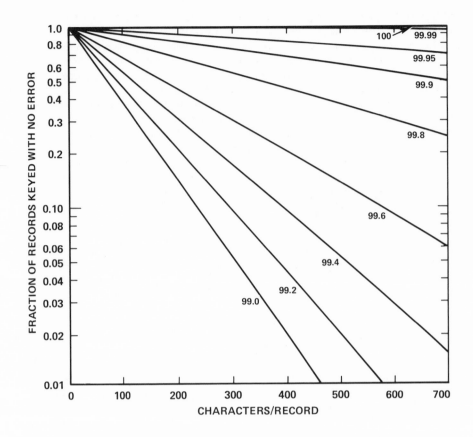

Fig. 1. Effect of Keyboarding Accuracy on Keyed Records. Each graph is for a given keyboarding accuracy. The resultant plots show the fraction of records which might be expected to be keyed without error as a function of characters/record.

post-humous works about, and later editions of works by an author will be entered with death dates. These occurrences would, in the overwhelming majority of cases, create no difficulty in a manual system, as *Truman ... 1884-1972* would be manually interfiled with *Truman ... 1884-* by the filing clerk. The same would no doubt happen in the case of Walsh, Edmund A.[5] In an automated system we would inevitably create a new author.

Add to these cases the wholesale chaos wrought by changes to the cataloging rules. The ALA rules published in 1949 were superseded by the Anglo-American Code in 1967, leaving behind a residue known as superimposition. This policy is in the process of being abandoned by The Library of Congress, causing another round of resolution of form and entry. Closely related are changes to the LC subject heading structure. These are instances which, in general, affect both manual and automated systems alike.

There is, however, another category, which primarily affects automated systems. In the last five years there have been some interesting changes to the LC subject heading structure; the general subheadings of the form *Hist. and Crit.* were converted to their spelled out form, as were the abbreviations *U.S.* and *Gt. Brit.*[6] We are now in the process of grappling with a wholesale change to chronologically subdivided headings, in which all such headings will be supplied with explicit dates. These changes, while only annoying in a manual system, usually present severe problems for automated systems.

Authority File Maintenance

In summary we have two basic problems which must be addressed when considering maintenance of a machine readable catalog: (1) the need to guarantee consistency at any given time, and (2) the need to provide a method of rapidly and accurately changing this structure as circumstances dictate. Providing answers to these questions might be said to be a distinction between a cataloging system, and one which provides only cataloging reference assistance. In the latter, an interface is provided to an off-line manual catalog maintenance system, while in the former, the catalog itself is included in the overall system.

An established method of guaranteeing cataloging consistency generally exists in most manual systems. Libraries usually maintain one or more manual authority files. An authority file is just that, the authority which defines the manner in which certain forms will be used. Authority files may consist of separate files of subject headings used in the catalog, they may be embedded in the official catalog as the authority for personal names, or appear in any number of different forms. For a discussion of the possibilities see Maruice Tauber's book, *Technical Services in Libraries.*[7] [8] A cataloger when preparing a record for an item to be added to the collection will reference these authority files to insure that he is adding it within the context of what already exists. He will also take care to update the authority files when he must create a new form.

Thus, we would find a ready made solution to the dilemmas posed earlier, if we were to render this file machine manipulable, and used it to govern the bibliographic file. Before we can use this file to control the catalog we must consider its own intrinsic maintenance requirements. To a degree unexperienced in a bibliographic file, an authority file consists of a highly complex set of interrelationships.

This brings us to a consideration of the third function which a catalog must perform: provide information regarding its own organization. Since the form of a term chosen by a cataloger may not necessarily coincide with the thought processes of a user of the catalog, some translation mechanism must be provided. For instance, the user must be led to often little expected wonders such as, *Registers of Deaths* see *Registers of Births, etc.,* or *Virgil* see *Vergilius Maro, Publius.* There are also the purely instructional kinds of references, in which the user is directed to a more specific heading which he might not have considered—the *see also* reference.

The cross reference structure just alluded to—both direct *see* and *see also*—must be controlled if we are not to have blind references in the catalog, or a cross reference leading to yet another cross reference. The *see also* reference is monstrously misused in catalogs which have been in existence for a considerable period of time. When usage changes, such as in the change from *Spanish America* to *Latin America,* many libraries, rather than submitting to the expense of converting all of the *Spanish America* cards, will simply establish a new sequence under *Latin America* and connect the two with *see also* references. Tauber points out that such an artifice is perhaps not so bad if it happens once to a heading, however, after a few iterations it tends to overburden, and render useless the cross reference structure of the catalog.[9]

There is another type of heading which is used in the catalog for purely informational purposes—the general note. An example might be the following note from the NYPL catalog: *Trans ... A word beginning with this prefix is filed as one word regardless of punctuation. (i.e. Trans World and Trans-World are filed as Transworld.)*[10]

Textual notes associated with a valid heading, also serve as a guide to the catalog. A distinction is made between notes for the cataloger, and notes for the public (scope notes). The former are usually a guide to the use of a heading of interest only to the cataloger, e.g. the *"Divide like..."* notes. These actually never appear in the public catalog, but are found in the working authority file. The scope notes are intended to guide the public in the use of the catalog. These sometimes take the form, *"Here are entered works on ...".* These notes consisting, in general, of free text usually present no control problems.[11]

By control I mean that the alteration, deletion or change of a term should automatically be reflected everywhere else it is used. We could conceive of a machine based authority system in which all of the reciprocal references were maintained manually. Indeed most authority lists currently in use are maintained in this manner. This, however, is a gross underutilization of the capabilities of the machine.

As a first prerequisite in the manipulation of an authority file we should have the capability of maintaining all of the cross reference linkages following additions, deletions or changes. In order to minimize human intervention, and insure integrity of the file all of the concomitant changes brought about by the alteration of a heading should be effected automatically. For example, let us assume that we have: *Documents see Archives; Preservation of Historical Records see Archives* and *Public records - Preservation see Archives,* and if for some reason we wished to change the established form, *Archives,* then we should expect the system to reflect that change automatically in each of the three headings which reference *Archives.* The number of references can become quite large, especially with early authors, and names derived by transliteration, e.g. our own authority file contains 11 cross references to Voltaire.

Since the authority file must provide the framework for the catalog, we must exercise great care over its own internal consistency. Again, we could require that this consistency be maintained manually, but it more simply and accurately done by machine. These considerations include guaranteeing that a heading is not established twice, once as a cross reference and once again as a valid heading, or simply established twice as a heading. Thus, attempts to alter a heading into a form which conflicts with another heading, a cross reference or general note must be prevented. An attempt to add a *see from* tracing to a heading must be prevented if it (the *see from*) conflicts with a valid heading already on the file. The addition of a *see from* tracing should itself automatically create the cross reference record; both in the interests of efficiency and in order to insure consistency. There is a more difficult area of conflict which we will consider following a discussion of subdivided headings.

Whenever a subdivided heading is established in a manual authority file there is usually an attendant attempt made to establish all of its higher level headings if they do not already exist. Further, if a geographical place name is used as a subdivision for the first time, it too is established. Such an approach can prove extremely valuable in an automated system, as all of the ancillary establishment can be effected by programming logic, necessitating no additional keyboarding or proofreading. Let us assume that we are attempting to establish, *Music - France - History and Criticism - 20th Century,* then we should expect to automatically generate:

> *Music - France - History and Criticism*
> *Music - France,* and
> *Music,*

in addition to the original heading. Since *France* is itself a valid place name, we should also expect to establish it.

This technique is an invaluable aid in building the file. We can further take advantage of this process to make several other consistency checks before permitting the form to either be added to the file, or to be accepted as an alteration to an existing form. We can check each of the generated headings for possible conflict with a cross reference, or general note. We can also extend this same validation procedure to the generated place name. If any component is found to be in conflict, we would then reject the entire set of generated headings. As an example, if the heading presented above had used *Gaul* in place of *France,* and we already had the cross reference, *Gaul see France,* on the file we would dismiss the entire set of headings. Similarly an error condition would be detected if the heading had been *Music drama - ...,* and there was a reference, *Music drama see Opera.* The alternative to dismissing the entire set of headings would be to effect an automatic transfer of the improper component to its correct form. This has not been the approach taken at NYPL. We felt that, the inherent complexities aside, it was more prudent in a batch environment to reject the entire set of headings when an error was detected.

Authority/Bibliographic File Interface

Up until this point I have been trying to speak about authority systems in pretty general terms. The system described is, however, essentially the one we implemented, and have been using since 1970 at NYPL. The system we developed is both batch and tape oriented. As a result there are additional features which an authority system should support not included in the description just given. I shall return to them later, but for the moment I should like to consider the interface between authority and bibliographic files. For the purposes of this discussion, I should like to drop the conditional mode, and talk specifically about the present NYPL system.

The first requirement of an authority file is that it verify the use of all common access point data used in a bibliographic record. This includes all of the access points in the record with the exclusion of those which are single item dependent (title page form of title, tag 245, and variant titles, tag 740). In terms of MARC tags these include all of the form 1xx, 4xx, 6xx, 7xx and 8xx (see figure 2). Tag 240, uniform title, presents certain unique problems. Establishment of such a title in disembodied form on an autority file would prove quite akward in practice, as it is often difficult to identify without being appended to an author. Consider *[Symphony, No. 4 Op. 90, A Major]*. If not attached to Mendelssohn such a uniform title is virtually meaningless. The solution adopted at NYPL has been to attach the uniform title data to an author.[1][2] The separation is maintained by a unique delimiter created for this purpose.

Verification of data used in a bibliographic record is effected via an alphabetic match. This presents a problem. If we require that the match be precise (character for character) the cataloger is required to perform a great deal of unnecessary work. By the same token we wish the match to be as unambiguous as possible. The solution we have adopted proceeds by requiring only that the cataloger spell the form correctly. That is, he need not concern himself with punctuation, diacritical marks, subfield delimiters or extraneous word spaces. In fact, if any of these accoutrements are entered with the bibliographic record they are ignored in favor of the version of the heading on the authority file. Figure 3 shows the construction of several match keys. The necessity of constructing this key in the most literal manner is illustrated by contrasting it with the filing form which would have been created by each heading.

In the interests of consistency, catalogers are not required to supply the two digit suffix to the MARC tag, as this too is controlled by the authority file. The tag structure of authority fields in a MARC record is quite interesting in that the final two digits serve to characterize the form:

    X00 - Personal name,
    X10 - Corporate name,
    X11 - Conference name,
    X51 - Place name,
    X30 - Uniform title heading,
    X40 - Title, and
    X50 - Topical subject.

X00 Personal name

| 100 | 400 | 600 | 700 | 800 |

X10 Corporate name

| 110 | 410 | 610 | 710 | 810 |

X11 Conference name

| 111 | 411 | 611 | 711 | 811 |

X51 Place name

| - | - | 651 | - | - |

X30 Uniform Title heading

| 130 | - | 630 | 730 | 830 |

X40 Series title (240 and 740 are excluded)

| - | 440 | - | - | 840 |

X50 Topical Subject

| - | - | 650 | - | - |

Fig. 2. Authority tags used in MARC monograph records.

Alphabetic Match Key

90 byte alphanumeric key derived from first 80 characters of established form plus binary key from data beyond 80 characters.

Filing Form

Alphanumeric form derived by algorithm from established form, categorization, delimiters, and language codes. Form is 80 bytes in length, contains 106 characters in compressed 6 bit notation.

EXAMPLES

Händel, Georg Friederich, (d) 1685-1759

HANDEL_GEORG_FRIEDRICH_1685_1759

HAENDEL_GEORG_FRIEDRICH____1685_1759

Gustaf (b) VI (c) King of Sweden

GUSTAF_VI_KING_OF_SWEDEN

GUSTAF_____6_KING_OF_SWEDEN

Anti - Reformation

ANTI_REFORMATION

ANTIREFORMATION

France (x) - History (y) - Revolution

FRANCE_HISTORY_REVOLUTION

FRANCE_HISTORY____6789_3201

The West (x) - History

THE_WEST_HISTORY

WEST_HISTORY

Fig. 3. NYPL authority record.

Thus, we have a ready made system for categorizing forms on an authority file. By using such a scheme we are able to maintain a single authority file for all categories of names, uniform titles, series titles and subject headings. This structure also permits us to insure that a form is uniformly categorized no matter how it is used in a record. For example, the same corporate author might appear as a main entry, subject entry, or added entry. In all cases the same authority record would be referenced, and in all cases we can be sure that it will appear as 110, 610 and 710 respectively. Maintenance of consistency of categorization can prove of critical importance when producing a divided catalog. If a tag suffix is provided as input in a bibliographic record it is ignored in favor of the data in the authority file.

Should the alphabetic match result in failure, a warning message is generated and the particular field placed in non-valid status. Should, on the other hand, the match prove valid, the form as it appears on the authority file is returned for review in the bibliographic record. In addition, an identifying serial number, assigned to the authority record is returned to the bibliographic record for the field in question. This neutral number was assigned to the authority record when it itself entered the system, and follows the form through all of its metamorphoses. In all future displays of the bibliographic record, authority data will be referenced by ID number, thus, we are able to automatically reflect any changes to the established form in all bibliographic records which use the form. In fact only the authority ID number has any significance in an authority field following a successful interface match. If any aspect of an authority field in a bibliographic record is altered, the entire verification process is automatically reinitiated, i.e. an alphabetic match is again sought. Figure 4 illustrates the linkage of a field in a bibliographic record to an authority record. Figure 5 shows an expanded view of a directory entry, and illustrates the manner in which the authority control number and match status are stored.

The matching process itself is somewhat complex. Since the purpose of an authority file is to control the use of term in a single place, it becomes desirable to have only one version of a name regardless of how it is used, or of the author's relationship to a work. Thus, we would not wish to establish an author several times simply because he might have been a translator, compiler, illustrator, editor, joint editor, defendant, appellant, etc., in various records. Thus, relator data need to be ignored in the matching process. Of course, these data must be retained, and appended to responses from the authority file. The system must note the presence of these non-authority data when requesting authority data for use in a bibliographic record by ID number.

Page analytics present even more complex problems. The series statement (field 4xx) is often of the form, In:, followed by a series title. This datum must likewise be ignored in the matching process. Further the series may be numbered, hence the volume information should also not take part in the matching process. The worst case is probably the one in which the series statement is of the form *In his:, In her:, In its:,* etc., followed by a series title. This is cataloging shorthand for a series entered under author, in which the author is the same as the main entry of the record. Here again it would do us little good to have a disembodied title such as, *Series in Theoretical Physics,* on the authority file if not attached to an author.

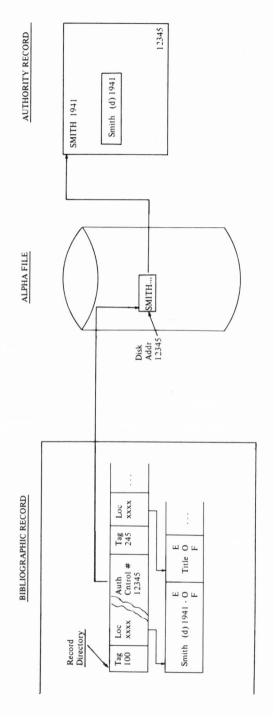

Fig. 4.

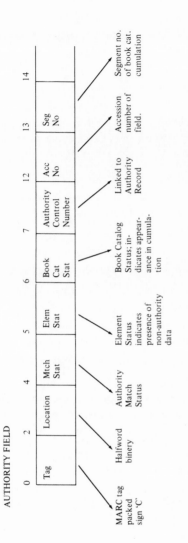

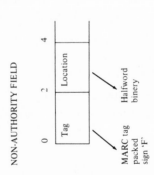

Fig. 5. Bibliographic record directory entry

Hence, in order to effect an alphabetic match we must ignore the incipit *In his:* and the volume statement, and combine the data in the 4xx field with that in the 1xx field. Of course when a match is found we must decompose the response and reappend all of the ignored data. Subsequent accesses by ID number will not go through the process of combination with main entry, however, the decomposition must still be performed. Similarly we must not lose track of any non-authority data associated with the field.

Since we maintain series titles on the authority file we can also control the call number of a kept together series in the authority record for the series title. Thus, for a previously cataloged series we do not require that a call number be entered as part of the bibliographic record, as it will be returned by the interface system.

In the verification process we must also examine the record type of the matching authority record. There are several types of authority records which are not permitted for use in cataloging: cross references, general notes and dual entries (we shall discuss the dual entry later). If a field used in a bibliographic record matches one of these record types, validation is not permitted and a diagnostic message is generated. An exception is made when we match a cross reference which references only a single valid heading. In that case, since there is no ambiguity, we effect an automatic transfer, accompanied by a diagnostic message. This technique has proven so powerful that we have set up a non-printing type of cross reference. Such cross references would never appear in a book catalog. They are only used to automatically trap and convert invalid headings.

As you will recall, following a first match, each authority field in a bibliographic record is controlled entirely by the ID number returned in the interface. This naturally permits us to access the latest version of all authority data whenever a bibliographic record is displayed. This would be true regardless of whether we were producing proof copy or a book catalog. In this manner all changes to authority records are automatically reflected throughout the bibliographic file.

Since access is by number, we can create an extremely powerful transaction. By placing a pointer in the numerical index to the authority file, we can effect a transfer of one heading into another. Such a transaction is extremely simple to use: one need only key a three character transaction code and two nine digit numbers. This will in effect coalesce two headings. Figure 6 illustrates this transfer operation in the index file. Such a transaction, of course, proves quite useful when a heading is inadvertently entered in more than one form. This does not occur too often in normal operation. However, its value in cleaning up an existing inconsistent file is immense. We have actually done this in cooperation with the Hennepin County Public Library. They had a file which consisted of 77,000 records converted in the course of two years. This file was replete with inconsistencies. In the course of two weeks, with the assistance of students, hired as temporary clerks, they entered 11,000 maintenance transactions against an intentionally "dirty" authority file. Of the 11,000 transactions, over 6,000 were transfers. They in effect performed substantial recataloging on the eve of publication of their catalog.[13]

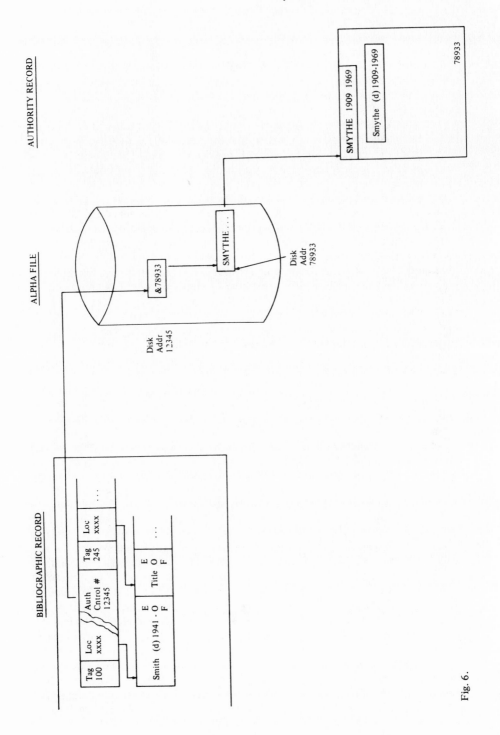

Fig. 6.

The Dual Entry

Of particular interest here in Canada might be a unique type of heading which we maintain on our authority file—the dual entry. This heading lies conceptually between a cross reference and a proper heading. It is controlled on the authority file just as a cross reference would be. The dual entry serves essentially as a synonym. One of the decisions made by NYPL when it decided to automate, was that all future cataloging would rigorously adhere to LC practice. This decision had to be amended for two of the special collections: Music, and Genealogy. They had a need for certain non-LC subject headings in order to produce special sequences in the book catalog. These headings are of such a form that they represent synonyms of proper LC headings. Thus, rather than adding non-LC data to the bibliographic record, or expending the added effort of having subject specialists modify LC cataloging copy, we provide for these cases by a linked record on the authority file. The establishment of a dual entry field in an authority record causes a sort of phantom tracing to appear in a book catalog. For example, on our authority file the heading, *Sonatas (Flute),* has associated with it the dual entry *Flute music.* The net effect is that whenever *Sonatas Flute* is used in a bibliographic record, two subject entries will be created in the book catalog; one under *Sonatas (Flute),* and a second under *Flute music.* Our purpose in doing this is to bring together all music scores for a given instrument in one sequence. You, of course, have the interesting requirement of producing bilingual cataloging. Figure 7 illustrates the linkage between two headings and their dual entries.

Additional Authority File Functions

Were you to examine an authority file of headings used in any library you would first be impressed with the number of times particular elements keep reappearing. Headings can be sub-divided *ad nauseum,* place names keep reappearing as subdividing elements in all manner of headings, similarly for chronological, and certain general subdivisions. Thus, it would appear highly desirable to have only one version of such common elements on the file and have it referenced, whenever used, by a pointer. In this manner one could change all occurrences of *Ceylon* in the authority file to *Sri Lanka* with a single transaction.

The inclusion of such a feature in an authority system would provide an extremely powerful tool for the control of bibliographic data. We were unable to include such a feature, in any reasonable way, in our tape based system. We are, however, in the process of converting our entire system to a direct access mode of operation at which time we shall include such functions. There are yet important technical questions regarding the extent to which a heading should be decomposed into a series of pointers. I am not convinced that the speed of existing direct access devices can support the number of pointers required in a completely flexible system. It is easy to predict that the storage capacity of DASD's will continue to increase, but, barring a breakthrough such as crystal storage, there is no evidence that a dramatic decrease in access time can be expected in the near future. Our current plans call for providing back and forth pointers between a heading and its next subdivision. We have not yet reached a firm design decision regarding place names. Although considerable storage economy could be achieved by reducing

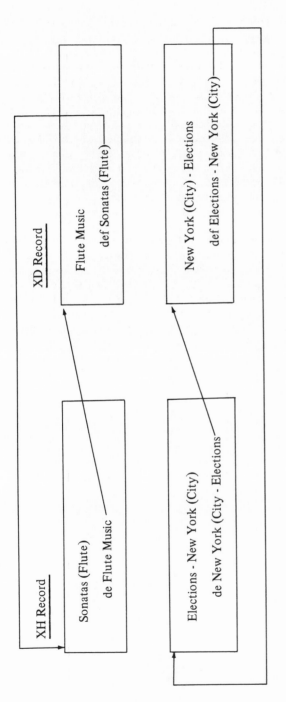

Fig. 7. Dual Entry.

other types of subdivisions to pointers we have decided that the access overhead is definitely not worth the advantages at this time.

In a network mode of operation an authority file must be capable of extending control over subsets of its own data. The prime requirement is that consistence be achieved within each subset, while at the same time being capable of drawing upon the common data for the mutual storage economy of all. Such a mechanism is of great importance even within a single institution such as NYPL, as NYPL is in effect two libraries—The Branch and Research Libraries. Although both subscribe to AACR practices there are differences of interpretation, e.g. Research uses *Homerus,* while the Branch Libraries prefer *Homer.* Further complicating the issue, within the Branch System we have a requirement to provide for both juvenile and adult cataloging. There are areas of conflict between juvenile headings and adult cross references. Thus, although we wish to maintain consistency within each of these files we do not wish to do it at the expense of storing separate authority files.

I believe the system we have developed at NYPL, thus far, should be ample proof of the feasibility of authority control in practice. I would also hope that I have managed to convey the importance of such a mechanism in maintaining the catalog of an individual library. Mechanical control over the data in a data base collected from several disparate sources, as in the collection of a national data base, is of even greater importance. Only in this way can we insure that we will be collecting a consistent coherent data base and not a chaotic machine readable collection of reference records.

Appendix

NYPL Authority File—Organization

File Organization

Physical Sequential

Access

Physical sequential access by alphabetic match key
Indirect access by control number via 'ALPHA' index file.

Record Types

XH - Heading
XS - Cross Reference
XN - General Note
XD - Dual Entry

Heading Types

00 - Personal name
10 - Corporate name
10j - Corporate Political jurisdiction
11 - Conference name
51 - Place name (incapable of authorship)
52 - Place name (capable of authorship)

30 - Uniform title heading
40 - Series title

50 - Topical subject

NYPL Authority Record—Heading

1. Record Type   **X H**

2. Match Key   Unique key derived from established form.

3. Authority Control Number   Serial number assigned to record upon entry into system. Access by item number by inverted 'ALPHA' index file.

4.	Established Form	Fully delimited form of heading.
5.	Categorization	Terminal two digits of MARC tag used to categorize form.
6.	Language Codes	Language code for filing. Two codes will be present when form is an author title combination.
7.	Filing Form	Filing form of established form. Derived by algorithm. Manual override provided. Two filing forms when author/title combination.
8.	Seen From (x tracing)	Text of seen from form. Linked to an XS record by alphabetic key. Field is repeatable.
9.	Dual Entry	Text of dual entry. Linked to an XD record by alphabetic key.
10.	See Also	Text of see also heading. Field is repeatable.
11.	Seen Also from (xx tracing)	Text of seen also from heading. Field is repeatable.
12.	Public Note	Text of public note or scope note. Field is repeatable.
13.	Cataloger's Note	Text of cataloger's note. Field is repeatable.
14.	Geographic Subdivision Note	Alternate form of place name to be used when heading is used as a subdivision.
15.	Series Call Number	Call number for a kept together series.
16.	Regionalization Number	Decision indicator for direct or indirect regionalization.
17.	Series Indicators	Series Title, Kept together decision, Scattered decision, Untraced Series decision.
18.	Indexing Indicator	Indexing decision indicator.

19.	Authority Source	LC or NYPL.
20.	Record Status	Valid, Active, Hold, Retain, Kill.
21.	Activity Dates	Date entered on file, date of last activity, release date, keyboard date.

Heading Generation

Music (z) - France (x) - History and Criticism (y) - 20th Century.

Generates:

Music (z) - France (x) - History and Criticism

Music (z) - France

Music

France

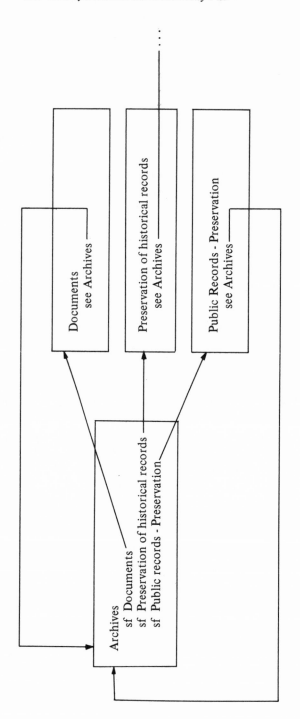

[Fig. 8. Established form and references]

Notes

1. Frances Ohmes and J. F. Jones. *The Other Half of Cataloging.* In: LRTS: 17 P. 320-329.

2. Ibid. P. 323

3. Ibid. P. 324

4. From counts made on the MARC file in July 1973 when it contained 329,354 records. It was found that there was an average of 3.39 authority fields per bibliographic record with a mean length of 34 characters each. Thus with an accuracy rate of 99.9% one could have expected 36,229 records to have at least one faulty common access point.

5. This could also prove to be a problem in a manual system, as the more complete form might be chosen to eliminate conflict in the catalog.

6. *Subject Headings Used in the Dictionary Catalog of the Library of Congress:* Seventh Edition, 1966, P. 600.

7. Maurice F. Tauber. *Technical Services in Libraries: Acquisitions, Cataloging, Classification, Binding, Photographic Reproduction, and Circulation Operations.* New York, Columbia University Press 1953, P. 137-139.

8. Ibid. P. 166-167

9. Ibid. P. 172

10. The New York Public Library. *Dictionary Catalog of The Research Libraries: A cumulative list of authors, titles, and subjects representing books and book-like materials added to the collections since January 1, 1971.* Supplement O-Z, April 1974, P. 428

11. Notes very frequently reference another heading, and hence good arguments could be made that they should be brought under mechanical control.

12. X30 type uniform title headings are established as independent entities.

13. Hennepin County Library, *Catalog,* introduction P. iv.

The Most Concise
AACR2

Michael Gorman

Editor's Introduction

Three years after the publication of *AACR2,* of which he was a joint editor, Michael Gorman published the *The Concise AACR2.* In the second work, he attempted to provide a useful abridgement of the full code. Shortly thereafter, Gorman became a regular contributor to *American Libraries,* and for the September 1981 issue, he wrote a single column called "The Most Concise *AACR2."* While the article may have been written tongue-in-cheek, it provides valuable insight into the fundamental assumptions of *AACR2.*

Gorman claims that *AACR2* was not written as a code for cataloging with computers, and he may well be correct: design of such a code entails a substantial study of just what a new technology means for catalog display. The truth of this assertion needs investigation, especially in light of the changing technologies used by the writers of codes presented in this volume. Panizzi wrote in the context of a manuscript slip catalog; Cutter wrote in the context of both printed book and card catalog; Lubetzky wrote with a card catalog in mind; and Taube dealt with the technology of a punched card sorter. It is important not to confuse computer technology with that of a punched card sorter. Boolean logic may make sense in terms of punched cards; it is less certain that it is sufficient in the online world without the additional capability of free text searching.

Gorman's rule for punctuation in the body of the description is derived from the International Standard Bibliographic

Description. The differences between it and the rule described in Lubetzky's "Principles of Descriptive Cataloging" are substantial. Although not always clearly stated, there are differences in their objectives of description, for example. The reader may want to consider whether the punctuation found in the ISBD is required for an online catalog, or is a historical relic dating from text search algorithms of the late 1960s, or is even a necessary means of reaching international understanding. On the other hand, the mandatory presence of the author statement (called "statement of responsibility" in *AACR2*) in the new code has a reason: given free text search capability, varying forms of name for an author can be located among catalog entries bearing identical main entry headings.

A long standing problem in discussions of cataloging theory has been whether an item being cataloged should be described as a member of a class of bibliographical objects, such as example of one of several editions of a work, or, instead, as an independent object. Because of the dichotomy in *AACR2* between the rules for description on the one hand, and the rules for entry and form of heading on the other, the preparers of *AACR2* seem to imply that what is cataloged should be viewed first as an independent object, and only later be related to other objects represented in the catalog. Although this approach appears to be new in cataloging, it is not clear that it makes a great difference in actual practice.

Rule 0.5 of *AACR2* states that since the catalogs of many libraries require no main entry, the rules for main entry are to be used "only as guidance in determining all the entries required in particular instances."* In "The Most Concise *AACR2*," Gorman opts for a catalog free from main entry. Baughman and Svenonius have questioned whether such a catalog can be constructed in the context of the full *AACR2*.†

If there is to be a new code written for the online catalog, what direction will it take? Will it be in directions suggested in this code? Part of the answer will lie in the perception of the capabilities of computer technology at the time a new code is written.

MC

Anglo-American Cataloguing Rules, 2d ed., prepared by the American Library Association, the British Library, the Canadian Committee on Cataloguing [and] the Library of Congress. (Chicago: American Library Association, 1978), 2.

†Betty Baughman and Elaine Svenonius, "AACR2: Main Entry Free?" *Cataloging & Classification Quarterly* 5(Fall 1984): 1-15.

Further Reading

Gorman, Michael. "Cataloging and the New Technologies." In *The Nature and Future of the Catalog,* edited by Maurice J. Freedman and S. Michael Malinconico, 127-36. Phoenix, Ariz: The Oryx Press, 1979.

Reprinted in this volume. Presents a revaluation of the objectives for cataloging codes after AACR2.

————. "Changes in Cataloguing Codes: Rules for Entry and Headings." *Library Trends* 25(January 1977):587-601.

Outlines the differences between older codes and AACR2.

Anglo-American Cataloguing Rules. 2d ed., prepared by the American Library Association, the British Library, the Canadian Committee on Cataloguing [and] the Library of Congress. Chicago: American Library Association, 1978.

The full AACR2.

Baughman, Betty. and Elaine Svenonius. "AACR2: Main Entry Free?" *Cataloging & Classification Quarterly* 5(Fall 1984):1-15.

Challenges the idea that AACR2 is readily converted to a code free of main entry.

The Most Concise AACR2

[Original] ed. note. Having recently completed a concise edition of AACR2, Gorman, unable to suppress the urge to condense the code even further, sent AL this version. In a heroic effort, he has squeezed the 640-page second edition into a few pithy rules.

Committed to cogent syntheses of complex concepts in librarianship, American Libraries presents—in handy bookmark form—the most concise AACR2 to date. (Gorman has hinted at a one-sentence AACR2.)

Rule 1. Describe the item you have in hand. Record the following details in this order and with this punctuation:

Title : subtitle / author's name as given ; names of other persons or bodies named on the title page, label, container, title frame, etc. —— Edition (abbreviated). —— Place of publication : Publisher, Year of publication.

Number of pages, volumes, discs, reels, objects, etc. ; Dimensions of the object (metric). —— (Name of series)

Descriptive notes

Examples of descriptions

i) His last bow : some reminiscences of Sherlock Holmes / A. Conan Doyle. —— London : Murray, 1917.
305 p. ; 20 cm. —— (Murray's fiction library)

ii) A white sport coat and a pink crustacean / Jimmy Buffett. —— New York : ABC, 1973.
1 sound disc ; 12 in.
Backing by the Coral Reefer Band.

iii) Little Ernie's big day / by Norma Eustace ; designed by Doris Manier. —— 2nd ed. —— Chicago: Little Folks, 1980.
1 filmstrip ; 35 mm. —— (Big day filmstrips)

If the item is a serial (periodical, etc.), add the numbering of the first issue before the place of publication and leave the date and number of volumes "open" as in this example:

Circulation systems review. —— Vol. 1, no. 1 - . —— New Orleans : Borax Press, 1980– v. ; 25 cm.

Rule 2. Make as many copies of the description as are necessary and add to each the name of the author and of other persons or bodies associated with the work.

Rule 2A. Give the names of people in their best known form.

Wodehouse, P.G.
Buffett, Jimmy
Harris, Emmylou
Seuss, Dr.

Rule 2B. Give the names of corporate bodies in their best known form.

Yale University
Coral Reefer Band
Newberry Library

If a corporate body is part of another body, give it as a subheading *only if* it has an indistinct (blah) name.

United States. Department of the Interior
F. W. Woolworth Company. Personnel Division
University of Michigan. Library.

Cataloging and the New Technologies

Michael Gorman

Editor's Introduction

By the time he reached his late thirties, Michael Gorman had established himself as an important figure in the history of cataloging through his creation of what is now the International Standard Bibliographical Description (ISBD). Later he was joint editor of the second edition of the *Anglo-American Cataloguing Rules (AACR2).* After completing most of his work on *AACR2,* Gorman presented his vision of the nature of a truly computerized catalog at institutes in 1975 and 1977 presented by the Information Science and Automation Division (ISAD)* of the American Library Association.

At the time Gorman wrote, catalogs were beginning to change from a fixed display, whether on cards or in book form, to a more easily updated and even portable form, in computer output microform or in online form. These changes in physical format entail not only a new form of display, Gorman claims, but also conceptual changes in the nature of the catalog. Existing catalogs, even though they were presented in new formats, were still conceptually in card form.

One of the first concepts to be revised is that of main entry. Main entry used to be the principal entry, the one to which references referred, in the bookform catalog. In card

---

*Now called the Library and Information Technology Association.

catalogs, main entry had the tasks of identifying the chief access to a bibliographic record and pointing to the work and edition in question in the subject portion of the catalog. Often it was also the repository of up-to-date information about the secondary entries, often called tracings, made for that record. One might argue that these functions could be logically distinguished in the bookform catalog's main entry. In an online catalog, however, main entry has no place as the repository of tracings. If computer algorithms were sufficiently advanced, main entry might not be the item to which references referred; if a heading other than the established one were requested, the computer could respond either by presenting all the records under the non-established but requested form of name or by presenting the records under the established form of name. In either case, main entry would no longer fulfill its traditional role.

Main entry has also fulfilled other functions, such as providing a standard form by which to identify a work. To eliminate confusion, Gorman invents the term *standard citation* to stand for an established way of citing a work or referring to a name in a catalog; standard citation provides "an indication of the standard manner of citing the name of each person and each body and the title of each work."† Variant forms of the name of a person or body are linked to one another in what Gorman calls a *package*. Packages of name forms are linked to packages of works, subjects, or even descriptions of particular physical items. Each package has a preferred form of name, title, etc. To the user, this standardized form need not be the only access; far from it: any access point will provide an identical amount of information.

Standardized citations can be varied in response to varying environments; Gorman cites as examples the different ways in which names of countries and prefixes to surnames are handled from language to language. In short, while standard forms vary from place to place, the technology of an online catalog is able to make the catalog receptive to all of them. Gorman points out, however, that standard citations are not always required; it may be surmised that their use would be limited to printed catalogs and subarrangement for materials under a given subject, for example.

---

†See reprint page 244 in this volume.

When reading Gorman's paper, one can readily appreciate that codes like AACR2 were not written with the revaluation of cataloging objectives Gorman has in mind. Rather, they were based on the conceptual structure of card catalogs. While a future machine cataloging code may have objectives differing from those described in Gorman, the compilers of such a code must almost surely undertake the reevaluation called for by Gorman.

If Gorman's idea of standard citation is taken seriously, much of the debate about codes free from main entry loses its point; it appears the debate has revolved around ambiguous definitions of *main entry*. On the other hand, if works can have standard citations, as Gorman seems to claim, then one must assume that it makes sense to talk of *works*. Many of the articles printed in this volume bear heavily on this point, especially those by Pettee, Verona, and Lubetzky ("Objectives").

The original printing of this article includes a summary of discussion among participants in the ISAD institute. One questioner asked whether economic constraints on the size of a microform catalog were sufficient to prohibit the provision of multiple full entries; references would then have to be used just as they are in card and book catalogs. Gorman accepted the existence of the constraints and pointed out that they will not exist in an online catalog in which the computer could take the referenced form of name and present the user with full information. It is in this light that Gorman's article should read.

One reason that the catalog envisioned by Gorman has not yet been implemented on a large scale is because of the present lack of fast-acting but transitory global change algorithms in online catalog systems today. But progress towards these procedures is being made, and the reevaluation urged by Gorman will surely be required.

MC

Cataloging and the New Technologies

My interest in the new technologies in technical services in libraries arises from the simple belief that technology, if intelligently applied, can bring three important benefits. It can improve the efficiency of our service to library users; it can enable us to spend our limited resources more sensibly; and it can improve the nature of the work of all employed in the library. The last of these advantages is too often ignored. In our precomputer systems much library work consists of mindless drudgery which is an insult to the intelligence of those who carry it out. Who would willingly spend their days filing cards in a card catalog? The ideal of a technically improved library system can be found in the words of William Morris written nearly one hundred years ago: "[W]ork in a duly ordered community should be made attractive by the consciousness of usefulness, by its being carried on with intelligent interest, by variety, and by its being exercised amidst pleasurable surroundings." (William Morris, *Useful Work versus Useless Toil,* 1885) I believe that that ideal is as valid now as then, and that it constitutes a primary factor in the appeal of the new technologies. Efficiency is not the only criterion, we must also pursue the improvement of the lot of the library worker.

An interesting aspect of the new technology is the widespread fear of change and cynicism about change among many people who might expect to benefit from it. This is, of course, due in great part to an entirely understandable reaction to the ills, real and imagined, that can be seen as resulting from many modern technical advances. I strongly believe that we must cultivate a more positive attitude towards change in the field of library work, and that this attitude must pervade all levels of librarianship. It is evident that library administrators and library educators have a great responsibility in this respect. Only when this more positive attitude is widespread can we begin to achieve the real benefits of the new technology, because only when new systems are enthusiastically applied by people who believe in what they are doing will a new era in librarianship be achieved.

A common attitude to the mechanization of library technical services is that the machine can be used to accomplish many of our current practices more quickly.

Reprinted by permission of the American Library Association from *The Nature and Future of the Catalog,* ed. Maurice J. Freedman and S. Michael Malinconico, pp. 127-36; published by Oryx Press, copyright © 1979 by the American Library Association.

In my opinion this approach is incorrect, and the use of computers to speed up and perpetuate outdated systems is a perversion of technology. I wish to show that the best use of mechanization will be founded on a complete reconsideration of all of our systems, an examination of what we are doing and why we are doing it. If this process leads to radical change, so be it. If it means the abandonment of cherished ideas of the past, then let us abandon those ideas. I must emphasize that this does not mean a supine acceptance of temporary technical and financial limitations of the present stage of automation. In this country it is scarcely necessary to point out that what human beings can imagine, human beings can do. We should think of the eventual possibilities of machine systems and what they can achieve, and not be diverted by short- or medium-term problems.

I intend to examine a number of the changes that the computer has made, is making, or will make to cataloging. I hope that these will demonstrate the extent and nature of those changes and show the direction in which we should be moving.

First, let us look at the physical nature of the end product of our work: the catalog. Too often the prevalent attitude towards the physical form of the catalog is that expressed by a student of mine in an essay which began "As well as normal catalogues there are book and microfilm catalogues." I will divide these forms into what I call the *old* forms (that is, the card and the book catalogs) and the *new* forms (that is, the microform catalog produced from machine-readable records and the online computer catalog). If we contrast these two categories, certain qualitative and quantitative differences become apparent. The old forms are either unique (that is, located in one place) or, in the case of the book catalog, expensive to duplicate and heavy to transport. The new forms can be made available in many places, both inside and outside the library. The old forms are perpetually and inescapably out of date. The new forms are capable of speedy updating and near complete currency. The old forms are inflexible in that they allow limited and highly structured access to information. The new forms, either because of their nature (as with the online computer catalog) or because of the cheapness of the material on which they are produced (as with microform catalogs) allow the possibility of many more points of access to information. The old forms arise out of previous technologies, and have the restrictions and limitations of those technologies. The new forms arise out of our current and emerging technologies, and do not suffer from those restrictions and limitations.

These changes in the physical form of the catalog have implications which go far beyond changes in form or even in improvements in speed and convenience to the catalog user. They should be seen as changing the nature of what we are doing, or, at least, as forcing a reconsideration of our cataloging practices. To take an obvious example, in a new catalog how does our old friend the main entry fare? To attempt to answer this question I must go beyond the physical form of the catalog and delineate the machine-readable catalog record of the future.

As with all emerging technologies, the computerization of catalog records has had to develop both technically and conceptually. It has had to go through various stages, each of which is both a prerequisite of, and paradoxically a hindrance to, the next stage. It is only now, after 15 years, that we can see the shape of computer records of the future. Those records will be true products of their technology, as opposed to what we have now—a computer record which amounts to little more than an electronic version of a familiar and much-loved

artifact measuring approximately three inches by five inches. The developed catalog record that is emerging is multilayered and multidimensional. It uses computer
technology to achieve far more than the mere mechanization of catalog entry
production. (See Diagram 1.) You will see from this diagram that information
relating to a particular item, which is at present contained in machine records as a
single unitary set of information, is presented in the developed machine system in a
number of *linked packages* of information. So, there are individual packages
relating to the names of a person, to the names of a corporate body, to the titles of
a work, to a subject, and to the description of a particular physical item. These are,
as is shown in the diagram, linked to each other when they apply to an item or
group of items. To take a fairly simple example, we can imagine a user who is
searching for information about a particular edition of Dante's *Divine Comedy*. The
user can approach the system by name, by title, by subject, etc. In this instance,
let us imagine that the approach is by one of the forms of name by which Dante is
identified—ALIGHIERI. This name would give access to the package of information
relating to Dante. This package will include two important pieces of information.
First, that the standard form of citation for Dante is DANTE ALIGHIERI. Second,
that that name is linked with a number of works, among which is one sometimes
identified as the DIVINE COMEDY. The work package contains the information
that the standard title for the work is DIVINA COMMEDIA. It also contains links
with packages describing particular manifestations of the work. The user would
then be presented, on a screen or in a print-out, with the information about the
standard citations of the work and descriptions of those editions which were
English translations entitled the DIVINE COMEDY. This process of assembling
and presenting information is done automatically within the machine system by
program and it is done extremely quickly. The user is only aware of the way in
which the assembled information is presented to him or her. The example I have
used is extremely simple. Other packages relating to the work and its manifestations
are also present in the system. For example, there will be links to individual parts of
the DIVINE COMEDY (INFERNO, PURGATORIO, etc.); to series in which
items have been issued; and to the subjects, names, and titles of the work, its parts,
and of the series.

I do not wish to discuss the mechanisms by which this developed record
works, but to concentrate on it conceptually. In looking at this diagrammatic
representation of the system, we can see the essential difference between it and
catalog entries or bibliographic records found in previous systems. Because of the
way in which the developed record is structured, it is possible to approach information from any level, and by way of any access point within one of those packages.
For example, if a series package is associated with subject packages, information
relating to that series will be retrieved in a subject search. It is here that the multi-
dimensionality of the developed machine system lies.

I embarked on this somewhat lengthy description of a system with a question
about the main entry. In fact, I believe that the idea of the main entry as a particular physical entity in the catalog arose out of our previous technologies. What
remains of the main-entry idea is the fact that the developed machine system, if it
is to be capable of carrying out all its functions, allows for, and indeed demands,
an indication of the standard manner of citing the name of each person and each
body and the title of each work. In the example I used there is a standard citation

DIAGRAM 1

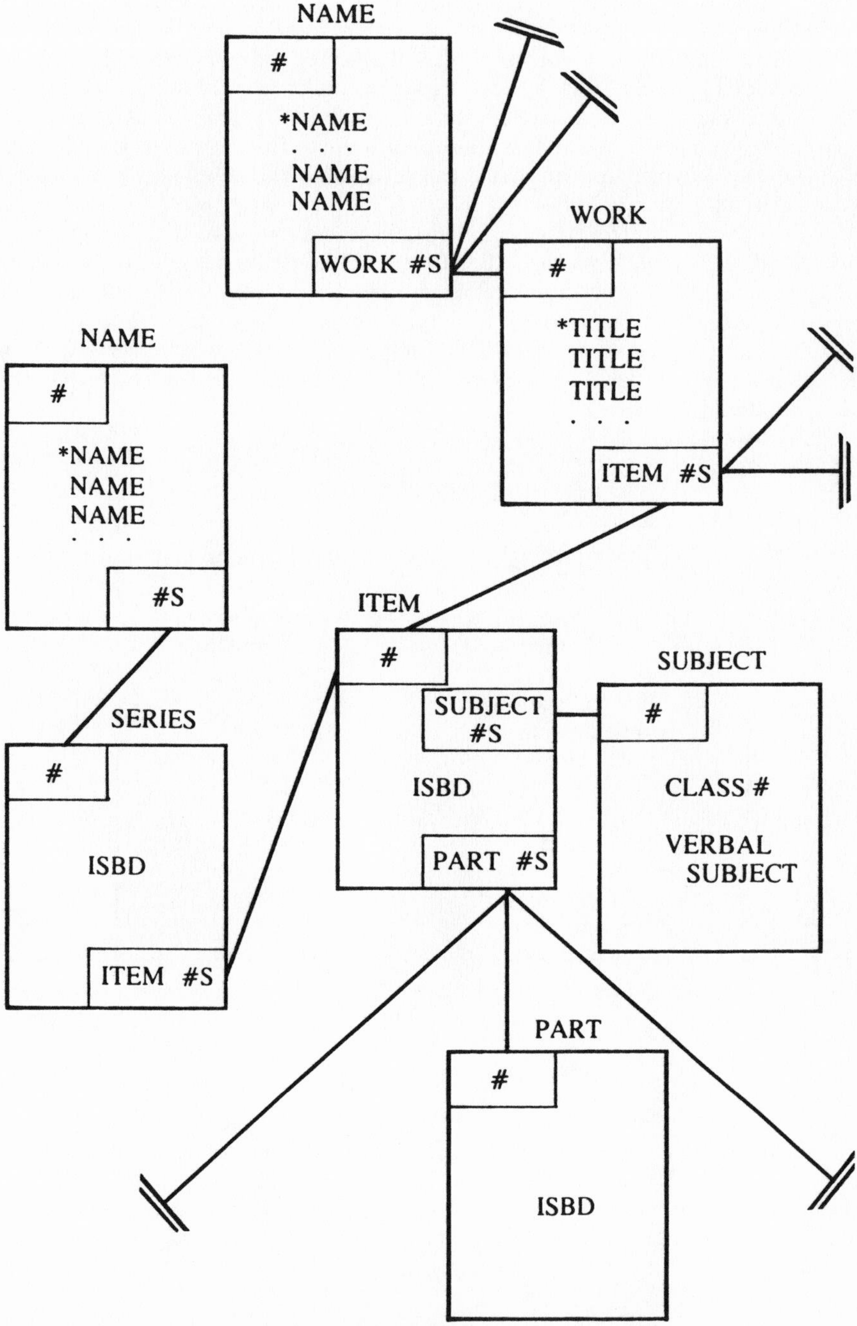

NAME

```
┌─────────────────────────┐
│ ┌───────┐               │
│ │ #     │               │
│ └───────┘               │
│   *NAME                 │
│    . . .                │
│   NAME                  │
│   NAME                  │
│         ┌───────────────┤
│         │ WORK #S       │
└─────────┴───────────────┘
```

WORK

```
┌─────────────────────────┐
│ ┌───────┐               │
│ │ #     │               │
│ └───────┘               │
│   *TITLE                │
│   TITLE                 │
│   TITLE                 │
│    . . .                │
│         ┌───────────────┤
│         │ ITEM #S       │
└─────────┴───────────────┘
```

NAME

```
┌─────────────────────────┐
│ ┌───────┐               │
│ │ #     │               │
│ └───────┘               │
│   *NAME                 │
│   NAME                  │
│   NAME                  │
│    . . .                │
│              ┌──────────┤
│              │ #S       │
└──────────────┴──────────┘
```

ITEM

```
┌─────────────────────────┐
│ ┌───────┐               │
│ │ #     │               │
│ └───────┤ SUBJECT       │
│         │ #S            │
│         └───────        │
│   ISBD                  │
│                         │
│         ┌───────────────┤
│         │ PART #S       │
└─────────┴───────────────┘
```

SUBJECT

```
┌─────────────────────────┐
│ ┌───────┐               │
│ │ #     │               │
│ └───────┘               │
│   CLASS #               │
│                         │
│   VERBAL                │
│   SUBJECT               │
│                         │
└─────────────────────────┘
```

SERIES

```
┌─────────────────────────┐
│ ┌───────┐               │
│ │ #     │               │
│ └───────┘               │
│   ISBD                  │
│                         │
│         ┌───────────────┤
│         │ ITEM #S       │
└─────────┴───────────────┘
```

PART

```
┌─────────────────────────┐
│ ┌───────┐               │
│ │ #     │               │
│ └───────┘               │
│   ISBD                  │
│                         │
└─────────────────────────┘
```

THE DEVELOPED MACHINE RECORD

for Dante and a standard citation for the *Divine Comedy*. As the link between them will contain an indication of their relationship (in this case, that of primary responsibility or *authorship*), the standard citation for the work emerges as DANTE ALIGHIERI. DIVINA COMMEDIA. This enables the machine system to fulfill all the remaining useful purposes of the main-entry idea. Individual items can, however, be equally accessed by any variant forms of that name or of that title. What has happened is that we have been released from the tyranny of the idea that there is only one place in which full information is to be found, and that there is only one way in which an item should be approached. We are left with the concept of standard citation.

The likely contents of two of the packages of information are: (1) a name package and (2) a work package. (See Diagram 2.) The replacement of the main-entry idea by that of a standard citation can readily be seen. In the name package there is a place for the preferred form of the name. In the work package there is a place for the preferred form of the title. Each package will contain links which not only connect one package to another but also define precisely the nature of the relationship between them.

DIAGRAM 2

NAME PACKAGE	WORK PACKAGE
Control number	Control number
Preferred form of name	Preferred title
Other forms	Other titles
Different spelling	. . .
Romanization	Additions
Standard	Language
Others	Date
Pseudonyms	Etc.
Real name	Linking numbers
Dates	
Full forenames	
Cutter number	
Linking numbers	

It is evident that the work of the cataloger in preparing these packages is very different from the work involved in preparing conventional catalog entries. (See Diagram 3.) Diagram 3 illustrates a different symbolic representation of the developed machine record. In this diagram a complete aggregation of related information is presented, rather simplistically, as a set of building blocks. Using this analogy, the task of the cataloger can be seen as that of constructing new building blocks and fitting them into an existing structure. These new modules will be standard descriptions of items newly acquired, new subject packages, new name packages, and new work packages. Once these are created, the cataloger must perceive the links between new and existing packages, and build them into the system. Familiar injunctions such as "Enter under . . ." seem to have been lost. In fact, in many applications the choice of main entry (or standard citation) is unimportant. A standard description will be accessible by a number of characteristics, each of which has equal validity. As far as the user is concerned, all access points are main access points because they all provide an equal amount of information. In other applications the choice of standard forms is very important, so this task remains when constructing multipurpose records.

DIAGRAM 3

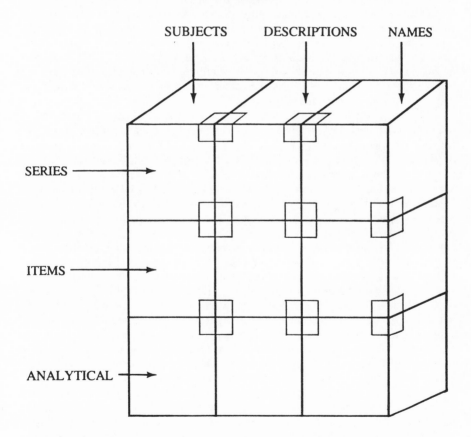

MODULAR NATURE OF THE DEVELOPED MACHINE RECORD

Diagram 3 also demonstrates the multidimensional nature of the developed machine record. The subject of a series, an item, or a part are equally accessible, as are the names associated with a series, an item, or a part. The user can approach information either (in terms of this diagram) horizontally, that is, at one level containing subject, name, and descriptive information; or vertically, that is, by category of information irrespective of level. The catalog no longer has to concentrate on one level of information to the complete or partial exclusion of all others.

We have seen that the work of the cataloger is different in that these packages of information are prepared individually, but it is the same in that such work demands as much, if not more, professionalism and commitment to standardization as before. There is one further important difference between such work and conventional cataloging; this lies in the fact that the element of repetition that our present system demands is all but eliminated. Once a package of information is established and its links to other packages are made, it remains as the package for that name, subject, item, etc., and subsequent work connected with the same data consists simply of citing the control number for that package in the appropriate field. Thus the machine system can be used to eliminate busywork and to leave the cataloger with the task of establishing new information in a standard manner, that is, the truly professional task. To return briefly to the quotation from Morris, I believe that this aspect of technological change goes a long way towards the realization of the ideal of "useful" work.

Another change that technology can bring to cataloging is the possibility of resolving what have hitherto been considered irreconcilable problems. Take, for example, Russian names. (See Diagram 4.) No one has yet come up with a satisfactory solution to the problem of whether one should use a romanized form of name or the *popular* English form of name. Another instance is the difference between the English and North American practices in adding dates to personal names. In English practice they are added only when there is a conflict; in North American practice they are added, when available, in anticipation of conflict. Another instance is that of the choice between pseudonyms and *real* names of persons. Other instances of unresolved or partially resolved conflicts of this type abound in our precomputer cataloging codes. Using a developed machine-readable record these problems can be resolved. First, the question of whether one uses the systematic or *popular* form of name for a Russian: In the developed machine system, each of these forms will be present, and each will be accompanied by an indication of the type of name. A particular printed catalog using that record could select, by program, the form which is preferred for that catalog. Even within one library one could use the systematic form for a general catalog and the *popular* form for a reading list. The other example, that of dates added to personal names, is resolved by the fact that, in the name package I showed you, the dates are held separately. These dates are recorded when the package is created (or subsequently) and remain in the package only to be printed when conflict occurs. In that way, the irreconcilable problem in our premachine systems—the necessity to record dates and use them or not to record them at all—is overcome. They are recorded in all instances, but only used in instances where they are relevant and necessary. Again we see that the impact of technology is to alter the cataloging task and to alter the nature of the decisions that the catalogers have to make.

DIAGRAM 4

Romanization
> EVTUSHENKO, Evgenii Aleksandrovich
> or
> YEVTUSHENKO, Yevgeny Alexandrovitch

Dates
> FUTZENHAMMER, Shamus
> or
> FUTZENHAMMER, Shamus, 1871-1970

Entry element
> GOGH, Vincent van
> or
> VAN GOGH, Vincent
> or
> ?

An impact of computer technology which has already occurred is the systematization of the description of library materials. This was brought about by the introduction of *International Standard Bibliographic Description (ISBD)*. I do not wish to discuss the merits or demerits of this particular way of systematizing description, but to make some deductions from its occurrence. The *ISBD* has been through a lengthy process of development. It will be seen that the second edition of *AACR* contains a complete scheme for the description of library materials based on *ISBD*. A fundamental aspect of *ISBD* is that the description is formalized in two ways. First, in the standard order in which the elements of the description are presented. Second, in the formalized punctuation that is used to separate one element of the description from another. This formalization was intended to have two purposes. The first was to enable the automatic translation of human-readable data into machine-readable data. Fairly simple programs can be used to recognize the various elements of the description. The second, and to my mind, much more important, purpose was to aid the human comprehension of descriptive data. Here we can see the interaction of machine systems and cataloging standards: The desire to make information more understandable to the user meets the necessity in the machine system for pieces of information (in this case elements of descriptive data) to be clearly delimited. Some people have said that this implies some kind of sacrifice of standards and the imposition of alien conventions on cataloging. I would reject both of these assertions as it seems to me that the systemization arises from an increased desire to communicate and from an enhanced understanding of the interaction of cataloging and machine- and human-readable systems. This interaction is entirely desirable and furnishes a good example of the sort of cooperation and growth that should take place in the future.

The *ISBD* system is widely used throughout the world and in our own English-speaking cataloging community. No such universal system exists for the formulation of headings and uniform titles, though there has been much discussion of the possibilities of such a system. There are a number of reasons why this universal system does not exist. The most important reasons are that the differences between different codes are far greater as far as access points are concerned than they were as far as description was concerned; and the fact that the question of the choice and form of headings is perceived to be far more important in its implications than the question of description.

We have, I would suggest, arrived at a point where many of the differences regarding access points are either resolved or on the point of resolution because of the introduction of machine systems. In a developed machine system a name package can carry a number of preferred forms of name, each of which is accompanied by an indication of the environment in which it is preferred. For example, the name package for the government of the U.S.A. can include the forms *United States, Etats-Unis,* and *Estados Unidos* with an indication that these are the preferred forms in an English language, French language, and Spanish language environment, respectively. Thus the machine can be used to resolve a fundamental problem in international standardization. There still remain certain problems that cannot be resolved by the manipulation of name packages. One problem which is representative of these is the question of standard entry element for persons with family names that include a prefix. Some codes enter all such names under the part following the prefix, others (as in the case of *AACR*) base the decision on the language of the person bearing the name, and others base the decision on the nationality of the person. There are two ways to solve this problem. We can either aim at complete international agreement on entry elements or we can use the computer to arrive at a solution acceptable to all. This second solution presupposes that there is no one way to enter such a name. The cataloger's task is to recognize and code each element of the name, and to add other necessary indications. Programs can then be used to cite the name in the form appropriate to a particular output. (See Diagram 4.) If we take the example of the name VINCENT VAN GOGH, we find that it consists of three elements: a forename VINCENT, a prefix VAN, and a main element of surname GOGH. The cataloger would add codes to each of these and an indication of the language of the person, the nationality, etc. An *AACR* program would use the indication that the person's language was Dutch to assemble the name for printing in the form GOGH, VINCENT VAN. Other systems would use different programs to achieve different results.

The implication of all this is that we no longer need an international code of cataloging rules, whether based on the Paris Principles or not, because of the introduction of machine systems. We no longer need a single solution to each problem. The machine allows us to choose between a range of options, in a standard and controlled manner, and permits these options to be selected by program depending on the purpose for which a particular record is used. To return to a prevailing theme of this paper—the impact of technology on the work of the cataloger—the cataloger is then entrusted with the task of analyzing data and ensuring that alternative treatments are possible. He or she is no longer required to decide on one solution, and is therefore no longer presented with the kind of invidious choice that our present rules demand.

My last instance of the changes being brought about by technology is that which is commonly, though inaccurately, known as alphabetical filing. Modern filing rules, such as those developed by John Rather for the Library of Congress and those being developed by the American Library Association and by the British Library Filing Rules Committee, are much simpler than their predecessors. This simplicity depends, to a great extent, on a principle which states that one should file a character as it is and not as if it were something else (Diagram 5). For example, the number 3 occurring in a title is filed as a number, in with other numbers, and in an order dictated by its numerical significance. One does not file it as if it were *t-h-r-e-e* or *d-r-e-i* or *t-r-o-i-s*. This change has resulted from a reconsideration of all our filing practices which itself resulted from the use of the computer in filing. This does not mean that it would be impossible to file 3 as if it were a word, in fact such a thing is perfectly simple. What it does mean is that the use of the computer in filing has made it necessary to look at our filing practices and to ask ourselves why we file one thing as if it were something else. The conclusion that most of us have come to is that such a practice may have had some validity in the past but has no validity now. It now seems a manifest absurdity to say that if this elephant were an orange, it would file in such-and-such a place. This is an illogical premise upon which to base an agreement. An elephant is not an orange, it belongs with the elephants and not with the oranges. Why, again, have we chosen to file names beginning with *Mc* as if they began with *Mac*? The answer is that they (almost) sound the same. Why base an aberration in arrangement on sound? These are awkward questions which the process of mechanizing filing poses. I do not wish to argue for one filing arrangement or another, though I do believe that the simpler the arrangement and the fewer the rules, the more chance users have of finding information speedily. I wish merely to point out that the reconsideration of filing practices which was necessitated by the introduction of computer filing has been a healthy and fruitful process. It has made us examine every aspect of the process, to stop doing things out of habit, to retain those principles which are logical and comprehensible and to discard those which are simply the accretions of the years. I strongly urge that the type of reconsideration we have given to filing practices should be applied throughout the whole range of cataloging practices.

Technology can bring three important benefits. The first of these is an improvement of the efficiency of our service to library users; for example, the user of a developed machine system can approach information at many levels and from many access points. The second benefit is that we are able to use our limited resources more sensibly; for instance, using a machine to arrange entries is more efficient and more cost-effective than using people to carry out that task, also the elimination of redundant and repetitive work of all kinds is something that tends towards efficiency and cost-effectiveness. The third benefit is the improvement of the nature of the work of those engaged in cataloging and other technical services. I hope I have demonstrated that the advent of the computer does not imply the abolition or the lessening of standards, that it does not imply the reduction of cataloging as a professional task, and that there is as much room for standards and for expertise in a computerized system as there ever has been. Furthermore, that the computer can be used, and is already being used, to eliminate drudgery, busywork, and useless toil in library systems.

DIAGRAM 5

Filing

1 man . . .
2 femmes . . .
3 groschenoper. . .

or

dreadnought . . .
3 groschenoper . . .
Drell, Heinrich

and

trespasser . . .
3 femmes . . .
Trondheim . . .

I would like to close now with another quotation from William Morris in a vision that he had of the future: "All work which would be irksome to do by hand is done by immensely improved machinery; and in all work which it is a pleasure to do by hand machinery is done without." (That was, alas, from Chapter 15 of William Morris's *News from Nowhere,* 1890.)

The Catalog as
Access Mechanism:
Background and Concepts

Patrick Wilson

Editor's Introduction

Patrick Wilson, a professor at the Graduate School of Library and Information Studies, University of California at Berkeley, began his career teaching philosophy. When he turned to library and information science, he began to examine under a philosopher's microscope some of the basic tenets of his new field, particularly those pertaining to bibliographic control. In the following selection, Wilson looks at what catalogs are supposed to do and how well they do it. He begins with Cutter's statement of the objectives of the catalog.

Cutter's first objective is that a catalog should enable us to find a book, of which either the author, title, or subject is known. But, observes Wilson, most libraries do not help us to find a book in the sense of finding its actual location. For this, in addition to catalog information, we must know whether the book is out on loan, lost, in storage, etc. Only libraries with online catalogs incorporating circulation information can effectively fulfill the finding function of the catalog.

But there are other difficulties relating to the finding function of the catalog. As Wilson reads Cutter, his first objective addresses only books, and, even more specifically, books within a given library. Books, however, are physical objects; it is a mistake to believe users are interested in these.

Rather, they are interested in the texts that are embodied or manifested in them. Further, users' interests are not necessarily limited spatially; that is, they may be interested not only in what is immediately accessible in a given library, but also in what can be obtained by recalling books, fetching them from storage, or ordering them on inter-library loan. The catalog is an access tool, and accessibility (finding) admits of degree.

Wilson also finds problematic Cutter's second objective, which is to show what the library has by a given author, on a given subject, or in a given kind of literature. Most catalogs do not assemble all the works of a given author. For instance, it is usually too costly to make analytics, to make access points for all authors making distinct contributions to a given publication. The question of which access points to make raises a corollary question of what should be taken as the basic cataloging unit. The Anglo-American cataloging rules for entry are based on the stated assumption of the primacy of the work.* Wilson questions the tenability of taking the work as the basic cataloging unit on the grounds that often there is no operational way of distinguishing the texts of a given work: when is a translation so putative as to no longer be a translation? A philosopher's question, it may be argued; however, failure to address in a straightforward way the definition of *work* has led to inconsistencies in cataloging practice, particularly in treating kinship relations (such as translations and editions) among families of texts.

It would appear, then, that we are far from achieving the objectives of the catalog as stated by Cutter. Wilson, however, sees no cause for concern in this. The bibliographic universe, he observes, is self-organizing. There are many ways to discover books. The library catalog is only one component of a vast and complex bibliographic apparatus. As such, it need not be the sole or definitive guide to the bibliographic universe.

ES

Anglo-American Cataloguing Rules, 2d ed., prepared by the American Library Association, the British Library, the Canadian Committee on Cataloguing [and] the Library of Congress (Chicago: American Library Association, 1978), 277.

Further Reading

Wilson, Patrick. *Two Kinds of Power: An Essay on Bibliographical Control.* Berkeley: University of California Press, 1968.

Wilson looks at the purposes and means of bibliographical control and, in so doing, uncovers difficulties in such bibliographic activities as describing what constitutes the bibliographic universe and determining the subject of a book.

See also Verona, "Literary Unit Versus Bibliographical Unit" and Lubetzky, "The Objectives of the Catalog," both of which are reprinted in this volume and touch on the objectives of the catalog and the concept of *work*.

The Catalog as Access Mechanism: Background and Concepts

I want to consider what catalogs are supposed to do; how and to what extent they do it; and what differences it makes to our notions of goals and methods when we think of an online catalog instead of a card, book, or microform catalog. I take the standpoint not of a cataloger, which I'm not, but of one interested in the whole bibliographical universe and the various ways in which we try to organize and exploit it. By *bibliographical universe,* I mean the whole body of public records of talking and writing. Published records are central, but we can consider unpublished records as part of the bibliographical universe if they are accessible to the public. Records of activities other than talking and writing—of painting and drawing and composing music, for example—are outside my scope. Insofar as people's talking and writing has permanent effect, it does so in two quite different ways, one very concrete and one quite abstract. Concretely, some marks are made on paper, or some traces left on a piece of magnetic tape; abstractly, a certain string of words has been produced—a certain text. For historical purposes the original manuscript or other original physical record is of enormous importance, but from another standpoint, the crucial thing about what one says or writes down is simply that it specifies a definite sequence of words, a definite text, that can appear again and again in different physical manifestations. The words are not likely to be new; only the particular choice and order are new—and they may not be very new. The text may incorporate strings of words that resulted from one's own or other people's prior performances; it may be almost nothing but others' strings of words, cut up and stuck end to end with a bit of transition supplied. The first published appearance of the text, the first edition, if there is one, may be the only appearance; for most texts the first edition is also the last. If this were so for all texts, life would be easier for catalogers. But the first appearance may be just the beginning. The same text may appear again and again, separately or as part of a longer string, as in an anthology. And the text may serve as the basis for the production of new related texts that constitute new *versions* of the old text: rethinking and correcting mistakes lead to revised versions of the initial text; expansion and elaboration to enlarged versions; simplification and contraction to abridged versions; recasting in other styles or literary genres to adaptations; addition by someone else of critical

Reprinted by permission of the American Library Association, "The Catalog as Access Mechanism: Background Concepts," by Patrick Wilson from *Library Technology and Technical Services* 27:1, pp. 4-17 (Jan.-Mar. 1983); 1983 American Library Association.

apparatus to critical editions; and, of course, translation into other languages. Others may produce their own texts that expound the first text, that imitate it, that summarize and criticize it, that attempt to refute or defend or improve on it, and so on indefinitely. These can be called *derivatives* from the first text. Once in the bibliographical universe, a text can become an ancestor of a huge family of other texts related to it in an immense variety of ways and degrees; and any of these near and remote relatives, versions and derivatives, might have one or many published appearances, and start its own family of related texts. This universe of texts, each making one or more published appearances and in one or more versions, is the world to which the catalog is to give entry.

You'll recognize this talk of text and published appearance as something like the familiar distinction between *literary unit* and *bibliographical unit* or between a *book* and the *work* it contains.[1] Some such distinction is inescapable. I prefer to talk about texts and related texts: versions and derivatives, than to talk of works or literary units. I know how to tell if two publications contain the same text or not—they do if they contain the same sequence of words—but I'm not sure I know how to tell if two publications contain the same work or not. The trouble is that we seem to be required to make an either/or decision: either two texts are texts of the same work or they are not. But the relations among texts are endlessly complex; there are so many possible gradations and shadings of relationship, that I find it quite hopeless to look for a general rule or principle according to which I could make that either/or decision. How much can a text be revised before it becomes a different work? How exact does a translation have to be to count as a translation of the same work? I think there is no general way of answering such questions, and thus doubt the possibility of clarifying the notion of a work. There may be a useful distinction to be made between work and text, but I don't know what it is. For now, we'll simply do without the notion of a work.

The bibliographical universe is in a certain sense a self-organizing world: there are organizing devices internal to the world. We think most readily of the big independent periodical indexes, abstracting services, published catalogs, national bibliographies, comprehensive subject bibliographies as constituting *the* bibliographical apparatus. These are designed to be instruments of bibliographical control, by which I mean instruments of discovery, allowing first the discovery of the very existence of a text or book and then the discovery of where copies can be found. The bibliographical universe is not under effective bibliographical control until anyone can discover those of its inhabitants that will suit his or her purposes, whatever those purposes may be. A serious explorer of the bibliographical universe may manage to avoid use of those big independent bibliographical works, relying instead on the network of references within the nonbibliographical literature; there is more than one way to skin a cat, and the big formal bibliographical works are not the only means of discovery. One might have satisfactory bibliographical control of the universe of texts without relying on the formal bibliographical apparatus at all. But in fact that apparatus is often essential as a means of discovery of other elements in that universe. Now just what place is the catalog supposed to have in the whole array of bibliographical instruments? The catalog of a particular library is just one more piece of bibliography among thousands of others. What is it supposed to do that the other bibliographical works don't, or don't do so well? What does it do that wouldn't be done, or wouldn't be done so well, if you didn't have it but did have everything else?

If we want to know what a library catalog is supposed to do, the best place to start is Cutter's classic statement of the "objects" of a catalog, which has been repeated with minor modifications by practically everyone who discusses the nature of the catalog.[2] Cutter says, and everybody agrees, that the first objective is to enable a person to find a book of which either the author or the title or the subject is known. Three questions arise in my mind at once. First: seriously, Is the catalog to enable us to find a book? Then it should tell us where the book is. Up to now, it has not generally done so. It has given a theoretical location: a call number. But the books that I want seem rarely to be at their theoretical locations; they're on loan, in process, lost, in storage, misshelved, or waiting to be reshelved. To find the actual location, one has to consult circulation records which, with luck, will tell one where the book actually is or, at least, when it is expected to be returned to the library. Up to now, one has often had to consult at least two files to find out where a book was; the catalog gave only the theoretical location. The situation changes when the catalog goes online; now the two separate files could be merged, and the single catalog could tell you, if not precisely where in space the book was, at least what its current status was. Now the catalog would come closer to being able to do what it was supposed to do.

But which books are these that the catalog is supposed to enable me to find? The books *in* the library? No, of course not, the books that the library *has*. But is that quite right? Isn't it somewhat narrow-minded? Isn't it true that what happens to be "owned" by a particular institution is only a part of what's actually *available* at that place? The library can supply me with a book it doesn't own but borrows from another library. If the library owns a book but it's not actually available and won't be available for weeks or months, it may be able to provide me with a copy that it doesn't own. I recently read an LC copy of a book, all the local copies of which had disappeared. Why limit the catalog to things owned but perhaps not actually available? Why not extend it to cover things available through the library, whether or not owned by the library? The fact that things available from other sources are not instantly available is nothing to the point, for half the books the library owns that I want aren't instantly available either. Only the noncirculating library can come close to guaranteeing that the things the library owns will be instantly available in their theoretical locations; but even it can make available things it doesn't own, after some delay. Why tie the catalog to the notion of ownership? One good reason is that almost everything in the bibliographical universe is potentially available at any library; if the interlibrary lending system is working as it should, I ought to be able to get almost anything after perhaps a long wait. And so the local catalog should list everything that anyone is willing to lend; and that would make it a big catalog, impracticably big. But does that mean an impossible catalog in principle? Surely not; a stratified catalog, divided into zones of accessibility, in which you first look in the local zone, then move to a next-proximate zone, then to a further one, is in principle perfectly possible, and would be a better tool for finding a book than present catalogs limited to what's locally owned.

Finally: Find a *book*? Why a *book*? Well, of course we want to enable people to find phonograph records and newspapers and so on; the catalog need not be limited to books. But that's not the point. Books are not the only things identifiable by author and title and subject; so are the texts that books contain. I may know perfectly well what text I want without knowing what book or books, if any, it appears in. Don't we want to say that the catalog is meant to allow one to find copies of texts? You can't just find a text; it has to appear in some physical form. But if it's the text that one is looking for, and if the same text appears in different books or in nonbook formats, one may not care at all which published appearance one gets so long as it contains the right text. This is a real difference, not just a question of words; a good book-finder may not be a good text-finder.

While it sounds good to say the catalog is supposed to enable us to find copies of texts, in fact our catalogs are not designed to do so except in a limited variety of cases. *Very* roughly, it will do that for long texts but not for short texts. If the text I want happens to occupy an entire book, I can find it in the catalog, provided I can recognize from the description that it *is* the text I'm looking for. If it occupies only part of a book, I *may* be able to find it in the catalog; I can do so if this part has been separately listed in the catalog (that is, if an analytic entry has been made), or if I find a description of the book that enumerates its contents. But unless the book is a collection of texts by the same author, I may never find it in the first place. Contents notes don't help if one can't find the catalog record in the first place. We don't set ourselves the goal of allowing discovery in the catalog of periodical articles, single contributions in collections, single speeches in Congress, or the like. That is what periodical indexes and other bibliographical works are for. The basic unit for the catalog is not the text but the separate publication, the bibliographically independent publication. Our basic unit is indeed the book, when it's not the serial publication treated as a single multivolume book. As far as texts are concerned, we're mostly concerned only with texts that happen to occupy all or most of a book, and since books can be small or large, a short text may after all appear in the catalog and a longer text not appear. So if we happen to have two published appearances of the same text, one as the sole content of a book, and one as part of an issue of a periodical, or in several issues of a periodical, the first appearance will show up in the catalog but the second one won't. Our choice of basic cataloging unit has the consequence that enormous numbers of texts are not locatable through the catalog without first using some other bibliographical work, to find what book or serial they are in. And it has the consequence that of the different copies of the same text in the library, some will be discoverable directly through the catalog, others discoverable only by an indirect approach through other bibliographical works. This is the standard practice, and I don't quarrel with it; but I do want to point out that it makes a cleavage of the bibliographical universe that is hard to describe briefly and accurately, and that must be quite mysterious and even irrational to the unindoctrinated user of the library.

The strangeness of the situation becomes more striking when we turn to another group of objectives of the catalog. In Cutter's formulation, the catalog is to show what the library has by a given author, or on a given subject, or in a given kind of literature. Note the exact wording: the catalog is to *show what the library has*. This is appealingly direct and to the point. It's exactly what one might have expected a catalog to do. Cutter didn't say that the catalog was to show what *books* a library had, but simply: *what* it had. He didn't say the catalog was to *help* one *find* what the library had, but to *show* what it had. This objective has been quoted approvingly for a hundred years, but we don't really mean it. It's not our real objective—not, at least, if the objective is understood as it normally would be understood, to mean that one meant to show *all* that one had. We certainly don't reveal all that we have by a particular author, and don't even aim to do so. We don't show all that we have on particular subjects, and don't even aim to do so. In the case of subjects, it's not just a matter of ignoring relatively short texts. Showing what you have means being explicit; if part of a book discusses a certain subject, and if you describe the book using terms applicable only to the whole book, you're not being explicit about the part. If the part discusses, say, the topic of metaphor, but the book is described as a whole as being about language, you haven't shown that you have that discussion of metaphor. We don't aim to show, to reveal explicitly, all the separate or distinguishable contents of a book.

This is all right, or at least understandable. But it has odd consequences. A naive user might legitimately expect that, if you've got two copies of the same text in your library, you'll list both; you certainly wouldn't list one and hide the other. This is such a basic and intuitively reasonable expectation that we might call it a principle: the Principle of Parity, say. The same text appearing in different circumstances of publication should be treated the same in all of its appearances, at least to this extent: if you show one, show them all. But we don't observe this principle. Cutter himself did have a rule requiring analytic entry for any part of a book that also appeared as a separate; we've forgotten that rule.[3] Cutter's rules themselves appeared as an appendix in a government report on public libraries; they've also appeared separately, in several versions, as the entire content of a small book. The former appearance will be ignored by the catalog, the latter will be recognized. Parity is not a cataloger's principle.

The same Principle of Parity applies to subject description, though it can take any of several forms. For example: if you have two texts that give the same amount of information about a subject, then show both if you show either; don't show one and hide the other. Alternatively: if you have two texts of equal importance for the study of a subject, show both if you show either; don't show one and conceal the fact that you have another equally important one. That has a corollary: for heaven's sake, don't list a small inferior work and conceal a large important work. Now you may immediately object: that's a matter of value judgments, and we can't expect the catalog to reflect value judgments (except insofar as it reflects value judgments involved in book-selection decisions). If anything has got to be value free and neutral, it's the catalog. Just so: and for just that reason, the catalog is unavoidably a terrible guide to what the library has on a subject. It grossly violates the Principle of Parity in this evaluative version, but nothing can be done about that because to do anything would require evaluation, and we don't evaluate. But the other version of the Principle, in terms of quantity of information (or quantity of text) is also grossly violated: a slight monograph will be listed, a huge treatise that incidentally has twice the amount of material on the same topic will go unrecognized as having anything to say on the topic. This is a consequence of the basic rule of subject cataloging, the rule of specific entry: a work all about a large subject is so described, the smaller subjects included in its scope are not explicitly shown. The rule is a sensible one, but adherence to it automatically results in violations of the Principle of Parity. We can of course say that we expect any intelligent person to realize that not all of the material on a subject will be in books of which that is *the* subject, and that he or she will have to look elsewhere to find what may actually be better for the purpose at hand. And to help in that further search, we provide a systematic set of cross-references that can be followed up. This is so, and a persistent and ingenious catalog user can make good use of that apparatus of cross-references. But providing some help to the persistent and ingenious catalog user is a far cry from showing explicitly what the library has. The catalog is selective, first in what it exhibits at all, second in what it tells about the things it does exhibit. The selectivity is defensible, but we really must not keep saying simply that the catalog shows what we have by an author or on a topic: it shows some of what we have. We'll come back later to the question of whether it ought to show more.

The big questions to answer when designing a bibliographical instrument are these: first, what's to count as one item, and what items, so counted, are to be included (the question of unit and scope); second, what information is to be supplied about each item; third, what information will allow one to find an item— how things are to be accessible, how organized, indexed, arranged (the question of access). We've been discussing the first of these, unit and scope; let's turn to the others.

The big difference between conventional card or book or microform catalogs, on the one hand, and online catalogs, on the other, is in access and display of information. Until now, decisions about access took the form of decisions about entries: main entry, added entries. An item appeared at a given number of places in the catalog—under the name of the author, under the title, under the name of a series, for example. At each appearance, the same descriptive information might be given, or, as was the case when Cutter was writing, the full information might be given only once, and only partial information given otherwise. That tedious old notion of the main entry made sense then; the main entry was the entry giving full information. With the advent of the unit card system, the notion dwindled to a ghost of its former self, as the notion of the entry you would make if you were going to make only one. (This is an oversimplification, but not by much.) But in a computer environment the notion of main entry seems to lose all meaning. And the notion of entry itself is transformed. The question is not where and how an item is to appear in a fixed list, but how it can be made to appear: first, what signals will produce a record, and second, what different forms the record can be made to take when it appears.

To emphasize how the notion of entry changes in a computer environment, let me remind you of the OCLC search keys. (In fact, it seems to me that the independent development by OCLC of its search keys was decisive in altering the notion of the entry.) The sequence of letters "bell, dean" is one way of making records for Saul Bellow's novel *The Dean's December* appear; another way is "dea,de,,". It sounds very odd to say that Bellow's novel is entered in that OCLC catalog under "bell, dean" and under "dea,de,," but that's in fact what it amounts to. Search keys or search statements or, as we might say, cues that will retrieve a record are the computerized catalog's analogs or equivalents of entries in manual catalogs. The record for an item may be physically stored in just one place, but that one place is not the item's one entry; it's not an entry at all but the source of entries. Or rather: the question that used to be put as one of selection of main and added entries becomes transformed into the question of permissible search requests, of the kinds of instructions to a machine that will make a particular item appear. Simultaneously, the question of how much information to provide for each entry changes; the possibility of asking for different amounts of information (short, medium, full, as Cutter would say) means that the question is now what different amounts and formats of information we will allow the user to make appear. That finally does in the notion of main entry, for if one has the option of getting full information no matter what search request or cue one uses to make the item appear, then every entry is main entry, and the notion of main entry loses all point.

Instead of deciding what entries to make, then, we have to decide what kinds of search keys or search statements or cues and combinations of cues will suffice to retrieve a record. The great practical difference that the computer makes is (1) in the enormous increase it allows in the number of different elements of information that might be used as cues; (2) in the possibility of combining cues using the Boolean operators *and, or,* and *not*; and (3) in the possibility of automatically changing the access system without altering the basic bibliographical records themselves. There are so many new possibilities that if a system designer were to ask: Which of the possible kinds of search capabilities would you like us to build into the system?, it's hard to imagine how one could resist saying: We want them all, now. Naturally, we'll want to be able to do what we could do in the old catalogs: if there was a point in making entries under author's name and title and editor and series in the old catalogs, the point is presumably still valid, and we'll want to be able to make a record appear by specifying author or title or editor or series. It would be odd and disappointing to find that an online catalog gave us less access than did the old system of main and added entries. But we want to be able to retrieve a record using partial information and combinations of partial cues: author's surname only (instead of full name) plus some word or words from the title (not the exact title with all words in the right order); those cues plus publication data, or plus approximate publication date; part of a surname plus other cues; and so on. We want to be able to exclude things: to ask for works not written in Bulgarian, not published after 1970, and so on. The question is, How much of the full combinatory capacity of the computer, working on what part of the range of elements in the full description, are we to make use of? If that is a radical transformation of our old question about how many entries to make for a particular record, it is still the same question at heart: how to make the records accessible. I can think of no general principle that one could use to help decide that question except the Principle of Generosity: the more the merrier. Or, to put it more solemnly: maximize the chances of finding what one is looking for, given the information one starts with. Minimize the restrictions on use of whatever information one has. If we take that line, the question of access converges on the question of description; if you're going to supply a piece of information in the full description of an item, why not let one who happens to have that piece of information use it in trying to get that item to appear? If it's worth giving at all, why isn't it worth using for retrieval purposes, as one part of a search request? Clearly not very many of the possible kinds of complex search requests are going to be used often; simple search requests using authors' names and partial titles are going to be the popular ones,

I would expect. But from the point of view of the user, not the system designer, the desirable thing would be to allow the user to use whatever information he or she had to start with, in trying to locate particular items: to maximize accessibility.

I want to interrupt the story at this point to caution against too much satisfaction about the possibility of altering the access system automatically without changing the basic records. The passage of time causes problems for a catalog, some of which are all too familiar, some of which are, I think, unduly neglected. People change their names; organizations change their names too, as do serial publications. New versions of old texts appear. New things are written about. Old things get new names, terminology changes. This last kind of change is one that looks to be easy to cope with in an online environment; with automated authority control, changes of terminology are easily dealt with. But there is a kind of change that cannot be accommodated so easily. The establishment of a new subject takes time; subject catalogers wisely wait for a while to let terminology settle down, though the easier it is to change terminology, the less reason there is for waiting. But during the wait, and even before one recognizes that there is something to wait for, people have been producing books that in retrospect can be seen to be best described by terminology that was not then available. After you finally recognize the category of, say, popular culture as something that can be the subject of a book, you might ask: How have we been describing books on this subject up to now, when we lacked that subject heading? The introduction of a new category, not simply a new name for an old category, should be the occasion for a retrospective look at what has previously been done, for the chances are that some of the old work is in error, given the new vocabulary. Recataloging is in order. But, so far as I know, it is not established practice to reexamine old cataloging in the light of new vocabulary. Corrections may be made for accidental reasons: a new edition of an old work, a need to correct old author entries. But systematic review of old subject cataloging, I think not. Now as terminology changes and new categories are introduced, over time the amount of misdescribed material is bound to increase; the accuracy of the subject catalog declines, the quality is gradually degraded. This is something that automatic procedures cannot eliminate. There is no automatic recognition process for misdescribed works.

We've got rid of the notion of entry or, rather, replaced it with the notion of permissible search request. In particular, we've got rid of main entry, and so are rid of those wearisome debates about whether main entry should always be under title, and those difficult decisions in particular cases about whether main entry should be under personal or corporate author. Good riddance! Now, might not the notion of authorship be thrown out too? Mr. Gorman has recently managed somehow to persuade the library profession that corporate authorship is a bad idea and should be entirely, or almost entirely, discarded (except for certain 'emanations' from corporate bodies). That was a most surprising feat. It occurs to me that a profession that can do that ought to be able to take the next small step and toss out the idea of personal authorship as well. I hasten to say that I'm not suggesting abandonment of authority control. We want to be able to pose search requests using personal names with the assurance that we will retrieve things appearing with any form of the name of the same person, and that requires standardization on names, or links among different forms of name used by the same person, that might be automatically activated when any particular form is used in a search request.

But we might keep authority control while abandoning authorship, by which I mean, ceasing to do anything to indicate explicitly that a person *is* the author of a particular text. This will, I hope, sound shocking; are not our catalogs firmly based on the authorship principle? If we want to allow a person to find a book of known authorship, how can we do so without identifying authors *as* authors? In fact, however, I think our catalogs are not firmly based on the authorship principle. We do not really inquire into the question of whether a personal name on the title page is the name of the author of the book. We take things at face value. Authorship really means purported authorship. When we learn that a text purportedly written by a late president of the United States was actually written by his assistants, we don't rush out to change the catalog records; that president is still the purported author. The managed textbooks that are written by anonymous hacks and that appear under the names of eminent professors would be listed, with a clear conscience, under their title-page purported authors. We recognize pro forma authorship, as when the twentieth edition of a text containing hardly a word set down by the original author is still ascribed to the original author, depending on the appearance of the title page. We're not really serious about authorship, and that is quite right; title-page names are the names likely to be used by those looking for the texts, and hence are the ones to worry about. No, we are not serious about authorship; and why take seriously the job of establishing purported authorship? A bibliographical record might now simply contain a title-page transcription, and the proper names contained in that transcription made searchable; this might easily be done without taking any position on the question of whether a name is the name of the author. What difference would it make? We would allow people to search by specifying a personal name alone, or personal name and title; in either case those things (and maybe more) would be retrieved that would have been retrieved if we allowed them to search for items of which some person was the author. We can, I say to forestall instant objection, distinguish between personal names as subjects and personal names as nonsubjects, "bibliographical" personal names, all without explicitly indicating authorship. As far as I can see, dropping explicit indication of authorship would be no great loss. But it may be helpful and thus desirable to specify different fuctions or roles played by individuals, and allowing one to search for works of which an individual is the purported author without also retrieving those of which he is the purported editor or translator or introduction writer. The Principle of Generosity would favor this. Still, it is worth reflecting on how little we do in fact depend on the notion of authorship. We proceed, more and more, on the basis of quite another principle: the Principle of Maximum Feasible Superficiality. As much as possible, we take things at face value. I do *not* say this is a defect.

Let us return for a moment to corporate authorship. Absent the need to decide on main entry, the debate over corporate main entry disappears. If we drop the notion of authorship, the notion of corporate authorship disappears as well. As with personal names, corporate names appearing in a title transcription or elsewhere might be made searchable without explicitly indicating any particular functional relationship between corporate body and text. But if we want to assign function or role indicators to personal names, distinguishing purported authors from purported editors and the like, why should we not assign them to corporate names too? In particular, the role indicator of purported authorship? For this good reason, it will be said, that an organization as an entity cannot write a book; only people, singly or in groups, can write books. I suspect that the rejection of corporate authorship is in part based on a romantic view of personal authorship. In scientific journals, for instance, the appearance of a personal name at the head of a journal article does not imply, hardly begins to suggest, that the person named did any writing; it only implies that the person had some unspecified role in doing the piece of research that is reported in the article. Mary Leakey wanted her name taken off a paper not because she hadn't actually written any of the work (of course she hadn't; she had lent the actual writers some bones), but because she disapproved of the content.[4] Authorship no longer really implies writing, and purported authorship needn't imply purported writing. The ways in which an organization might very seriously be eligible for authorship are explored deeply in Michael Carpenter's book *Corporate Authorship;*[5] I want to supplement that book by arguing, briefly, that since we don't take personal authorship seriously (and shouldn't), we needn't take corporate authorship seriously either, but we needn't take it any less seriously. For us, in practice, authorship is mainly a matter of name prominently displayed on title page; and it needn't make any difference whether the name looks like the name of an individual, or a committee, or a project, or an event, or a corporation, or a government department. To attribute a role to an organization or group need no more imply any theory about what part different members of the group played in the putting together of a string of words, than attribution of the role of author to an individual has to imply a theory about what the person actually did. In other words: role attribution without commitment—superficial role attribution. The notion of corporate authorship is not dead; if one wants a deep analysis of what it seriously means, that's available; without deep analysis, we are justified in using the notion as superficially as we use the notion of personal authorship.

Let us return to the question of subject description. One of the first things one is likely to think of, when contemplating a computer-based catalog, is that now we should take the occasion to begin revealing more of the content of our collections. Subject analysis is shallow; it often amounts to little more than paraphrasing the titles of books in a formalized vocabulary and syntax. The vocabulary and syntax are that of the Library of Congress subject heading system; they needn't, of course, be that. There are plenty of alternative ways of formulating short formalized descriptions of content, the PRECIS system being the most talked about. But the point is that whatever system you employ, short descriptions of overall subject matter just don't reveal much explicitly about content. And so one might say: now is the time to deepen the indexing, to make more of the content of the texts directly accessible. Lots of alternatives suggest themselves; for instance, a layered content description: first an overall summary of content; then a set of descriptions of separate parts or aspects of the content; then a further set of descriptions of smaller parts or aspects. Given a search procedure that allowed one to search in different layers, sticking to the top layer if one wanted, going deeper if one wanted, this would greatly increase retrieval capability, it would enlarge the amount of material on a topic that was explicitly shown as such. Should we not be working on plans to do just this?

I wouldn't try to prevent anyone from producing a more deeply indexed subject catalog, but I'd like to argue against doing it. My reasons have to do, first, with the kind of bibliographical control that is most important to library users, and second, with the way we ought to be thinking about the subject component of the catalog. Let's look at the user first. For most users most of the time, I suspect that it is fair to say that, when they're not looking for a particular item they already know they want to see, they're looking for something *good*. Years ago, I put it this way: that the kind of power one would most like to have is power to get the best textual means to one's particular goal or end.[6] Years of trying to find reasons to doubt that have left me still of that belief. Light users of libraries want something they will find good to read; serious users want the ones that will serve them best to accomplish some purpose. I wanted recently to catch up on what had been going on in the study known as behavioral decision theory; of course what I wanted was a *good* survey of recent work: authoritative, up to date, clear, well-written, by someone who was fair to all parties, and so on. I wanted the best account I could get. The kind of bibliographical control I wanted was not the ability to discover everything there is that fits the bare topical description of what I'm looking for, but the ability to get the good ones and be spared the bad ones. There's another and related matter: as often as not, what I'm looking for is something I can describe only in functional terms—I want something that would help me see or understand or solve something. I'd like to be able to say what's bothering me, and then ask: What is there that would help me in this situation? I don't care what the subject matter is, who the author is, how old it is, I will take anything that will be of help. I don't know where to look in a list of subjects, for as far as I know the things that might help might be anywhere.

If I'm right about this, then the two things that make a text most interesting to me are things that we won't or can't provide in the catalog. We won't say anything about value; even if we did, we might well say the wrong thing, for the value in question is relative to an individual's situation and purposes. The other point is harder to grasp, I think. From the point of view of the user who wants materials that will help solve or at least clarify his problem, the cataloger approaches materials from the wrong end.[7] The catalogers go book by book, and about each one ask: What is this particular book about? But to be of real help, they'd have to start not with particular books but with particular questions or problems, and ask about each book, What if anything might this book contribute to solving or clarifying this particular problem? Doing that would be an effort to organize materials functionally, by their relationship to particular problems. The cataloger doesn't and can't do that, has rather to take each book in sequence and describe it internally, and consequently produces an instrument that is fatally flawed from the serious user's point of view.

We can't provide evaluations, and can't organize materials functionally, in terms of uses to which they can be put rather than topics they're about. We're stuck with content description in terms of subject matter and form. Should we at least do as much of that as we possibly can? Granted that we can't provide the kind of bibliographical control that would be most desirable, shouldn't we provide as much as possible of a second-best sort? I'd argue that we should not, that you don't compensate for a basic flaw in the instrument by making the instrument bigger and bigger. I'm talking now only about subject catalogs and subject cataloging. If it were proposed to make more of the discrete texts in a collection available by author and title, to provide more analysis but confine the analysis to bibliographical description, with no subject analysis other than what is automatically provided by title words, then I would say, by all means let's do it. But if it comes to deeper subject cataloging, I say, forget it. In fact, go in the other direction. Abandon the idea that all the items entered in the database have to be provided with subject cataloging data; abandon the idea that the online catalog has to have the equivalent of a complete subject catalog as a subcomponent. Do subject cataloging selectively. Redefine the role of the subject catalog; rather than being a device to show everything the library has on a subject, which it never has done, think of it as having a different purpose: to serve as a readily available, convenient, universal bibliography, highly selective, confined to things on hand (not, then, expanded in the direction of being a subject index to everything available through interlibrary loan), and confined to big units—books; not a list of best books, but of books thought worth having on the premises. In some libraries of course, for example an undergraduate library in a university, it comes close to being a list of recommended books; and as a universal though shallow bibliography, a subject catalog would be no worse if it were still more selective, excluding things unlikely to be of interest except to specialists. Say that it's universal, not in including everything you have but in excluding no topic in advance; say that it's not meant to be complete but to provide useful starting points for one approaching a new and unknown topic, or for one who wants just one sizeable chunk of text dealing with that topic. Recognize and say that further and deeper inquiry will quickly have to abandon the subject catalog and turn elsewhere, to specialized bibliographies and indexes, and, above all, to the self-organizing apparatus of footnotes and bibliographies in books and articles. And that inquiry will then be led back, to the author and title components of the catalog, to find the particular items first discovered elsewhere. Thought of in this way, the relative shallowness of subject indexing is not a defect, and deeper indexing would not be a merit.

The upshot of all this is, as far as I'm concerned, that the unique contribution of the catalog is, after all, just what most people have always agreed it had to be, to help locate copies of books and texts that may have been learned about elsewhere. It has to be a local finding device. Its service as a convenient selective guide to the subject contents of the collection is secondary to this. It is in many ways a superficial bibliographical instrument, but this should cause no embarrassment; it is not meant to be, and should not try to be, the complete and definitive guide to the bibliographical universe, but an essential local supplement to the complex apparatus of means of discovery. In its revolutionary new online form, that's what it will still be. But if all goes well, it will be an excitingly flexible and comfortable piece of the bibliographical apparatus.

Notes

1.   Eva Verona, "Literary Unit versus Bibliographical Unit," *Libri* 9:79-104 (1959); Seymour Lubetzky, *Principles of Cataloging, Phase I: Descriptive Cataloging* (Los Angeles: Institute of Library Research, University of California, 1969).

2.   Charles A. Cutter, *Rules for a Dictionary Catalog*, 4th ed., rewritten (Washington, D.C.: Govt. Print. Off., 1904).

3.   Ibid., p. 83 (Rule 194b).

4.   Donald C. Johanson and Maitland A. Edey, *Lucy* (New York: Simon & Schuster, 1981), excerpted in *Science 81* 2:48-55 (March 1981).

5.   Michael Carpenter, *Corporate Authorship: Its Role in Library Cataloging* (Westport, Conn.: Greenwood Press, 1981).

6.   Patrick Wilson, *Two Kinds of Power: An Essay on Bibliographical Control* University of California Publications, Librarianship, 5 (Berkeley: Univ. of California Pr., 1968).

7.   Cf. Raynard Swank, "Subject Catalogs, Classifications, or Bibliographies? A Review of Critical Discussions, 1876-1942," *Library Quarterly* 14:316-32 (Oct. 1944), esp. p. 331.

Index

Codes of cataloging rules are generally products of corporate bodies. Because the forms of heading for such works vary greatly, they have been gathered under the main heading "Catalog codes." For similar reasons, references to catalogs of libraries are gathered under the heading "Catalogs."

Examples have not been indexed unless they are part of a lengthy discussion taking place over a number of pages or are otherwise memorable.

With few exceptions, acronyms have been preferred for the names of corporate bodies.